BEHOLD THE PROMISED LAND

John Hopkins Studies in Atlantic History and Culture
Richard Price and Franklin W. Knight, general editors

Richard Price, *The Guiana Maroons: Historical and Bibliographical Introduction*

O. Nigel Bolland, *The Formation of a Colonial Society: Belize, from Conquest to Crown Colony*

Douglas Taylor, *Languages of the West Indies*

Kenneth Evan Sharpe, *Peasant Politics: Struggle in a Dominican Village*

Roger Bastide, The African Religions of Brazil: Toward a Sociology of Interpenetration of Civilizations. Translated by Helen Sebba

Margaret E. Crahan and Franklin W. Knight, editors, *Africa and the Caribbean: The Legacies of a Link*

Tom W. Shick, *Behold the Promised Land: A History of Afro-American Settler Society in Nineteenth-Century Liberia*

Behold
the
Promised
Land

A History of
Afro-American Settler Society
in Nineteenth-Century Liberia

Tom W. Shick

The Johns Hopkins University Press
Baltimore and London

To my family, who believed in me the way only family can

This book has been brought to publication with the generous assistance of the Andrew W. Mellon Foundation.

Manufactured in the United States of America

Maps drawn by the Cartographic Library, University of Wisconsin, Madison.

The Johns Hopkins University Press, Baltimore, Maryland 21218
The Johns Hopkins Press Ltd., London

LIBRARY OF CONGRESS CATALOGING IN PUBLICATION DATA

Shick, Tom W.
  Behold the promised land.

  (Johns Hopkins studies in Atlantic history and culture)
  Bibliography: p. 181
  Includes index.
  1. Liberia—History—To 1847. 2. Liberia—History—1847-1944. 3. Afro-Americans—Liberia—History. 4. Afro-Americans—Colonization—Liberia.
  I. Title. II. Series.
  DT633.S47 966.6'201 79-22960
  ISBN 0-8018-2309-9

Sketch on title page by Emmy Simmons (1975) represents a settler home in Arthington.

Contents

Illustrations

Maps

Tables

Preface

Oil in Nigeria, Cubans in Mozambique, and liberation struggles in Zimbabwe and Namibia are among the contemporary realities on the African continent that attract the notice of the American press and public. Ironically, Liberia, the oldest republic in Africa and a country whose cultural, political, and economic fortunes have been linked to the United States for more than a century, remains shrouded in obscurity for most Americans. Few Americans other than those who have lived there for a time—as missionaries, Peace Corps volunteers, employees of American companies, or members of the official American Embassy community—know the details of Liberia's history. Still fewer believe it has any significance for their lives. The particular nature of American-Liberian interdependence derives from the experiences and actions of Americans who left the United States during the nineteenth century to settle permanently in Liberia. The immigrants were all Americans of African descent, and this was not a mere accident of history. Their destiny on African soil was a direct consequence of American race relations in the nineteenth century and later.

The issue of slavery in America has lost much (although not all) of its emotionalism over the years since the Civil War. The Republic of Liberia, however, remains as a symbolic reminder of the past, for it was not so long ago that this small country carried the enormous burden of representing the Promised Land for people of African descent in the New World. Driven by slavery and racism to leave their homes in America, the nineteenth-century immigrants retained vivid memories of the racial rejection that had brought them "back to Africa." As settlers, however, they could not discard their American cultural baggage and totally immerse themselves in African life. Instead they evolved a distinctive settler society with both African and

American characteristics. They faced the challenge of rebuilding their lives in Africa within a context of intense internal and external pressure.

This, then, is a book about men, women, and children who became settlers in the land of their forebears. It tries to capture the quality of their experience while setting it within an international context. In many ways it is as much a part of Afro-American history as it is of Liberian history.

Since 1969, when I began the research for this book, a number of influences have affected the discipline of history in fundamental ways. Historians have begun to adopt interdisciplinary approaches to historical problems with increasing frequency and sophistication. For example, some historians have used psychological theories of personality development to provide stimulating insights in biographical studies. Others have used oral traditions, linguistic theory, and anthropological evidence to reconstruct the past of nonliterate societies. Quantitative analysis, an innovative methodological technique, has altered the direction of much recent historical research. The new quantifiers have rescued data previously considered too voluminous to be manageable and have provided an interesting approach to the history of nonelites.

While the discipline of history has undergone general methodological changes, the area of Afro-American history has faced a critical point. The black-studies movement raised fundamental issues and called loudly for new perspectives. The result has been a new emphasis on the motives, drives, and circumstances of the Afro-American community, in short, a new reading of Afro-American history from the inside out. This has helped to liberate Afro-American history from its longstanding position as a marginal backdrop to general American history. Many of the same questions have led to a trend away from the ethnocentric bias that once made African history preponderantly the history of Europeans in Africa.

This book was shaped in its formative stages by the influence of these developments on historical methodology. I used traditional archival sources in the United States, England, and West Africa extensively. These sources were augmented, however, by the analysis of quantitative data and field research that included the collection of family genealogies. My goal has been to understand the evolution of Liberian settler society, which drew heavily on the American traditions of the immigrants. The mutual assimilation of culture in Liberia between these immigrants and the indigenous people suggests possible generalizations about the overall process of westernization in nineteenth-century Africa. Like the Creoles of Sierra Leone and the Afro-Brazilian returnees to Dahomey, Nigeria, and Togo, the Afro-American immigrants to Liberia were agents of social change who shared a racial identification with Africans. Their experience fits a larger pattern that was important to West African coastal society of the time. References to the comparative dimension are found in the chapter footnotes, and my own thoughts on the subject are in the last chapter. My primary purpose, however, is to provide the general reader with a history of Liberian settlers that blends individual experiences into the matrix of social dynamics that constituted Liberian settler society.

Many individuals have made this book possible by offering to me valuable advice and encouragement. I welcome the opportunity to acknowledge the generous support of others. Jean Herskovits and Leonard Jeffries, Jr., introduced me to African history while I was an undergraduate at the City College of New York. I am grateful for their unwavering faith at a time when other extraordinary events occupied everyone's mind. Philip D. Curtin supervised my graduate training at the University of Wisconsin. I join a generation of Wisconsin graduate students who benefitted from his rigorous professional standards. I wish to thank him for his sustained support and willingness to give me the necessary latitude and advice to get the job done. Jan Vansina, William A. Brown, and Stanley K. Schultz ultimately read the manuscript when it was still in dissertation form. Their suggestions and comments helped me to both strengthen arguments and enhance the clarity of my prose. They have my sincere thanks.

The field research for this book was made possible by a generous grant from the Social Science Research Council. The University of Wisconsin Comparative World History Program provided timely support that enabled me to process quantitative data. The University of Wisconsin Cartographic Laboratory prepared the maps contained in this book, underwriting the costs involved. I am pleased to express my gratitude for these sources of funding. Although it is unlikely that this book could have been completed without the above support, I alone am responsible for what appears in the pages that follow.

I have had the good fortune of having the resources and intellectual climate of the University of Wisconsin, Madison, as my academic home. I am grateful for the support and encouragement of the Afro-American Studies Department and the African Studies Program and of the staffs of the University of Wisconsin Memorial Library, especially David P. Henige, African bibliographer, and of the Wisconsin State Historical Society.

I began research for this book using the facilities of libraries and archives across this country. Many professionals aided me by answering my inquiries and bringing to my attention sources that proved invaluable to me. Sylvia Render, of the Library of Congress, and James Walker and Debra Newman, of the National Archives, were especially supportive and have my sincere appreciation.

During the fifteen months I spent in West Africa many individuals gave freely of their time and expertise to help me with my agenda. In Liberia,

Siata Barclay, Major M. Branch, Dean Anna E. Cooper, D. Musulen Cooper, Dennis and Vivian Derryck, Leonard DeShield, Elwood Dunn, Matilda King, S. A. Morris-Kainessie, Clarence and Lillie Norman, R. Vahnjah Richards, Blake Robinson, Clathan Ross, Africanus Schaacks, Roger and Emmy Simmons, and Eugenia Simpson-Cooper are among those who helped most. I received the cooperation of Dr. J. Melvin Mason, then president of the Liberian Research Association, and Director Augustine D. Jallah, of the Liberian Government Archives, under the Ministry of Foreign Affairs. At the University of Liberia several persons provided encouragement, stimulation, and friendship. Drs. Mary Antoinette Brown Sherman, S. Jabaru Carlon, Jeanette Carter, Zamba Liberty, and Jane J. Martin maintained an active interest in my work. Mrs. Ruth Armstrong, of the University Library, facilitated my use of important resources there. I accomplished much more than I could have expected because of the dedication and dependability of Melvin Morris-Kainessie, my research assistant. Lawrence Breitborde, David Brown, Stephen Hlophe, William Siegmann, and Jo Mary Sullivan were fellow researchers who gave me the benefit of their perspectives on Liberian history.

I was fortunate to meet Counselor Christian Abayomi Cassell in Monrovia. He graciously shared both his intimate knowledge of the Liberian past and the specific and important history of his own family, and he permitted me to examine his rare collection of Liberian newspapers and books. His commitment to preserving the record of Liberia's history through personal efforts was immediately evident and inspiring.

During a month of work in Freetown, Sierra Leone, I received generous assistance from the archivists, librarians, and the staffs of the Sierra Leone Government Archives and the Fourah Bay University Library. My special thanks to Dr. John Peterson, then director of the African Studies Institute at Fourah Bay University, for giving me the courtesy of the Institute and the status of visiting research associate. Wayne R. Williams and his family extended the very warmest hospitality by offering a spare bedroom in their home in Leicester Village.

The following individuals read all or parts of the manuscript and took time to react with comments, suggestions, and criticisms: Marjorie Bogen-Forsythe, Allen Bogue, Steven Feierman, Lawrence Glasco, Fred Hayward, Robert A. Hill, Svend E. Holsoe, Stanley I. Kutler, Richard A. Long, Nell I. Painter, and Peter H. Smith. I hope each will see where I have leaned on his or her wisdom and forgive me where I have failed. I would like to thank Svend E. Holsoe, of the Department of Anthropology at the University of Delaware, for his generous assistance to me over many years. His spirit of scholarly cooperation and extensive knowledge of Liberia are well known by those of us who share a research interest in the country. I am especially indebted to him for bringing to my attention the rare portrait of Edward James

Roye that appears in this book. To Alex Haley and the members of the Kinte Library Project, my thanks for the opportunity to share in that historic venture, which contributed immeasurably to my own work.

Franklin W. Knight and Richard Price recommended this book for inclusion in the Johns Hopkins Studies in Atlantic History and Culture series. The book has benefitted immeasurably from the expert attention of the professional staff at The Johns Hopkins University Press. Henry Y. K. Tom, social sciences editor, guided me along the road to publication, and Joanne Allen, manuscript editor, used a sensitive editorial pencil to improve the quality of the final product. To all of the above I am grateful.

A special thanks to attorney Joseph D. Shine, of Charleston, South Carolina, for the many courtesies he extended to me in the final stages of preparing the manuscript for the press.

Finally, my own network of extended-family ties sustained me over the long road that this research carried me. My debt to them is beyond adequate expression.

Part One/Context

Afro-American colonization was an issue that excited the emotions of Americans in the nineteenth century. More often than not, the Republic of Liberia figured prominently in American public debates on the subject, for it was this small West African country that symbolized an alternative to racial integration in America. Euro-Americans, through the American Colonization Society, planted the seeds for a new society. Afro-Americans, through immigration, cultivated that which was sown. The motivations for building this settler society in Africa were deeply rooted in the context of American life in the nineteenth century.

1/Colonization and the Afro-American Community

For two hundred and twenty-eight years has the colored man toiled over the soil of America, under a burning sun and a driver's lash—plowing, planting, reaping, that white men might roll in ease, their hands unhardened by labor, and their brows unmoistened by the waters of genial toil; and now that the moral sense of mankind is beginning to revolt at this system of foul treachery and cruel wrong, and is demanding its overthrow, the mean and cowardly oppressor is mediating plans to expel the colored man entirely from the country. Shame upon the guilty wretches that dare propose, and all that countenance such a proposition. We live here—have lived here—have a right to live here, and mean to live here.

—Frederick Douglass, *The North Star*,
January 26, 1849

The parallel development of egalitarian principles and chattel slavery was the most important contradiction in American society before 1865. The colonial demand for independence during the Revolutionary War period intensified an obvious moral dilemma.[1] The English lexicographer and literary critic Samuel Johnson touched on the sensitive issue when he publicly wondered, "How is it that we hear the loudest yelps for liberty among the drivers of negroes?"[2] Although clearly germane, his stinging remark produced no audible rejoinder. "Revolutionary slaveholder" was a contradiction in terms that invited such sarcastic comments. Few patriots were more troubled by this than Thomas Jefferson, the leading philosopher of the Revolution. Jefferson, the champion of the natural rights of man, nevertheless harbored deep doubts about their applicability to African slaves. He recognized the evils of slavery—he even spoke out against them—but he worried privately that emancipation would have serious racial implications for Euro-Americans. In 1782 Jefferson mentioned one solution to this quandry that was just then gaining some support in America: "Among the Romans emancipation required but one effort. The slave when free, might mix, without staining the blood of his master. But with us a second [step] is necessary, unknown to history. When freed, he is to be removed beyond the reach of mixture."[3] By

3

the time Jefferson's view appeared in print in 1787, the substance of his point
had already crystallized the concept of colonization.

Those Americans who, like Jefferson, were willing to concede that
slavery was a potential bane on the new nation saw the scenario in broader
terms. If human bondage was eventually to end, what would protect society
from the greater dangers of miscegenation, which might follow abolition?
Colonization offered an attractive solution. If slavery and the slave trade were
morally wrong, why not simply reverse the course of history by returning
emancipated slaves to Africa? To its supporters colonization was more than
just a policy of expedient deportation, since it implied the building of a new
society on African soil. Benefits would accrue to both sides: America would
remove the alleged cause of increasing societal stress, and Africa would receive the advantages of Christianity and civilization from its returning descendants. This was the basic premise of colonization, which became the focus
of great debate during the nineteenth century.

The aftermath of the Revolutionary War provided the first opportunities
for the implementation of colonization schemes. Although the American
patriots secured independence from England, the institution of slavery remained a vexing problem. Rather than abolish human bondage, the founding
fathers agreed to a series of compromises that ensured its continued survival.
Slavery was given legal recognition when the Constitutional Convention
met in 1787 to draft the nation's basic laws. Although never mentioning it
explicitly, four clauses in the Constitution provided direct protection for
slavery in American life.[4] The revolutionary furor clearly did not destroy the
legitimacy of slavery as a domestic institution. It did, however, contribute to
an increase in personal manumission by southern slaveholders and to the prohibition against slavery within the jurisdiction of states in the North.[5] Both
activities increased the size of the free Afro-American population. The growth
in the number of Afro-Americans living outside the controls of slavery gave
additional immediacy to the challenge of developing a concrete program of
colonization, for many Euro-Americans believed that the possibility of a
federal act of universal and unconditional emancipation increased with every
measure that expanded the size of the free Afro-American community.

The earliest American criticism of slavery came from within the Church,
where the divine sanction to the institution found some vocal disbelievers.
It is not at all surprising that colonization proved appealing to antislavery religious leaders. The Reverend Samuel Hopkins was one such promoter of
colonization during the late eighteenth century. Working from his community
base as pastor of the First Congregational Church of Newport, Rhode Island,
Hopkins proposed a voluntary plan to send freed slaves back to Africa. He
stressed the evangelizing potential of his idea. In 1773 Hopkins enlisted the
cooperation of another Congregationalist minister, Ezra Stiles, to raise funds

necessary to send a small number of emancipated slaves to West Africa. His plan called for religious training of the selected individuals prior to their departure. Thus Hopkins envisioned them spreading the Christian gospel in the land of their nativity.[6] Hopkins's unwavering commitment to colonization was sustained by genuine emigrationist sentiment within the New England Afro-American community. A coincidental convergence of interests had developed. Many Afro-Americans had already expressed their desire to return to their homeland through individual and group petitions to state legislatures. This emigrationist sentiment provided support for Hopkins's belief in the practicality of colonization. Although war terminated this specific project before it could be carried out, Hopkins continued to articulate the virtues of colonization until his death in 1803.[7]

The first celebrated repatriation of Afro-Americans to the African continent came in the second decade of the nineteenth century.[8] The effort was the brainchild of Paul Cuffee, an enterprising Afro-American Quaker. Cuffee was a prosperous New England trader and the owner of a small fleet of whaling ships. He had become involved in the struggle for the political rights of free Afro-Americans in the state of Massachusetts. Ultimately, however, Cuffee turned his attention and energies to Africa, in particular to the British colony of Sierra Leone. Cuffee believed that Afro-American emigration to Sierra Leone would help to build a black Christian nation in Africa and also suppress the nefarious slave trade. He asserted his racial sentiment by declaring that "as I am of the African race, I feel myself interested for them, and, if I am favored with a talent, I think I am willing that they should be benefitted thereby."[9] In December 1815, largely at his own expense, Cuffee transported thirty-eight Afro-Americans to Sierra Leone. He died on September 7, 1817, and thus did not realize his hopes of generating greater enthusiasm for his activities among free Afro-Americans. It is ironic that Cuffee's accomplishment did not immediately inspire similar projects by other free Afro-Americans of means; instead it encouraged Euro-Americans to reconsider the old proposals of Samuel Hopkins.[10]

When news of Paul Cuffee's voyage began to circulate in America, it rekindled the flame of colonization in other states. Charles Fenton Mercer, of Virginia, introduced a series of resolutions that were passed by the Virginia Assembly in 1816. The resolutions called on the federal government to find a territory in the North Pacific in which to settle Virginia's free Afro-Americans and those thereafter emancipated. Mercer, in sponsoring the resolutions, informed the Assembly that "many thousands of individuals in our native State . . . are restrained from manumitting their slaves . . . by the melancholy conviction that they cannot yield to the suggestions of humanity without manifest injury to their country."[11] He believed that the free Afro-American population endangered the peace of the state and reduced the value of slave property. Thus Mercer called for colonization as the best way to remove obstacles to widespread emancipation in Virginia.

Robert Finley, a teacher and religious leader from New Jersey, outlined his own view on colonization in a letter to John P. Munford, of New York, in 1815. Like Mercer, he pointed to colonization as a solution to America's race problem. Finley, however, added to the argument his notion of other likely benefits: "Could they [Afro-Americans] be sent to Africa . . . we should send to Africa a population partially civilized and christianized for its benefit; our blacks themselves would be put in better condition."[12] Robert Finley acted upon his convictions by participating in a colonization meeting in Princeton, New Jersey. At the meeting a resolution was passed urging the New Jersey legislature to use its influence to secure the adoption of some deportation scheme by Congress. While Mercer and Finley both advocated colonization, neither man had a concrete plan to propose. Even where proposals did exist, the financial means for executing them continued to be elusive.[13]

The flurry of discussion and resolutions about colonization finally culminated in a national meeting. Leading Euro-American advocates of colonization came together in Washington, D.C., in December 1816. The conferees agreed to form the American Society for Colonizing the Free People of Color of the United States, a national organization that quickly became known as the American Colonization Society. Among the influential founders of this society were Robert Finley, Samuel J. Mills, Henry Clay, Francis Scott Key, and Judge Bushrod Washington. The stated purpose of the new organization was to consider the expediency and practicality of "ameliorating" the condition of the free people of color in America by providing a colonial retreat, either on this continent or in Africa. Henry Clay, chairman of the Washington meeting, noted that the question of emancipation or abolition of slavery was purposely avoided to ensure the cooperation of slaveholders like himself.[14] The society eventually sponsored the "planting" of a colony in West Africa, which in 1847 became the independent Republic of Liberia.

The occasion of the signing of the American Colonization Society charter was to be a rare moment of euphoria for the assembled advocates of colonization, an euphoria seldom repeated during the life of the body. Years of individual advocacy by a handful of stalwarts had finally brought about the formation of a national organization devoted to the principle of colonization. Prominent politicians, religious leaders, and professional men—in many cases slaveholders themselves—gave their blessing to the society. The hopes of the participants for developing a nationally coordinated colonization project were understandably high. The founders were optimistic that if the project were successful, they could then convince the federal government to provide the means necessary to take colonization to its logical conclusion, namely, the removal of all Afro-Americans from the United States. Almost before the founders could make the return journey to their homes a chorus of negative reactions issued forth from the more articulate members of the free Afro-American community. In city after city throughout the North free Afro-Americans met to pass resolutions opposing the colonization idea.[15] The society was given notice that its plans for social engineering were not shared by many of the potential recipients of its so-called benevolence.

Afro-American leadership, by and large, continued to withhold endorsement of the American Colonization Society or its goals despite attempts by the society to clarify what it considered as misunderstandings of its motives. David Walker expressed the sentiments of many of his peers when he declared, "America is more our country than it is the whites—we have enriched it with our blood and tears . . . and will they drive us from our property and homes, which we have earned with our blood?"[16] Had Afro-American attitudes towards emigration changed so drastically since the days of Samuel Hopkins? The answer can be found in the relationship between colonization and the continuation of slavery. Colonization had become an anathema to the antislavery movement. Abolitionists, particularly outspoken Afro-Americans, considered colonization to be a vicious scheme designed to perpetuate slavery by removing the bondsman's natural ally from America. Thus any Afro-American who dared to endorse the American Colonization Society or even to express approval of the principles of emigration and colonization was cast in the light of a traitor forsaking his enslaved brothers and sisters.

Public attacks were instrumental in forcing the officials of the American Colonization Society to devote inordinate energy to defending their organization. Claiming the support of thousands of free Afro-Americans, radical abolitionists like William Lloyd Garrison charged the society with conspiracy. A bitter propaganda battle ensued to win the minds of free Afro-Americans.[17] What method was most likely to achieve the liberation of slaves? The abolitionists argued that slavery could be destroyed through a campaign of moral suasion that exposed the evils of the institution to the American public. They felt that national moral outrage would cause clamor for universal emancipation that could not be ignored. The role of the antislavery movement was to generate that moral outrage within the country. Most Afro-Americans were fully committed to this approach. Some, however, held the belief that slavery would never end until the capacity of the African race to manage its own affairs had been demonstrated to the world. To them the uplifting of the African race could only be accomplished outside of America; once there were strong, independent Negro states, the days of slavery would be numbered. Thus there were mavericks in the Afro-American community who saw emigration as a necessary means to an end, and they were not willing to abandon their convictions simply because the American Colonization Society existed.

The advocates of Negro nationalism faced a formidable task in trying to convince free Afro-Americans of the correctness of their stance on emigration. They undertook the effort even while lacking agreement within their own ranks as to the best destination. Central America, Haiti, Canada, and Africa all had strong promoters. Even the National Emigration Convention, held in Cleveland, Ohio, in August 1854, did not succeed in achieving concensus on one location for all emigrationists to rally behind; however, it authorized investigative expeditions to Central America, Haiti, and West Africa to determine prospects for emigration to those places.[18]

The concept of Negro nationalism owed its development to those who argued its merits in speeches, pamphlets, and books. Martin Robinson Delany, physician and editor of *The Mystery*, a Pittsburgh weekly newspaper, made his contribution to Negro nationalism in 1852, when his book *The condition, elevation, emigration, and destiny of the colored people of the United States politically considered* was published. Delany tried to demonstrate that the free Afro-American community in America suffered from the same policy of political degradation that oppressed slaves and that consequently, although America was their birthplace, they remained without the security of the full citizenship rights accorded Euro-Americans. Delany argued that only emigration could lead to the elevation of the race. At the time, Delany, like most of the free Afro-American leadership, found emigration to Liberia undesirable. Unsure that the motives of the American Colonization Society were in the best interest of Afro-Americans, he stressed the advantages of Central and South America for emigration.[19] In later years Delany came to reconsider Africa as the place for building a "Negro Republic" and agreed to lead the expedition authorized by the National Emigration Convention to Nigeria in search of a suitable site;[20] however, he still refused to endorse the American Colonization Society colony in Liberia.

Ten years after Delany's treatise appeared in print, an appeal for emigration to Liberia was made by another—perhaps the most brilliant—advocate of Negro nationalism, Edward Wilmot Blyden. Blyden was born on the island of St. Thomas in the Caribbean in 1832, came to America in search of an opportunity to study theology in 1850, and after failing to gain admission to several schools because of his race, emigrated to Liberia in 1851.[21] In an address directed at Afro-Americans, Blyden began by quoting from the Bible: "Behold, the Lord thy God hath set the land before thee: go up and possess it, as the Lord God of thy fathers had said unto thee; fear not, neither be discouraged."[22] Following this reference to the Israelite mandate from God, Blyden outlined the responsibility of people of African descent living in the Diaspora. He declared that their role was one of "rolling back the appalling cloud of ignorance and superstition which overspreads the land, and to rear

Figure 1. Edward Wilmot Blyden, c. 1850

on those shores an asylum of liberty for the downtrodden sons of Africa wherever found."[23] Blyden maintained that the mandate for Afro-Americans to return to the African fatherland was from God. He noted the providential nature of their sojourn in slavery. For slavery, no matter how grim, did succeed in placing some of Africa's children in circumstances that prepared them to return to Africa and spread Christianity and civilization among their African kin. Moreover, Blyden stressed that the feeling of alienation so common among descendants of Africa in the Diaspora was fortuitious: It provided the motivation to return to Africa in search of political and social rights denied in New World societies. Finally, Blyden pointed to the continued survival of Liberia against overwhelming odds as the clearest evidence that Providence stood behind the effort, and he thereby beckoned the descendants of Africa in America to follow the example of the early pioneers and emigrate to Liberia.[24]

Never one to avoid the challenges of criticism, Blyden answered directly the charges that Afro-American settlers maintained a distinction between themselves and the indigenous Africans. He asserted that unlike other emigrants to foreign lands, who strive to advance their own immediate interests in the most expedient way and at the expense of any indigenous groups, the Liberian emigrant had a far nobler goal: "Our work is moral and intellectual as well as physical . . . our prosperity depends as much upon the wholesome and elevating influence we exert upon the native population, as upon the progress we make in agriculture, commerce and manufacture."[25] Thus it was Blyden's view that the Afro-American objective should be to achieve assimilation with Africans in Liberia rather than assimilation with Euro-Americans in the United States. To drive home his point, while making his fundamental contribution to the ideology of racial nationalism, Blyden observed: "When alien and hostile races have come together, one has had to succumb to the other; but when different people of the same family have been brought together, there has invariably been an improved and powerful class."[26]

Blyden was certainly a champion of the Liberian experiment. He was deeply committed to the idea that Afro-Americans should serve the cause of African redemption by returning to their racial homeland. In all of his writing, however, Blyden tended to minimize the cultural differences between Africans and their distant New World cousins. He retained faith in the power of racial affinity to overcome the cultural estrangement of Afro-Americans to Africa.[27] Such optimism was to be expected from a leading proponent of racial nationalism, but was it realistic in the nineteenth century? What kind of society were Afro-Americans coming from, and how would their American past influence their African future? Would the western cultural experiences help or hinder their adaptation to life in West Africa? These were relevant questions for the evolution of Liberian settler society. Exploring the cultural milieu of the emigrants prior to their departure helps to explain how they perceived themselves and their mission.

Contrary to popular opinion, the United States was never the primary importer of African slaves. The most recent estimate of African slave importation to the Western Hemisphere suggests that some 12 million slaves were imported over the course of five centuries. Beginning in the 1400s African slaves were taken largely from West Africa and the Angola region of Central Africa. Less than 5 percent of that total number were imported directly to the United States.[28] Yet despite the United States' relatively low level of importation as compared with that of other slave societies, the Afro-American population experienced exceptional growth in the United States. Until 1850 it had average annual growth rates of from 2 to 3 percent, doubling the population size every generation before the American Civil War (see table 1). The growth pattern was marked by more births than deaths rather than by any significant surge in importation. The native-born Afro-Americans represented the majority of the slave population even before the American Revolution. On the eve of the Civil War "all but one percent of U.S. slaves were

Table 1. Afro-American Population and Annual Growth Rates, 1790-1860

Year	Population	Average Annual Growth Rate (%)
1790	757,000	–
1800	1,002,000	2.80
1810	1,378,000	3.19
1820	1,772,000	2.51
1830	2,329,000	2.73
1840	2,874,000	2.10
1850	3,639,000	2.36
1860	4,442,000	2.00

Source: Reynolds Farley, *The Growth of the Black Population: A Study of Demographic Trends* (Chicago, 1970).

native-born and most of them were second, third, fourth, or fifth generation American."[29] Thus most Afro-Americans were exposed to the influences of Euro-American culture through a long period of residence in the land of their captivity. They tended to adjust to their new environment more rapidly, for example, than did their counterparts in the Caribbean.[30]

But did exposure to Euro-American culture, even over several generations, necessarily mean that Afro-Americans were completely divorced from their African heritage? For many years scholarly opinion assumed as much. The institution of slavery in America suppressed the obvious cultural expressions of African slaves. Under conditions of bondage they were unable to retain their languages, to continue important aspects of their material culture, or to practice their traditional religious beliefs. Thus the view that slavery stripped Africans of their cultural heritage had great currency among scholars until it was challenged by Melville J. Herskovits and Lorenzo D. Turner, among others. Herskovits and Turner argued, on the basis of extensive field research, that Africanisms—specific African cultural forms retained in the shape of either reinterpretations or syncretisms—still survived among New World populations of African descent after slavery had ended.[31] With the two points of view placing the issues in clear relief, subsequent scholarship has begun to resolve the question by stressing the dialectical relationship between the forces of acculturation and those of African cultural retention.[32] John Blassingame, for example, made just this point in *The Slave Community:*

> In spite of his disadvantages when compared to his Latin American counterpart, the American slave was able to retain many African cultural elements and an emotional contact with his motherland. This contact, however tenuous, enabled the slave to link European and African forms to create a distinctive culture.[33]

It is certain that knowledge of the Afro-American population, from which emigrants to Liberia were drawn, must go beyond mere statistics. The Liberian settlers included both emancipated slaves and members of the free Afro-

American community; both mulattoes and those of unmixed race; both urban and rural dwellers. The implications for Liberia of these and other variations among Afro-Americans cannot be safely underestimated.

Slavery and Afro-Americans

Virtually all nineteenth-century Afro-Americans were slaves at some point in their lives. By 1800 most slaves toiled on large plantations owned by wealthy planters in the rural South or Southwest. They were primarily field hands, cultivating staple crops like tobacco, sugar cane, or cotton. But even slavery had its variations. Slaveholders belonging to the planter class were in the minority. At least 88 percent of all slaveowners had fewer than twenty slaves; 72 percent, fewer than ten; and nearly 50 percent, fewer than five.[34] The more modest slaveholders often found it necessary to work side by side with their bondsmen in the fields, and often they employed the labor of their own families as well. Thus for some slaves—though admittedly not for most—life on a small rural farm was an alternative experience to the plantation regime stereotyped in Margaret Mitchell's *Gone with the Wind*.

Slavery also flourished in towns and cities. Urban centers grew in response to the combination of economic opportunities and favorable geographic locations in various places throughout the South. As the cities developed, their slave population increased as a result of the hiring out of skilled slaves on a contractual basis.[35] In many cities with industrial operations, skilled slave labor was highly valued. Richmond, Virginia, for example, relied heavily on slave labor in its tobacco and iron industries. Lott Cary worked as a common laborer at the Shochoe tobacco warehouse in Richmond in 1804; he sailed for Liberia seventeen years later, by then a skilled tobacconist.[36] By the nineteenth century, Afro-American craftsmanship was well-respected. Master cabinetmakers, like Tom Day of North Carolina; wrought-iron workers in Louisiana; and the many coopers, goldsmiths, tanners, and other artisans are some examples.[37]

Even on rural plantations slaves were not exclusively unskilled laborers. Slaves were used in all phases of plantation work, and certain jobs involved specialized training. When Mary Jones, of Walthourville, Georgia, needed shoes for her plantation workers in 1863, she chose to have a slave trained as a shoemaker. In a letter to her son she mentioned that "Robert leaves for Mount Vernon tomorrow, and kindly offers to take Tom with him, where he will work for four months at tanning and shoemaking, and by fall, I trust, will have gained sufficient knowledge to make the plantation shoes." Four months later Mary Jones was able to inform her son that the slave Tom "has quite the air of a *graduated tradesman*, and is tanning and making last preparatory to making shoes."[38]

The diversity of skill available in the slave community was of special relevance to the colonization movement. The American Colonization Society first concentrated on inducing members of the free Afro-American community to emigrate to Liberia voluntarily.[39] But once slaveholders were assured that the society posed no serious threat to the institution of slavery, many opted to use the organization for removing some of their slaves. Some slaveholders obviously saw a chance to rid themselves of old and unproductive dependents. Among the planter class, however, colonization was generally considered as a safe reward for faithful service. This attitude was consistent with the paternalism of prominent southern planters.[40]

General John Hartwell Cocke, of Bremo Bluff, Virginia, typified the paternal impulse that permeated the colonization movement. In 1833 he freed one of his slaves expressly for removal to Liberia. The general considered Peyton Skipwith worthy of emancipation and colonization because of his long and faithful service. Cocke also made a point of mentioning a few additional reasons for emancipating Skipwith. Peyton Skipwith, a skilled artisan, was a converted Christian who followed the principles of the temperance movement.[41] Slaveholding Southerners like General Cocke who endorsed colonization considered skill acquisition, conversion to Christianity, and morality as positive attributes for potential slave emigrants to Liberia. Thus along with the unlettered and the unskilled, there were more highly assimilated Afro-Americans among the Liberian immigrant population.

Free Afro-Americans

The earliest immigrants to Liberia were characterized by their status as "free people of color" in America. These pioneer immigrants played a key role in the formative years of Liberian colonization. Free Afro-Americans in the United States had increased in number from 59,466 in 1790 to 186,466 in 1810. By 1860 the U.S. Census Bureau reported a free Afro-American population of 488,000, of which 44 percent lived in the South Atlantic states and 46 percent were settled in the North.[42] Free Afro-Americans tended to reside in and around cities. There they took advantage of the relative anonymity of the urban environment and also the economic opportunities. Forty-seven percent of this population was urban by 1860, which meant, for example, that "they out-numbered slaves ten to one in Baltimore and 9,209 to 1,774 in Washington."[43] Cities like New Orleans and Richmond also had large communities of free Afro-Americans. Over time, members of this group accumulated property and maintained social connections with each other of lasting value.[44]

One conspicuous mark of the free Afro-American community was the high percentage of mulattoes. A precise statistical calculation is not possible;

however, sufficient qualitative evidence attests to the presence of persons with mixed racial ancestry among free Afro-Americans. Manumission was frequently the means used by slaveholders to offer a better life to their own mulatto offspring. The mulattoes were usually products of illicit relationships between slaveholders and female slaves. This was especially true in the gulfport area of the Lower South, where earlier Spanish and French influences contributed to a more relaxed racial climate. So common were extramarital unions across racial lines that the custom, called *placage*, achieved respectable status.[45] Other parts of the country had similar—albeit less accepted—social phenomena.

Euro-American fears of miscegenation—*placage* and other, similar practices notwithstanding—mounted in direct proportion to the growth of the Afro-American population. These fears were expressed within the evolving standards of the legal system. As early as 1640 the Virginia General Court set a precedent for the punishment of interracial coitus in the case of Hugh Davis. Davis was ordered by the court "to be soundly whipped, before an assembly of Negroes and others for abusing himself to the dishonor of God the shame of Christians, by defiling his body by lying with a Negro."[46] Where laws proved ineffective, informal social sanctions castigated violators. One man petitioned the American Colonization Society for permission to emigrate to Liberia. "My wife is a Quadroon of New Orleans," he declared. "We have been married five years and have two children, who being only one-eighth African, are blue-eyed, and flaxen haired; and nearly as 'pale-faced' as myself. Still, they are *coloured* and that is a word with tremendous import in North America!" Although he was established in his community, his neighbors constantly reminded him of his "transgressions against National feeling," and he feared "bequeathing to (his) children a hopeless degradation! I will go anywhere," he concluded, "to avoid so hateful an alternative."[47] The mulatto segment of the free Afro-American population symbolized the worst fears of a race-conscious society and were thus victimized for their complexion.

Lighter skin color may well have been the most visible manifestation of "free people," but it was certainly not the only one. The pressures of racism forced them to develop survival techniques of enduring significance. A fundamental response to racism by free Afro-Americans was the formation of separate religious institutions. The appearance of itinerant preachers moving from plantation to plantation was the start of the trend toward Afro-Americans' control over their assimilation of Christianity.[48] Eventually separate church congregations were formed in urban areas. Initially such churches were organized when Afro-Americans faced exclusion or discrimination from Euro-American churches. Segregated and denied any role of leadership in the ecclesiastical structure, Afro-Americans chose religious independence whenever the option was possible. It is not surprising that the free Afro-American community led the way.[49]

As free Afro-Americans worked to gain institutional control over their religious lives, they made similar attempts to solve secular problems through organizational unity. Their need for racial unity was compelling in a society that found few reasons to appreciate their presence.[50] Free Afro-Americans generally recognized "social uplifting" as the way to erase the stigma of slavery. Thus benevolent societies, fraternal orders, and self-help organizations mushroomed wherever Afro-Americans lived as freemen. The development of grass-roots leadership was the most significant by-product of this activity. In every case, the organization's goal was to provide protection, support, and encouragement to individual members.

As these different organizations functioned to meet various needs, the issue of color became a matter of conflict. The Brown Fellowship Society of Charleston, South Carolina, formed in 1790, limited membership only to mulattoes. Subsequently the Humane Brotherhood, in which membership was immediately restricted to "free Dark Men," was organized in the same city.[51] The divisive conflict reappeared in other situations. When the separatist African Methodist Episcopal Church held its first election to fill the position of bishop, Daniel Coker was nominated on the strength of his education and talents.[52] Some church leaders objected to Coker, however, because he was a mulatto. The controversy over his color was probably instrumental in his decision to withdraw his candidacy and emigrate to Liberia in 1820.[53]

Color distinctions among Afro-Americans were based on attitudes towards status in the larger society. William Kellogg, a North Carolina mulatto, was afraid to emigrate to Liberia because of "the prejudice that exists between Blacks and Mulattoes in the United States." He decided that he would rather remain in America and stay in "the hands of my superiors than [fall] into the hands of my inferiors." Kellogg was willing to consider emigration only to a separate mulatto colony, and he reminded the Euro-American officials of the American Colonization Society that there were "a great many mulattoes within these United States, who are stronger allied to the white man than they were to the Blacks."[54] Sociologist C. Eric Lincoln explained the situation well when he stated that "in the context of a distribution of status and power that implied the freedom of all white men and the susceptibility to chattel slavery of all Negroes, color became the visual rule of thumb, for the assignment of 'place' or status. . . . It is no less ironic for all its inevitability that Negroes, who were (and who remain) the prime subjects of color discrimination, adopted color as an index of social worth."[55]

The pioneer settlers and subsequent immigrants to Liberia all shared the legacy of American slavery. Some arrived straight from the plantation fields, while others came after living on the margins of American society as freedmen. In either case, as settlers they were confronted with a new and unfamiliar reality in Africa. When novelist Richard Wright migrated from Tennessee to Chicago in the 1930s he was struck by the strangeness of his new surroundings. Wright found that his responses to northern urban life were conditioned by his southern background.[56] Some one hundred years earlier, Afro-American immigrants to Liberia had reacted in similar ways. Although they left America in search of denied opportunities, the settlers could not escape the imprint of their American background.

Part Two/Transition

Afro-American immigration to Liberia might well be viewed romantically as a kind of homecoming. Returning to the land of their forebears had a certain Biblical quality about it. Certainly the immigrants thought so. They believed that their fate would have a profound influence on African people the world over. The immigrants discovered, however, that the transition from life in America to life in Africa was far from smooth. It would severely test the depth of their religious and political commitments.

2/Mortality and Mission

At present we would request our friends not to be discouraged. The Board laments the unfortunate issue of this
first effort, but they had no right to calculate upon the
absences of those disasters, difficulties, and disappointments, which attend all human affairs, and which are
ordered, or permitted, to attend them, for purposes we
may not see, we cannot see, we cannot doubt . . . . To these
dispensations of the Almighty we bow in submission and at
the same time resolve to go in the path of duty.

—Minutes of the Board of Managers
of the American Colonization Society,
October 16, 1820,
American Colonization Society Papers

We should not content ourselves with what has been
accomplished, greater and wider fields of usefulness are
daily opening before us while the spirits of our fathers are
exultant over the realization of their hopes for which they
fought, bled and died to lay the foundation of our political
structure upon which we are to build and perpetuate. Let
us catch the inspiration that moved them to the noble task
of sacrificing life itself for the good of the race and look
forward not for today but for years to come when we
shall be called upon to stand more boldly among nations
on the battle ground for Africa's redemption.

—From the Inaugural Address
of His Excellency J. J. Cheeseman,
President, Republic of Liberia,
January 1, 1894

Once the American Colonization Society was formed in Washington, the
leadership tried to win the support of the federal government for its program
of Afro-American colonization. A consequence of the earlier slave-trade prohibition gave the society a way of approaching its objective. In 1807 a federal
law was passed making illegal the further importation of African slaves to the
United States. The American Naval Squadron then began to stop vessels in

the Atlantic Ocean to search for human contraband. Those ships discovered to be carrying slaves were then escorted to American ports, where admiralty courts tried the cases. As more and more ships were condemned as slavers, a problem developed, namely: What should be done with the recaptured Africans liberated by the legal proceedings?

Charles Fenton Mercer offered a solution that was compatible with the aims of the American Colonization Society. In 1818, in his capacity as congressman from Virginia, Mercer proposed a bill that would "transfer the responsibility for disposing of rescued Africans from the state to the federal government."[1] His legislative proposal called for the establishment of a government agency in West Africa where rescued Africans would be resettled. The president would be authorized to make all necessary arrangements, while Congress was to appropriate one hundred thousand dollars for the project. On March 3, 1819, the bill became law as "An Act in addition to the acts prohibiting the Slave Trade."[2] The American Colonization Society encouraged President James Monroe to interpret his mandate liberally. The society hoped he would use his authority to purchase territory for a colony. Such a colony could then receive Afro-American immigrants, as well as newly recaptured Africans.

Monroe pondered the implications of forming an American colony in Africa. His Cabinet advisors raised legal questions about the constitutionality of the United States buying territory in foreign lands. Their strong reservations forced Monroe to move cautiously. Finally he agreed to start the program, but only after the American Colonization Society accepted the direct responsibility for purchasing land. Once this technical distinction was clarified, Monroe considered the government role to be only facilitating the resettlement of recaptured Africans. In 1819 he announced that two federal agents and a representative of the American Colonization Society, along with a company of laborers and artisans, were being sent to Africa. The officials had orders to establish a government station on the African coast.[3]

Thus the first concrete step towards creating a colony in Africa to receive Afro-Americans was accomplished by sleight of hand. The American Colonization Society maneuvered the federal government into providing assistance to its program. The special problem posed by recaptured Africans set in motion the colonization of Afro-Americans. In any event, the society was delighted by Monroe's decision. It later honored him by voting to name the first permanent settlement of the colony Monrovia.

"Planting the Colony"

On January 31, 1820, hundreds of well-wishers gathered on a pier in New York City to witness the sailing of the ship *Elizabeth*. The typically cold winter weather did not keep people away, for they had come to witness the start of a very special endeavor. A company of eighty-six Afro-Americans had been organized by Samuel Bacon, a government agent, with the help of his assistant, John P. Bankson. The American Colonization Society had selected Samuel Crozer to accompany the group on their voyage. Although the federal government viewed the Afro-Americans as workers hired to construct a government station in Africa, no one at the pier had any doubts about their real purpose. The "workers" were free Afro-American volunteers from New York, Philadelphia, Baltimore, Washington, and Petersburg, Virginia. Women and children made up more than half of the company and this made its official designation even more questionable. Samuel Bacon's explanation of the composition of the company to a skeptical secretary of the navy was that the men refused to go without their families.[4] In reality, the company was the first group of pioneer settlers to emigrate to Africa under the auspices of the American Colonization Society.

The Reverend Daniel Coker was among the volunteer "workers" recruited. He knew not only the real purpose of the *Elizabeth* company but also its historic significance. Coker kept a personal diary of the experience, which gave a settler's perspective on that first attempt to plant an American colony in West Africa. The voyage began with both the settlers and their Euro-American companions in high spirits. At last the mission was underway! But harmony was not destined to characterize the remaining days at sea. Tensions developed as soon as the ship's captain and the agents tried to exercise authority over the settlers. Daniel Coker assumed the role of mediator in one tense situation that threatened to explode into an open rebellion. The captain and a settler became embroiled in an argument so intense that pistols were almost drawn. That evening Coker confided to his diary the emotional state that followed the incident:

> After things had a little subsided, Mr. Bacon came to me as I was waiting by the cabin door, bathed in tears, said to me, "Brother Coker, this is an awful judgment upon us; come, let us go below and have religious worship." We did so, with the emigrants. He said much to the purpose; after he was done, I spoke with them in his absence for about a half hour; I felt that it was not labor lost—it was a weeping time.[5]

Daniel Coker's comments must have had a more telling effect on the settlers than did Samuel Bacon's, for as time passed, the settlers pressured Coker to assume a more formal leadership role on their behalf. Despite the urgings of his supporters, Coker refused to lead a challenge against the authority of the Euro-American agents. He argued that it was "the height of ingratitude to manifest any distrust of the sincerity of the Agents, after such proof that they have given, not to say anything of their having left friends and the comforts of a civilized life."[6] At that point Coker's popularity among the settlers began to diminish rapidly. By the end of the passage to West Africa his steadfast loyalty to the agents had estranged him from many of his peers.

Reaching the coast of West Africa did not end the causes of disunity; in fact, the most trying times were still ahead. The *Elizabeth* landed in Sierra Leone after a passage of only thirty days. The entire company proceeded directly to Sherbro Island, where temporary shelter had been prepared by John Kizell. Kizell, who resided at Campelar, Sherbro Island, was a former associate of Paul Cuffee. Samuel Bacon described Campelar as "a village of about twenty houses built in native style, situated on nearly the east end of Sherbro Island."[7] The decision to stay at Campelar was a tragic mistake. The area was unhealthy because of the lack of fresh water and the low, swampy land. By May 1820, just five months after leaving New York City, all three agents and twelve of the eighty-six original settlers had died on Campelar.[8]

The conflicts that had surfaced during the ocean voyage reappeared with greater intensity as the death toll mounted on Sherbro Island. A growing number of settlers refused to accept any authority but their own; unity of purpose gave way to individual interests. Just before Samuel Crozer died he formally transferred his power as the society agent to the able Daniel Coker. Suddenly Coker had the authority to exercise leadership; unfortunately, he no longer held the respect of all the settlers. Thus faced with a crisis situation, Coker decided to evacuate to the British colony at Freetown everyone who would follow him. At Freetown the Governor permitted the demoralized and sickly survivors of Campelar to stay in the elevated section of Fourah Bay.

The first expedition to plant an American colony had ended in disaster. Yet both the society and the Campelar survivors still hoped to accomplish their goal. When news of the tragic events reached America, the society immediately prepared to dispatch a second company. Shaken by the experience at Campelar, Daniel Coker nevertheless continued to have faith in the ultimate rewards of sacrifice: "Moses was I think permitted to see the promised land but not to enter in. I think it likely that I shall not be permitted to see our expected earthly Canaan. But this will be of but small moment so that some thousand of Africas children are safely landed . . . ."[9]

The hiatus at Fourah Bay provided a time for introspection by the remaining settlers. The idealistic rhetoric of colonization undoubtedly paled before the reality of their first turbulant months in Africa. The days passed slowly; there were more deaths and no news from America. The settlers began to draw apart, and splinter groups were formed. The excuse given for these separations was religious. Daniel Coker worried about the pattern, but he tried to remain optimistic, hoping that "notwithstanding this . . . we shall get along in harmony."[10]

On March 8, 1821, the first, badly needed supplies and reinforcements arrived in Freetown on the brig *Nautilus*. The second company of settlers, however, exacerbated the problem of religious division. Before their departure from America the baptist members of the *Nautilus* company had agreed to form a church congregation. During their journey to Sierra Leone the congregation worshipped together under the leadership of the Reverend Lott Cary.[11] The American Colonization Society sent two Episcopalians, Joseph R. Andrus and Christian Wiltberger, to replace the deceased Samuel Crozer. Ephraim Bacon and Jonathan B. Winn, the new government agents, also arrived. When Andrus called a religious meeting of all the settlers at Fourah Bay, some refused to attend and instead organized a separate meeting. A frustrated Daniel Coker wrote in his diary: "O Bigotry thou art no friend to religion or colonizing. I cannot see why such pains should be taken to oppose the Episcopal Church. I fear that no good will result from this great and important undertaking. I feel it to be a duty to enter this on this journal and bear testimony against the spirit. I wish to see every one enjoy the privilege of worshipping God according to the dictates of their own conscience. But this spirit I must condemn."[12]

Although problems of conflict and disunity persisted, the arrival of the *Nautilus* did spur a renewed effort to find a permanent settlement site. Andrus and Ephraim Bacon traveled east from Freetown along the coast in search of land. On April 12, 1821, they signed a treaty agreement with King Jack Ben, of Grand Bassa, on the Grain Coast. The officials of the American Colonization Society in Washington received the treaty but refused to ratify it. The society's board of managers objected to a treaty article that stipulated that no one in the proposed settlement "shall be permitted by letter, signal or in any other way to give notice to ships of war respecting slave vessels on our coast, so as to cause them to be seized, nor shall they be permitted to use anything but persuasion to cause us to abandon the slave trade."[13] In a fit of pique, the society dispatched Dr. Eli Ayres to relieve Andrus of his authority as principal agent. Ayres arrived in November 1821 to find only Christian Wiltberger awaiting him in Freetown. Both Andrus and Winn had died, and Bacon had already left Sierra Leone in extremely poor health.

Ayres saw that the situation at Fourah Bay was deteriorating. He was determined to quickly find a suitable location for an independent colony. When the U.S.S. *Alligator* made a port call in Freetown, Ayres enlisted the aid of its naval commander. Lieutenant Robert F. Stockton agreed to transport the agent along the coast to facilitate his efforts to secure land. They proceeded along the coast, west of Grand Bassa, and, using both a threat and gifts, finally negotiated an agreement for land with the local inhabitants of Cape Mesurado. This agreement suceeded in winning the endorsement of the society managers in Washington.[14] Although a new beginning was under way,

Figure 2. Providence Island, Original Site of First Settler Arrival in Liberia on April 25, 1822.

the old problems of disunity did not evaporate. The relationship between the settlers and their Euro-American companions continued to be tenuous.

The Physical Surroundings

On April 25, 1822, the first Afro-Americans set foot on Liberian soil. After a solemn ceremony of thanksgiving, they named their temporary haven Providence Island. The agents organized immediately to occupy the adjacent mainland; there, in Monrovia, the first permanent settlement was carved out of the thick forest. The task of colonization was formidable by any nineteenth-century standard. Even after the first twenty-five years of immigration, the American Colonization Society could only claim that the colony included a few modest enclaves dotting a two-hundred-eighty-mile coastline. The new environment made the transition from America to Africa a constant struggle. Only the deep sense of mission among the immigrants kept the vast majority from abandoning the colony during its initial period of settlement.

In 1822 neither the society nor its agents knew anything substantial about the country they would call Liberia. Most contemporary maps simply identified the area as a part of the Grain Coast (see map 1). The settlers became familiar with the physical environment of their new home only after years of residence and exploration. New—often daily—experiences had to be

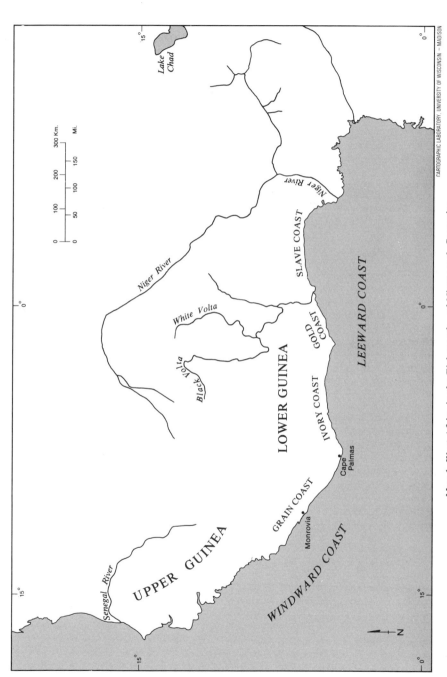

Map 1. West Africa in the Eighteenth and Nineteenth Centuries

faced by the settlers. The progress of the colony during the transition period depended heavily on accurate information about the surroundings.

The settlers soon discovered that travel would never be easy, even to areas that were not too distant. The ocean surf that pounded the shore was rough and dangerous. Even experienced ship captains were known to avoid stops there in favor of natural harbors further east. Although a number of rivers that flowed down from the interior reached the coast, lagoons and sand bars usually impeded direct access from the ocean. Moreover, beyond the coast most waterways were obstructed by frequent rapids and waterfalls. Overland travel was no less difficult because of dense vegetation. Liberia lies within the rain-forest belt of West Africa. High forest growth typified the coastal plain in the nineteenth century. Human occupation and agriculture altered the pattern in just a few places, causing secondary growth, or low bush, to replace the high forest.[15]

But travel was not the major preoccupation of the settlers at first. They had to lay the foundations for the settlement in anticipation of subsequent immigrants. Clearing the bush, constructing shelters, and building fortifications were the primary responsibilities. The prevailing climatic conditions of Liberia, especially the presence or absence of rain, hampered the progress of the work schedule. From April to November of every year there was heavy precipitation, averaging close to two hundred inches annually along the littoral. This rainy season was followed by a long dry spell, which usually lasted through March. During the dry season the harmattan brought the dry Saharan air flow across Liberia. Both temperatures and relative humidity levels were high throughout the year. This tropical climate pattern also affected the disease environment.

Twenty-four companies of settlers landed during the rainy-season months before 1847. They often found no adequate housing ready for them. Complaints about the spread of disease and death filled the pages of many of their letters to the United States. Lott Cary, an active settler leader, believed that "the sickness of newcomers hitherto has been greatly increased in consequence of the very unfavorable season of the year in which they leave America . . . . Send them out in the fall, and I think, that the sickness will be very light, and, in some constitutions, altogether avoided."[16] One society agent, Dr. J. W. Lugenbeel, noted that it was necessary for him to order some industrious settlers not to work in the rain against the best interest of their health.[17] Heavy rainfall also worsened the erosion and leaching of topsoil. Only with time and experience did the settlers learn to raise food crops with reliability.

Laterite and swamp soil were generally found on the Liberian coast. Both types were characterized by "a shallow layer of humus, by a low humus content, by high acidity and by deficiency in magnesium and calcium."[18]

Intensive agriculture would have required the use of fertilizers. Africans had already developed the technique of slash-and-burn cultivation to overcome the problem of poor soils. For the settlers on Cape Mesurado, agriculture was further hindered by the ubiquitous large, white rocks. One settler attempted to raise a crop of rice on the rocky, elevated ground of the Cape Mesurado promontory. "The industrious proprietor was unable to save enough rice to replace his seed."[19]

No problem was more devastating for the early settlers in Liberia than the disease environment. The tropical climate encouraged the spread of infectious diseases that left most individuals suffering from one or more physical ailments. The chronic disease that affected the lives of most settlers was malaria. The symptoms of malaria were physical debility, severe chills, and fever. The disease was so prevalent in the nineteenth century that Europeans called it African fever.[20] The actual cause of malaria was not discovered until the latter part of the century. Before the female anopheles mosquito was identified as the true vector of malaria by Sir Ronald Ross, many false theories were advanced. Suggested causes ranged from human effluvia and marsh miasmata to excessive personal habits of drunkenness and overeating.[21] Thus an understanding of the basic relationship between host, vector, and victim so important for effectively combatting malaria was lacking throughout most of the nineteenth century.

The impact of disease on Liberian settlers was expressed by the shockingly high mortality rate. Although 4,571 Afro-Americans immigrated to Liberia during the first twenty-three years, the Liberian census of 1843 reported only 2,388 persons living in that year.[22] High mortality from infectious diseases was largely responsible for the retardation of demographic growth during the period.[23] Society officials attributed over 45 percent of all deaths in the colony before 1844 to fever. Many persons died because there was no effective medical care. The society frequently appointed doctors as agents; however, they were forced to devote much of their time to nonmedical matters. Among the settlers less than a dozen persons had any recognized medical training.[24]

Most settlers were forced to rely solely on their own folk medicine. In the United States such knowledge had long offered the first line of defense against disease among Afro-Americans.[25] Herbs and other plants were used because of their recognized medicinal qualities. Liberian settlers also employed such techniques. As early as 1821 Daniel Coker mentioned in his diary that "fever tea" was used as a treatment for the symptoms of African fever.[26] The tea probably blocked dehydration and thereby reduced the body temperature of the patient. Years later, information about herbal remedies was still circulating among the settlers. News spread about one woman who had cured herself of dropsy in the chest with a mixture made by combining a boiled garden-parsley root with gin, which she administered in periodic doses.[27]

In the end, only their strong religious spirit of perserverance offered solace to the settlers in the face of a relentlessly deadly environment. During the transition period, 22 percent of all immigrants died in the first year of their arrival, while the central death rate for the adult population (ages 26 through 45) ranged between 60 and 90 deaths per thousand per year.[28] In every case these figures were translated into personal agony for individuals and families. It is little wonder that the very fact of survival has come to represent a clear sign of providential blessing in the national ethos of Liberia.[29]

The Human Environment

The complexity of the African human environment was initially bewildering to the settlers. Popular American stereotypes about Africans clouded their perceptions, but the demands of survival made real knowledge of African life and customs necessary.[30] The settlers gained an awareness of African cultural diversity only after the passing of time and many painful experiences. Their being strangers put them at a disadvantage.

Sixteen different African ethnic groups were living in Liberia by the nineteenth century. The settlers soon observed the linguistic variety among their new neighbors. In fact, three major divisions of the Niger-Congo language family made up the African population. Kru, predominant throughout the southeast, was spoken by the Glebo, Krahn, Kru, Bassa, Belle, and Dei (Dey). Mande, which predominated in the west and northwest, was spoken by the Mano, Dan (Gio), Kpelle, Loma, Bandi, Mende, Vai, and Mandinka (Mandingo). Finally, Mel was spoken by the Kissi and Gola, who lived in western Liberia adjacent to the Sierra Leone border (see map 2).[31]

Persistent migration from the northern savanna region accounted for the presence of Africans in Liberia. Virtually every group has retained oral traditions that emphasize the migration of ancestors. The Vai, for example, have traditions that explain their presence along the western coast of Liberia. Sometime in the fifteenth century the ruler of Timukutu sent the first of their group southward to hunt. Following their return, the ruler Va Kamara the Elder sent a larger party of hunters and warriors out under the leadership of his son, Small Va Kamara. This group succeeded in reaching the coast after a long and arduous journey through the forest. The traditions indicate an essentially peaceful acceptance by the Dei people already present there and the creation of the Vai Tewo chiefdom. It is quite probable that this tradition represents the consolidation of migrations by different Mande-speaking people in the savanna rather than one isolated event.[32]

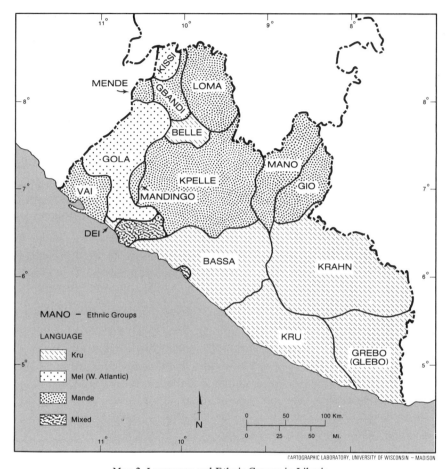

Map 2. Languages and Ethnic Groups in Liberia

   As more and more people moved into the Liberian forest, hunting and gathering activites were supplemented by agriculture. Rice cultivation was particularly important for many groups. In time, trade opportunities developed as well. The arrival of Portuguese traders on the coast during the sixteenth century provided a lucrative economic alternative for Africans. The coastal zone became the focus of competition and conflict among different groups. Trade networks emerged, which had an impact on political developments. The Mandinka, long noted for their commercial skills, took advantage of rising demands for scarce products. They established an extensive trading network across the ecological border of savanna and forest zones and then extended it to the coast. Trading systems like that of the Mandinka have been described by economic historians as trade diasporas. Small numbers of skilled traders served as cross-cultural brokers, facilitating the exchange of goods and services over long distances.[33] The Mandinka were active entreprenuers, but they also had other influences on the people among whom they lived and worked. As Moslems, they attempted to spread their religious beliefs and were particularly successful among the Vai. Contemporary reports suggest that Vai conversion to Islam came in the early 1800s.[34] The Mandinka were also skilled craftsmen, specializing in blacksmithing, weaving, and pottery. They often served local rulers as advisors, and they often used their high status to their own political advantage.

The major population movements within Liberia were more or less completed by the late eighteenth century. Trade interests directed towards the coast, however, did encourage secondary movements of conquest and consolidation by interior groups. The founding of the town of Bopulu, fifty miles north of Cape Mesurado, was motivated by such considerations. It was the forest counterpart to the savanna trading center of Musardu.[35] Control of Bopulu was in the hands of a confederation that linked a number of ethnically diverse peoples; among them the Mandinka traders had a prominent role.[36] The extent of the diversity was apparent in the rise of Bopulu's most powerful chief during the first half of the nineteenth century. Sao Boso (known as Boatswain by the Afro-American settlers) was, according to oral traditions, from the Mandinka clan called Kamara. He was raised, however, by a Bandi chief and thus claimed legitimacy through association as well as heredity.[37] From his position of power in Bopulu, Sao Boso controlled the trade to the western coast until his death in 1836. Large political states were not common in Liberia. The Condo confederation, centered at Bopulu, was a conspicuous exception, but even it suffered from the tendency towards decentralization. Factors related to the organization of traditional Liberian cultural life not only account for the absence of large territorial states but help to provide background for the dynamics of African-settler relations (discussed in detail in chapter 6).[38]

The most significant territorial unit in the daily lives of the African population was the town or village settlement. It was in such settlements, divided into separate quarters, that Africans resided, within related households that were usually polygynous. The town chief governed the affairs of his community in council with the quarter elders. The rights and responsibilities of individuals within the town varied according to their social status. In the nineteenth century at least three classes existed: freemen, pawns, and slaves. Among the freemen manifestations of wealth included wives, cattle, and slaves. In abundance, these scarce resources could be translated into power if offered in exchange for political allegiance. This process became the basis for a patron-client relationship.

The slaves and pawns were dependent classes; the degree to which the dependency was permanent distinguished one from the other. Famines, epidemics, and similar extraordinary events might force people to give up some of their rights as freemen in order to secure protection they could not provide for themselves. Under conditions of famine, for example, parents might pawn their children to more fortunate neighbors so as to guarantee their survival. Unlike slaves, however, kinsmen retained the right to reclaim pawned relatives. Once Afro-American settlers began arriving in Liberia, many Africans "pawned" their children to settler families so that they might be educated. Thus the ward system that evolved from this practice became an important channel of contact and communication between the settlers and their African neighbors.

The dispersed town settlements were linked by larger political organizations, or chiefdoms, which varied in size and duration during the nineteenth century. Chiefdoms were controlled by paramount chiefs, who rose to power by exploiting their ability to secure the allegiance of lesser chiefs. Political allegiance at the chiefdom level was often a fluid phenomenon, depending more on the personal charisma of individual chiefs than on any structural reality. A vital element of such charisma was the power that derived from ritual authority. Throughout most of Liberia ritual authority flowed from secret societies, most notably the Poro Society. Secret societies were powerful institutions of socialization and social control that relied on ritual authority to reinforce their sanctions. Separate societies existed for men and women. New initiates received specialized instruction during adolescence while secluded in "bush schools." Membership was lifelong and represented an enduring bond of association that transcended more limited ties of kinship or territorial affiliations. The mystery and the social role of African secret societies paralleled those of the settlers' fraternal orders. In both cases ritual leadership was generally, if not always, connected to political leadership.

Settler Society Profile, 1843

The early settlers grappled with the unfamiliar physical and human environment of Liberia. Their problems of adjustment to Africa were somewhat minimized by the establishment of small enclaves. The settlements of the colony stood apart from the African population for the most part. By choosing limited isolation, the settlers were able to reconstruct much of their former American life style. In time, compromises brought the settlers much closer to Africans; their initial isolation only delayed an inevitable process. A census of the colony taken by Society officials in 1843 gives a picture of the settler society prior to the creation of the republic.[39] The census refers to only one year; thus no inferences about change over time can be made on the basis of these data alone.

Table 2. Settler Household Status by Origin, 1843

Status	Origin Inside the Colony	Origin Outside the Colony	Total
Head of household	1	387	388
Non-head of household	651	1,349	2,000
Total	652	1,736	2,388

Source: U.S., Congress , Senate, *U.S. Navy Department, tables showing the number of Emigrants and recaptured Africans sent to the colony of Liberia by the government of the United States . . . together with a census of the colony and report of its commerce, &c. September, 1843: Senate Document No. 150,* 28th Cong., 2d sess., 1845.

The Liberian colony was marked by the influence of annual immigration. New immigrants joined the colony every year from 1820 until well into the twentieth century. Of the total population of 2,388 persons in 1843, 652, or less than one third, had been born in Liberia. That is to say, four years before the Republic of Liberia was founded, 73 percent of the population was foreign-born. This factor had far-reaching implications. For one thing, only one head of a family household in 1843 had been born in the colony (see table 2). The values of American life were passed down through the family structure and were reinforced with each new arrival from overseas.

The pattern of annual immigration also produced a distinct occupational hierarchy among the settlers. Until 1827 the society was able to send only free Afro-American volunteers to Liberia. The top of the occupational hierarchy comprised professionals and those who held appointed positions. This was a small elite, numbering only twenty-two persons in 1843, all of whom were former free Afro-Americans. After 1827 emancipated slaves and

Table 3. Settler Occupations by Education, 1843

Occupation	Education Educated	Education Literate	Education Semiliterate	Education Illiterate	Total
Agricultural	0	18	2	168	188
Appointive	6	2	0	0	8
Artisan	4	15	0	106	125
Commercial	13	21	0	14	48
Professional	18	4	0	0	22
Semiskilled	1	75	46	284	406
Unskilled	0	9	2	267	278
Miscellaneous	0	1	0	3	4
Total	42	145	50	842	1,079

Source: U.S., Congress, Senate, *U.S. Navy Department, tables showing the number of Emigrants and recaptured Africans sent to the colony of Liberia by the government of the United States . . . together with a census of the colony and a report of its commerce, &c. September, 1843: Senate Document No. 150,* 28th Cong., 2d sess., 1845.

Table 4. Settler Occupations by Sex Ratio, 1843

	Sex			
Occupation	*Male*	*Female*	*Unknown*	*Total*
Agricultural	184	6	2	192
Appointive	8	0	0	8
Artisan	49	75	2	126
Commercial	49	0	0	49
Professional	20	1	1	22
Semiskilled	274	127	11	412
Unskilled	175	101	4	280
Miscellaneous	3	1	0	4
Total	762	311	20	1,093

Source: U.S., Congress, Senate, *U.S. Navy Department, tables showing the number of Emigrants and recaptured Africans sent to the colony of Liberia by the government of the United States . . . together with a census of the colony and a report of its commerce, &c. September, 1843: Senate Document No. 150*, 28th Cong., 2d sess., 1845.

recaptured Africans were a part of the immigration process. Artisans and semiskilled and unskilled workers were as likely to be free Afro-Americans as they were emancipated slaves or recaptured Africans. Literacy as a function of education restricted the top occupational opportunities in the colony, but neither sex nor education was a barrier in any other category. (see tables 3 and 4).

The 1843 census listed seventy-eight different occupations—ranging from governor and supreme court judge to schoolteacher, seamstress, washerwoman, and laborer (see appendix A). Even though more emancipated slaves entered Liberia after 1843, there were still many skilled individuals in the population. In 1854 Colonel Montgomery Bell, of Nashville, Tennessee, liberated fifty of his slaves and paid their passage to Liberia. The men in the group were all skilled ironworkers. William McLain, of the American Colonization Society, noted that "they thoroughly understand the business, and have among them miners, colliers, moulders, and are fully competent to build a furnace for making iron, and carrying it on themselves."[40] The pool of skilled manpower was there; mortality and the pattern of dispersed settlements reduced the successful utilization of available human resources.

The American Colonization Society raised funds to support its colony in Liberia by organizing state auxiliary chapters. Some state auxiliaries insisted on using their contributions to organize separate settlements to accommodate emigrants from their state only. The Bassa Cove settlement, at the mouth of the St. John's River, was founded in 1834 on land purchased by the Young Men's Colonization Society of Pennsylvania.[41] The Sinoe settlement was founded in 1838 by the Mississippi State Colonization Society in order to relocate slaves from Mississippi.[42] The most elaborate effort by

Table 5. Settler Population Distribution by Settlement, 1843

Settlement	Number	Percentage
Coastal		
Bassa Cove	124	5
Edina	202	9
Marshall	142	6
Monrovia	912	38
Sinoe	79	3
Interior		
Bexley	135	6
Caldwell	311	13
Millsburg	220	9
New Georgia	263	11
Total	2,388	100

Source: U.S., Congress, Senate, *U.S. Navy Department, tables showing the number of Emigrants and recaptured Africans sent to the colony of Liberia by the government of the United States . . . together with a census of the colony and a report of its commerce, &c. September, 1843: Senate Document No. 150*, 28th Cong., 2d sess., 1845.

a state auxiliary was the Cape Palmas settlement, organized by the Maryland State Colonization Society in 1831.[43] Cape Palmas and Monrovia became the most important enclaves on the coast. The other settlements suffered from a lack of sustained financial support and limited numbers of immigrants (see table 5 and map 3). Monrovia was the first settlement, and it had the largest population. The 1843 census indicates that Monrovia was significant for more than its concentration of population.

The concept of central place helps to explain the role of Monrovia in relation to the other enclaves. Central-place theory first developed in the context of town geography.[44] As a theoretical approach to the study of spatial dispersion, its application can be much wider. For central-place theorists there is a basic ordering principal in human societies that is centralistic in nature. In geographical terms, this centrality is "the relative importance of a place with regard to the region surrounding it, or the degree to which the town exercises central functions."[45] Administrative and economic activities are among the important central functions. Thus multifunctional places that offer a wide variety of goods and services will become central places exerting influence and even control over other, functionally less diverse places within their orbit. To the extent that more than one place within a particular region possesses the ability to provide multifunctions, there will be competing central places.

Among the settler enclaves in Liberia, Monrovia was the central place, it had no serious rivals until after the republic was founded.[46] It had the advantage of being the administrative center for the colony and the most

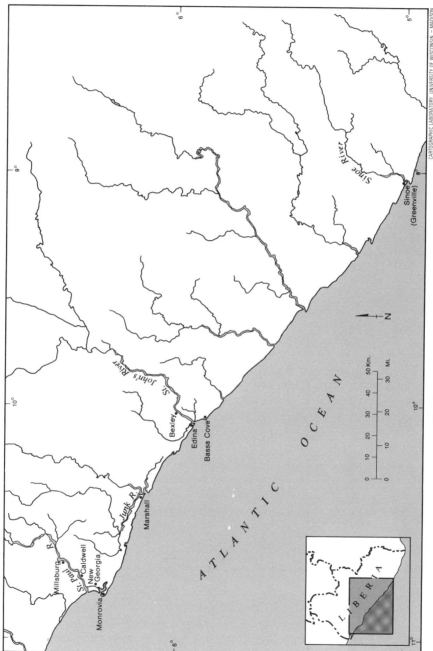

Map 3. Liberian Settler Enclaves, 1843

Table 6. Settler Occupation Distribution by Settlement, 1843

	Settlement									
	Coastal						Interior			
Occupation	Bassa Cove	Edina	Marshall	Monrovia	Sinoe	Bexley	Caldwell	Millsburg	New Georgia	Total
Agricultural	4	6	9	5	1	22	47	25	73	192
Appointive	0	1	0	6	0	1	0	0	0	8
Artisan	6	5	1	84	4	1	15	5	5	126
Commercial	5	8	7	18	2	1	4	4	0	49
Professional	0	4	1	11	1	1	2	2	0	22
Semiskilled	23	25	19	238	15	13	32	28	19	412
Unskilled	14	18	31	98	17	11	37	31	23	280
Miscellaneous	0	0	0	3	0	0	1	0	1	4
Total	52	67	68	463	40	50	128	95	120	1,093

Source: U.S., Congress, Senate, U.S. Navy Department, tables showing the number of Emigrants and recaptured Africans sent to the colony of Liberia by the government of the United States . . . together with a census of the colony and a report of its commerce, &c. September, 1843: Senate Document No. 150, 28th Cong., 2d sess., 1845.

active commercial community along the coast. Compared with other settlements, Monrovia attracted the most highly educated and thus most of the occupational elite. More than half of all professionals and artisans were living in Monrovia in 1843 (see table 6). The central place also attracts the dependent as well as the gifted. More than half of all Monrovians in 1843 were illiterate.

Society officials hoped for an even distribution of immigrants among the various settlements. The attraction of Monrovia was enigmatic, even to those officials resident in the town. In a letter to American Colonization Society, Dr. J. W. Lugenbeel described an incident he found difficult to explain: ". . . just before I was about to leave, several [settlers] . . . came to the government house, and entered a solemn protest against going any further than Monrovia. . . . No kind of argument respecting the greater advantage of a location in some farm district could prevail with [them]."[47] Lugenbeel was puzzled by the apparent appeal that Monrovia had for new settlers. "It is really astonishing that newcomers . . . should prefer to remain in this place, with one fourth of an acre of rocky land—a town lot; when they might have ten acres of as good land as any other in the world, in a much more healthy location, and altogether more pleasant than this place."[48] He could only offer his own impression:

> I cannot account for their strange choice in any other way, than by attributing it to ignorance, giving rise to fanciful notions excited by seeing some fine looking houses, occupied by well dressed persons, who live in pretty handsome style; and to the erroneous statements of lazy loungers, who try to persuade them to remain here, from self-interested motives; of which class of persons—drones in the community and obstacles to the prosperity of Liberia, Monrovia has more than its share.[49]

Other settlements were threatened with the loss of prospective immigrants by Monrovia's popularity. In 1850 a company of thirty-one settlers arrived on the ship *Edgar* bound for settlement in Bexley, Grand Bassa. Some Monrovians attempted to persuade them to remain in the town, and only the fact that their provisions had been sent directly to Bexley made them move on.[50] Two years earlier R. E. Murray, a prominent settler in Sinoe, had recommended that immigrants destined for Greenville be sent directly so that large numbers would not decide to stay in Monrovia.[51]

Agents and Settlers: Discord and Controversy

Colonial developments in Liberia produced an almost steady stream of complaints to the society managers in Washington. Most problems within the colony centered around settler resistance to the authority of appointed Euro-

American agents. Supervision by Euro-Americans was never part of the Afro-American concept of emigration and colonization.

The first major crisis occurred during the administration of Jehudi Ashmun.[52] Many settlers in Monrovia were dissatisfied with Ashmun's policy of allocating town lots. They accused him of favoritism in assigning choice spots. They also criticized his policy of rationing provisions from the colonial store. The discordant atmosphere led to a written remonstrance by the settlers which they sent to the board of managers on December 5, 1823.[53] Before the board could respond to the charges, however, angry settlers stormed the colonial storehouse and seized some of the provisions held there. Ashmun managed to survive this open act of rebellion against his authority, but his position was precarious. In April 1824 he was forced to leave the colony under duress. The administration of affairs was left in the hands of a respected settler, Elijah Johnson.[54] Ashmun wrote to the society from the Cape Verde Islands. He declared that only the mercy of God prevented a tragedy of blood similar to the devastations of Santo Domingo. He called upon the society to remain firm in its commitment to provide good government for the colony. There can be no doubt that to Ashmun continued good government meant continued Euro-American supervision.[55]

Recognizing the gravity of the situation, the board voted to send the Reverend Ralph R. Gurley to Liberia to investigate the problem and make recommendations on behalf of the society. Gurley's observations led him to blame the breakdown of authority on a few troublemakers; he blamed the trials and tribulations incidental to the founding of a colony on a remote and uncivilized shore and on the inability of those in power to restrain the first tendencies towards insubordination.[56] He was able to reestablish order; he even persuaded the settlers to accept Ashmun back as the principal agent. Ashmun retained his position until 1828, when poor health forced him to leave the colony; he died en route to America. The discontent that led to the storehouse confrontation, however, continued to plague Ashmun's successors in office.

The problems between settlers and agents were exacerbated by the dynamics of life in a small, enclave community. Personal conflicts often led to bitter resentments within the community. Joseph Blake, for example, wrote to the board charging that their agent Joseph Mechlin had seduced his wife, resulting in the birth of a mulatto child. After receiving no immediate reply, Blake wrote again demanding some redress from the board. He reminded them that had he acted directly and killed the agent, it would have been a "stigma cast on the Colony, that never could be rubbed off." Blake threatened to make the crime known to the whole world if the board did not satisfy him.[57] Unfortunately, the outcome of Joseph Blake's case remains unknown.

James Brown, another settler in Monrovia, wrote the board that although he believed in the principle of colonization, certain agents and their actions are 'calculated to chill my zeal."[58] To illustrate his concern, he mentioned agent John B. Pinney. Brown accused Pinney of making a statement that his education "had induced him to be prejudiced against Coloured Persons." The remark was overheard by emigrant passengers on the ship *Jupiter*, and upon arrival in Monrovia, word of it spread all over town. Further controversy plagued Pinney when he quarreled with a society physician, Dr. Todson. Brown said that the dispute so upset Pinney that the settlers lost faith in his ability to manage affairs and even questioned the soundness of his mind.[59]

John B. Russwurm also had difficulties with Pinney. He believed, however, that his settler enemies, Hiliary Teage and Jacob Prout, instigated the trouble.[60] In 1836 Russwrum left Monrovia to accept the position of governor in the Maryland settlement of Cape Palmas. While there, Russwurm reflected on the causes of disunity that seemed to infest the settlements. He cited the denial of more responsible positions to deserving settlers as a major cause of the difficulty. Russwurm also noted that with respect to Euro-American agents, the settlers had become "too enlightened to receive and respect everyone, whom the partiality of friends may think qualified."[61] Even the agents recognized the need for greater settler participation in the colonial administration. Mechlin believed, on the basis of his own experience, that "it would have the effect of influencing the minds of the more respectable free coloured population in our favor and induce many to emigrate who would otherwise remain unfriendly to the cause of African colonization."[62]

The turning point for settler self-governance in the colony began with the administration of Thomas Buchanan in 1839. Although the society still believed that Euro-American leadership was necessary, it now agreed to give the settlers a role in formulating local policy. A new constitution was accepted by the board of managers that created the Commonwealth Legislative Council, made up of settlers elected by their peers. The council met regularly with the governor to establish priorities for local policy. The creation of the council ushered in the beginnings of formalized settler politics. It provided the first opportunity for large numbers of settlers to perceive a vested interested in supporting the colonial administration. It also opened the door for political struggle when a different and potentially competitive power base developed in the colony.

The challenge to the colonial administration of Thomas Buchanan came from the independent missionary organization of the Methodist Episcopal Church, led by the Reverend John Seys. Missionaries supported by the Methodist Foreign Mission Board came to Liberia to work among the settlers and the indigenous people. Methodist settlers found economic security through association with the missionary stations. The Methodists also published a newspaper, *Africa's Luminary*, edited by Reverend Seys. A dispute between the Methodist missionaries and the Buchanan administration split loyalties within the colony. The issue was whether missionaries should be entitled to import goods into the colony for their work without the obligation of paying the established custom dues to the government treasury. The dispute reached the supreme court as the case of William N. Lewis, Collector of Customs, Port of Monrovia versus Reverend John Seys, Superintendent, Liberian Mission of the Methodist Episcopal Church.[63]

The customs case became more than a legal matter. The old problem of denominational differences threatened to polarize the settlers once again. The 1840 election of new council members became the stage for a political test of strength by two factions. An administration faction supported Governor Buchanan, while the Methodist faction stood solidly behind Seys. The resources of each faction were used to win additional adherents in order to elect new members to the council. Buchanan charged that Seys used money to influence voters to favor his position: "At Millsburg every voter was employed at unusually high wages on the [Methodist] Saw Mill and sugar plantation—and there *every vote* was polled for his friends."[64] One settler testified to the growing political pressures within the colony. He once worked as the colonial storekeeper but was no longer so employed. " . . . consequently I am not influenced [like many] by Money, for I earn a living by the sweat of my brow, tho a poor one only can be earned by one person for so large a family as I have in this Country, still my situation is far more preferable than if I were placed in a condition where my "salary" must govern the dictates of my conscience."[65]

The Methodists made efforts to organize opposition to the administration in settlements located away from the influence of Monrovia. Missionaries called public meetings, where anti-administration resolutions were passed and speeches attacked Buchanan personally. One settler told of being present when Reverend Seys declared that "the citizens ought to rise up and shake off this rotten system of tyranny and oppression."[66] Whether this particular allegation was true or not, actions were taken to run candidates opposed to Buchanan and his administration. In Edina, Amos Herring was one Methodist settler who was a candidate for a seat on the legislative council. He tried to get people to send representatives to Monrovia to defend the Methodist position against the Baptists and the government. The Buchanan faction won a majority of the council seats, despite the organized challenge of the Methodists.[67] The new council convened and moved to censure the Methodist missionaries for interfering with the affairs of government by propagating subversive doctrines and maintaining a spirit and actual stubborn resistance to authority.[68]

The election defeat of the Methodist forces did not suddenly end the bitter acrimony. The society board of managers continued to receive demands from the colony for the removal of all Methodist missionaries. Buchanan and Seys remained at loggerheads until September 3, 1841. On that day, Thomas Buchanan died, and Joseph Jenkins Roberts, a settler, was appointed as the new governor. Roberts managed to put the Buchanan-Seys feud behind the colony. The dynamics of partisan politics nevertheless remained alive in Liberia. Other issues would enflame the passions of settlers in later years. Settler unity would always be a fragile concept in Liberia—the stresses of a new environment made unity difficult to maintain for very long.

3/Establishing the Settler Standard: Settler Institutions

She came to Liberia with her parents the Ajons in 1853. She was imbued with the spirit of love and sympathy for the poor and needy, having by zeal and labors had erected Charity Hall, which for quite a number of years sheltered the poor and homeless. She was truly a Dorcas in the language of the Bible, "truly, she hath done what she could." Her works do follow her. She was a loving and affectionate wife, mother, relative and friend.

—Headstone inscription of
Maria Hawkins Williams, 1850-1922,
Palm Grove Cemetery, Monrovia, Liberia

The peculiar circumstances of the people of Liberia, demand mental and moral culture—well disciplined and balanced minds. And so limited are the means which they enjoy, for improvement, so few the facilities they possess for competing with other nations, and keeping up with this advancing age, that it becomes them to be inflexible in their endeavours and untiring in their efforts, adopting every measure that may be calculated to advance learning and science in our land.

—Philomath, in *Liberia Herald,*
November 17, 1852

The nineteenth century had its share of intrepid travelers who wrote about their unique adventures in faraway places. The American press carried traveler accounts, which helped to shape American public opinion about the larger world. As the debate over the merits of colonization raged in the United States, personal testimonies about the social experiment in Liberia appeared frequently in newspapers and journals. The American Colonization Society publicized all favorable reports in the hope that such news would encourage large-scale Afro-American immigration. Critics of colonization, on the other hand, called attention to unfavorable reports to support their rejection of the movement as folly. As a consequence, published eye-witness reports from Liberia tended to exaggerate either the vices or the virtues of life in Africa.[1]

Occasionally a perceptive and relatively impartial visitor reported on settler life in Liberia. Charles W. Thomas was one such person. His description of Monrovia in the late 1850s captured the quality of settler society.[2]

Charles Thomas came ashore at Cape Mesurado with the help of Kru men. His first impression was probably exactly what he had expected to find, for he passed through a small village near the water's edge made of "square, low huts, built of sticks and mud and thatched with grass."[3] Once Thomas entered the actual settler town of Monrovia, he was surprised to discover quite a different scene. Buildings that he considered "unpretentious, neat and comfortable" were everywhere. The presidential mansion and the homes of the commercial entrepreneurs especially caught Thomas's eye. He remarked that they were all stone structures, "tasty in appearance, and even luxurious in furniture."[4]

Monrovia was bustling with activity when Thomas arrived. A thriving commercial trade was evident. Many settlers were busy selling palm oil, rice, camwood, and animal skins to passing European and American ships. Thomas noted that several settlers had amassed considerable wealth by this means. Skilled artisans were plentiful in Monrovia and gainfully employed. Thomas noticed, however, that "those who had no trade nor the means of 'keeping store' are driven to farming."[5] Any careful observer would also have discovered that some settlers lived a marginal existence in the midst of apparent affluence. Thomas thought that some in this condition were simply too lazy to learn useful trades. It is interesting that he identified in this category the former barbers, waiters, and coachmen from urban America but not former plantation laborers.[6]

Although Charles Thomas considered only a few Monrovians to be wealthy, he described a general air of "society" that both pleased and worried him: ". . . we found a degree of refinement and taste for which we were not prepared. The people desire to live in comfortable and pretty houses, the ladies and beaux dress in fashion, and an aristocracy of means and education is already set up. The people generally dress above their means, extravagantly so, and the quantity of kid gloves and umbrellas displayed on all occasions does not promise well for a nation whose hope rests on hard and well developed muscles."[7] Thomas identified the "aristocracy of means and education" by its specific origins: "THE VIRGINIANS are said to be the leaders of the aristocracy . . . those who came originally from Maryland, Virginia, and Georgia, as a class, are more intelligent, more industrious, and more worthy than those who hail from points further North."[8] Charles Thomas was making a value judgment of major proportions. He implied that a small elite within the settler community created a standard that others strove to emulate. The only question that Thomas did not answer was, How did the standard of the settler elite encompass the entire community?

Figure 3. Joseph Jenkins Roberts, c. 1850

Settler Institutions

The social cement of the settler society began with family relations. The immigrants did not forget their relatives left behind in America, as their frequent correspondence poignantly illustrates.[9] For many, the bond of kinship became a vehicle for material as well as emotional support. The newly emancipated immigrants even asked their former owners for tools, seeds, money, and other necessities of life. They used familial terms of address and identification in these letters, which indicates their sensitivity to real and fictive kinship bonds; this possibly also demonstrates their determination to gain advantages by trying to exploit those bonds. Patterns of continuity and change in settler families extend the concept of Afro-American social relations into an international context.[10] The rapid rise of an elite in Monrovia, especially in economic affairs, was partially due to the vitality of family re-

Figure 4. Jane Rose Waring Roberts, c. 1850

lations. Had Charles W. Thomas known the family history of men like Joseph Jenkins Roberts and Colston Waring, he might have better understood the Monrovian aristocracy of wealth and means.

Joseph Jenkins Roberts was the oldest mulatto son of Amelia Roberts. Until 1829 the family resided in Petersburg, Virginia, where they were members of the free Afro-American community. They decided to leave Petersburg to start life anew in Africa, and they arrived in Monrovia on March 24, 1829. Before their departure Joseph had formed a commercial partnership with William Nelson Colson, a Petersburg barber and property owner. Once in Liberia, Roberts began to export African products to various American importers through Colson. On one occasion they delivered a shipment of camwood, palm oil, and ivory valued at $3,389.80 to the Philadelphia firm of Grant and Stone.[11] The lucrative enterprise was temporarily interrupted when Colson died, on his first business trip to Liberia, in 1835.[12] The company continued for some years, however, Nathan H. Elebeck, the brother of Colson's widow, representing her family's interest in the business (Elebeck reported directly to his sister on the continuing commercial activities of the company).[13]

The commercial success of Joseph J. Roberts paved the way for other members of his family to begin new careers. His brother Henry was able to return to America and study medicine. He came back to Liberia in 1848 to become one of the few medically trained settlers. John J. Roberts, another brother, married the daughter of Elijah Johnson, and by 1843 he and his wife, Elizabeth H. Roberts, were active as missionaries in the colony (see tables 7 and 8).[14] Joseph Jenkins Roberts's political activities eventually overshadowed his commercial accomplishments. He was twice elected president of Liberia, and he served as a diplomatic representative in Europe and America.[15]

Joseph Jenkins Roberts died a venerated statesman in 1876. The meaning of his life for his family was expressed in the terms of his will. It was through this instrument that his accumulated wealth was redistributed among the remaining members of his extended family. He left real property not only to his immediate family but also to the children of his brothers (see table 9). Roberts also provided for the establishment of an educational endowment for Liberia and thereby became the republic's first philanthropist.[16] Roberts clearly felt the responsibility of familial ties. His liberal bequests, however, were challenged by his only daughter, Sarah Ann Roberts. She petitioned the Monthly and Probate Court in June 1876 to set her father's will aside and declare her sole benefactor.[17] Although the court ruled against her petition, the action demonstrated another, less pleasant side of family relations in Liberia.

The free Afro-American community in Petersburg gave Liberia yet another commercially successful family in the nineteenth century. Colston Waring, a thirty-year-old minister, was among the passengers on the ship *Oswego*, which arrived in Monrovia on May 24, 1823.[18] Waring owned real estate in Petersburg valued at $1,037.50.[19] After liquidating his assets, he established a commercial firm in Monrovia with a settler partner, Francis Taylor. By the time of his death, in 1834, the business had become a flourishing enterprise. In 1830 the firm's business volume amounted to seventy thousand dollars.[20]

Waring died in Liberia on August 12, 1834, leaving his widow, four children, and a business, which was in part conducted by relatives. Harriet Waring sketched the life of her husband and their experiences in marriage in a letter to the American Colonization Society. She stated that her husband was born in Virginia on September 19, 1795, and was baptized on April 26, 1812, in the city of Norfolk, where he joined the Baptist Church. They were married on October 10, 1813, and then settled in Petersburg. Colston's move to Liberia was based on an offer to serve as a missionary of the African Bap-

Table 7. The Roberts Family Genealogy

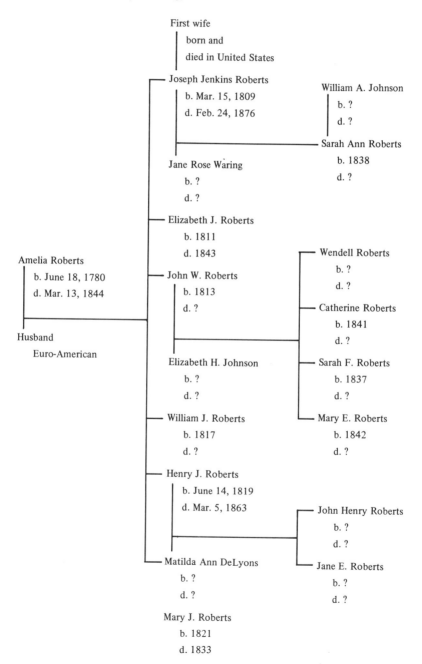

First wife
    born and
    died in United States

Joseph Jenkins Roberts
    b. Mar. 15, 1809
    d. Feb. 24, 1876

William A. Johnson
    b. ?
    d. ?

Sarah Ann Roberts
    b. 1838
    d. ?

Jane Rose Waring
    b. ?
    d. ?

Elizabeth J. Roberts
    b. 1811
    d. 1843

Wendell Roberts
    b. ?
    d. ?

Amelia Roberts
    b. June 18, 1780
    d. Mar. 13, 1844

John W. Roberts
    b. 1813
    d. ?

Catherine Roberts
    b. 1841
    d. ?

Husband
    Euro-American

Elizabeth H. Johnson
    b. ?
    d. ?

Sarah F. Roberts
    b. 1837
    d. ?

William J. Roberts
    b. 1817
    d. ?

Mary E. Roberts
    b. 1842
    d. ?

Henry J. Roberts
    b. June 14, 1819
    d. Mar. 5, 1863

John Henry Roberts
    b. ?
    d. ?

Matilda Ann DeLyons
    b. ?
    d. ?

Jane E. Roberts
    b. ?
    d. ?

Mary J. Roberts
    b. 1821
    d. 1833

Table 8. The Johnson Family Genealogy

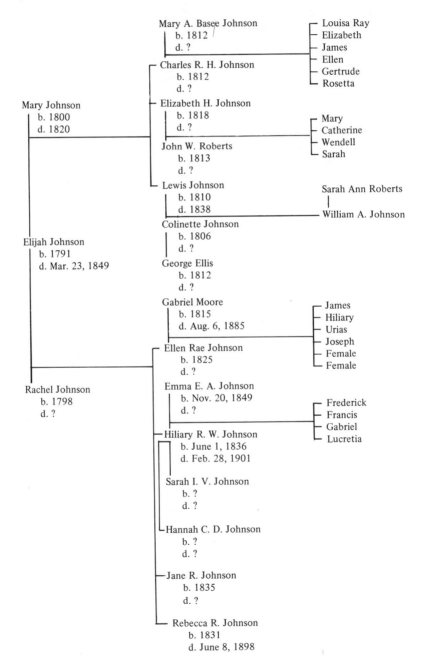

Table 9. Property Transfer in the Will of Joseph Jenkins Roberts

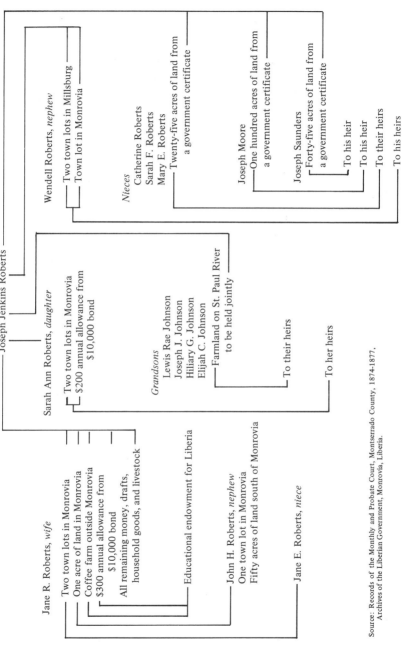

Source: Records of the Monthly and Probate Court, Montserrado County, 1874-1877,
Archives of the Liberian Government, Monrovia, Liberia.

tist Missionary Society of Petersburg. The society promised adequate support, but when it did not materialize, Colston become involved in commerce to support his family. "It was evident, he was not born a merchant, of which he was fully aware, but he was compelled in the first instance, to enter into the business of a commission merchant and afterwards continued it."[21]

The Warings and the Robertses, two elite families of Monrovia, were eventually linked by marriage. Jane Rose Waring became the wife of Joseph Jenkins Roberts. In this case marriage was a significant means for consolidating wealth and status among those at the top of the emerging Liberian social structure. But only a relatively few immigrants were able to translate modest gains in America into commercial businesses in Africa. Many were emancipated slaves with no previous experience with freedom or its demands. Once in Liberia, they too had to adjust, but with few advantages. The family structure nevertheless continued to function for them, as it did for free Afro-Americans.

John Hartwell Cocke emancipated Peyton Skipwith in October 1833. Skipwith's family was also freed, on the condition that they all emigrate to Liberia. One month later, after their manumission papers were properly executed, the Skipwith family sailed on the ship *Jupiter* with fifty-two other immigrants, primarily from the state of Virginia. The voyage was without incident, and the company arrived in Monrovia on January 1, 1834.[22] Tragedy struck the Skipwith family repeatedly during their first year in Liberia. Peyton's wife, Lydia, and two of his six children, Felicia and Napoleon, fell victims of African fever. Peyton himself was suffering from several ailments, and doctors advised him to leave Monrovia if he wanted to recover his health. Peyton described the grave situation in a letter to John Cocke: "I embrace this opportunity to write you these few lines to inform you that I am not well with a blindness of nights so that I cannot see. All the information that I can get from doctors is that I must stop laying stone. I have lost my wife she died on July 2d 1834. . . ."[23]

The likelihood of death due to disease was very great for most settlers during their first year in Liberia. In the years before 1844, 21 percent of all immigrants died within twelve months of their arrival. The survivors described the health problems during this initial period as part of the "seasoning process." The mortality rate was significantly lower among those who had survived at least two years, the annual number of deaths never rising above 3 percent.[24] Although initially Peyton Skipwith experienced more than his share of grief, by 1836 he was able to write: "The idea of being in a new country with a large family of helpless children, who could depend only on me for support, and I being so indisposed as to be of no use to them nor myself having no means and the prospect of their suffering made me feel distressed and greatly so, but thanks be to God my health and sight is recovered and that awful gloom is gone and I feel satisfied with my present home and desire no other."[25]

Through all the heartache of adjustment, Peyton had to provide economic support for his family and build a permanent home. A talented stonemason, he was one of eighty-four artisans living in Monrovia in 1843. The opportunities for employment were good at that time. Peyton discovered, however, that payment for work performed usually was made in trade goods like cloth, tobacco, powder, and pipes. He complained that it was necessary to exchange these goods for staples like flour, meat, and cooking oil, usually at a loss.[26] Peyton also discovered that his skills were in demand in another way. Young men offered themselves as apprentices to artisans, willingly exchanging their labor for the knowledge of a trade. In 1839 John Faulcon, another slave of John Cocke's, became Peyton Skipwith's first apprentice. His service gave additional security to the Skipwith family. Peyton was soon satisfied with Faulcon's work, and four years later John Faulcon was listed in the settlement census as a stonemason.[27]

Peyton Skipwith's modest economic position enabled his remaining children to receive religious and educational training. They attended school, were baptized, and became members of the Baptist Church of Monrovia.[28] By 1841, the family seemed to have made the transition from America to Africa successfully. Peyton remarried and took on more apprentices. His second marriage was to a widow with two children of her own. Crisis once again struck the family, however, when Peyton died, in October 1849 (see table 10). The distribution of property became an issue among Peyton's heirs because family members survived from both marriages. At least one son, Nash Skipwith, believed that he would get nothing more than a rifle, and he held little hope that other members of the family would do any better. His pessimism turned out to be unwarranted, for five months later Nash Skipwith was living in his father's house—probably Peyton's most valuable material asset.[29]

The death of Peyton Skipwith created a void in family leadership for his survivors. His daughter Matilda became more assertive. She had married Samuel B. Lomax, an artisan, who had mastered several trades.[30] But death continued to stalk the family. Matilda's husband drowned on July 23, 1849, and her brother Nash died suddenly on October 27, 1851.[31] These untimely deaths left the family with many dependent children and no reliable source of income. Matilda tried to save the situation by remarrying, but the real aid to the family was the arrival of Peyton's brother, James P. Skipwith, from America. He was highly motivated and optimistic about life in Monrovia. James opened a bakery in town and also purchased ten acres of land, where he hoped to cultivate coffee, cotton, sugar cane, and groundnuts.[32] He was also a willing participant in the civic responsibilities of Monrovia. He voted in elections and served on juries during legal proceedings for the first time in

Table 10. The Skipwith Family Genealogy

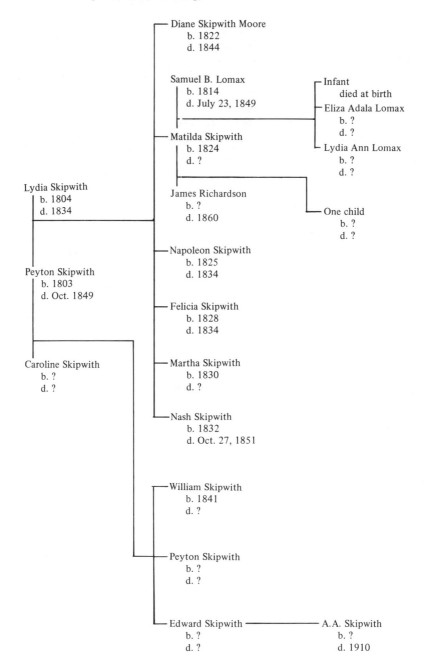

Diane Skipwith Moore
  b. 1822
  d. 1844

Samuel B. Lomax
  b. 1814
  d. July 23, 1849

Infant
  died at birth

Eliza Adala Lomax
  b. ?
  d. ?

Matilda Skipwith
  b. 1824
  d. ?

Lydia Ann Lomax
  b. ?
  d. ?

Lydia Skipwith
  b. 1804
  d. 1834

James Richardson
  b. ?
  d. 1860

One child
  b. ?
  d. ?

Napoleon Skipwith
  b. 1825
  d. 1834

Peyton Skipwith
  b. 1803
  d. Oct. 1849

Felicia Skipwith
  b. 1828
  d. 1834

Caroline Skipwith
  b. ?
  d. ?

Martha Skipwith
  b. 1830
  d. ?

Nash Skipwith
  b. 1832
  d. Oct. 27, 1851

William Skipwith
  b. 1841
  d. ?

Peyton Skipwith
  b. ?
  d. ?

Edward Skipwith
  b. ?
  d. ?

A.A. Skipwith
  b. ?
  d. 1910

his life. James Skipwith expressed his determination to stay in Liberia in 1860: "I find that a man must work both head and hands to make a living in this Country our work is almost like building the walls of Jerusalem we have to carry our tools all day in our hands and our Bibles at night yet notwithstanding it is the Best Country for the Black man that is to be found on the face of the Earth. God intended Africa for the Black race."[33] This period of promise for the Skipwith family was all too brief. On February 22, 1861, just three years after emigrating, James P. Skipwith died in Monrovia.[34] One visitor to Monrovia found Matilda living with her second husband and three children. "I called upon her and was disappointed to find her inhabiting a miserable shanty in a low, damp part of town, but she seemed and doubtless was thankful to Providence that matters were no worse."[35] The Skipwith family experience was bittersweet, standing in sharp contrast to the experiences of the Robertses and the Warings. The family structure in each case, however, served as the common reference point for adjustment to the African environment.

Community Institutions

Settler life was based on more than family ties. Wider bonds of association were important, especially for nurturing a sense of community purpose among settlers. Religious affiliations were the most obvious expression of settler solidarity. Immigrants constructed churches almost as quickly as they built their own homes. Reports of religious revivalism in Liberia were frequent. In 1859 news reached America that scores of children and youths were being converted to Christianity. The report claimed that forty persons had joined the Methodist Episcopal Church, while the Baptists and Presbyterians also received many new devotees.[36] Religious leaders led the way in extolling settlers to work together for the common good.

The recognized common good was the establishment and maintenance of a distinctive settler life style. Christianity was but one element of a "civilized" culture that the settlers struggled to preserve. The immediate influences of African society, many of which they considered negative, forced the settlers to maintain an exaggerated, often pompous alternative. The activities of community associations became the vehicle for displaying settler commitment to civilized life. Settler associations were primarily concerned with providing relief to the poor, social and moral upliftment, and mutual economic advancement. Leadership tended to come from the elite of each settlement, their position in associations further enhancing their prominence. Membership, however, was drawn from all classes and thus became a significant bond of unity beyond the more limited ties of familial relationships.

Each association, regardless of its declared purpose, devoted great attention to public displays and ceremonies. Elaborate activities, for example, became the mark of all association anniversary celebrations. The Ladies Benevolent Society of Monrovia held its first anniversary ceremony in 1836. The members assembled at the home of their directress early on the morning of November 10. From there they formed a procession and marched in pairs to the First Baptist Meeting House. The women were all dressed in uniform colors, and they wore badges on their lapels designating their position of responsibility within the society. At the Meeting House the Reverend Hiliary Teage delivered an address, and Beverly P. Yates read the society's constitution. After the ceremony, which included testimonials and singing, the membership again marched through the streets of Monrovia. To climax the day's events, they returned to the home of the directress and "spent the evening with that sociability common on such occasions."[37] The various aspects of the Ladies Benevolent Society anniversary celebration were standard for all public ceremonies of settler associations. Each comprised an opening processional, an oration by a prominent citizen, music, prayer, and a concluding social reception.

Settler benevolence was in response to a pressing need. The frequent deaths of adult settlers left many children orphaned. These children, along with the sick and the disabled, made up a dependent class within each settlement. It was this class that the Skipwith family tried to stay above. As early as 1836 a prominent settler leader proposed that a workhouse be established on a public farm. All the poor that applied for assistance could be sent to this place. Those able to work would be put to work on public projects, and the sick would be cared for at the workhouse. The director of the workhouse was to be a man—a family man was preferred—of steady, industrious habits and good moral character.[38] Years later the Liberian legislature extended the concept of the workhouse by passing an act for the relief and employment of the poor. The act established county poorhouses, where all able-bodied males would be required to work on a farm connected with the establishment. Women would be provided with wheels, looms, and knitting and sewing needles, while children would be cared for by appointed matrons.[39] The government program was always too modest to serve all who needed help; however the private efforts of settlers supplemented the available government resources.

At first, churches organized benevolent societies to offer relief for the needy (see table 11). The Ladies Dorcas Society was created in 1843 by the Methodist Episcopal Church of Monrovia. It was inspired by the Biblical reference to a charitable woman.[40] The object of the society was to relieve the poor in Monrovia and elsewhere and clothe converted Africans in the neighboring towns. The society received a deed for two town lots in Monrovia, and they built an asylum for the poor on the property. Chapters of the

Table 11. Benevolent Societies in Nineteenth-Century Liberia

County	Founding Date
Grand Bassa	
Women's Missionary Native Church Aid Society	1889
Maryland	
Baptist Union Sisters of Maryland County	1889
Gentlemen's Mutual Relief Society of East Palmas	1887
Ladies Mutual Relief Society of Cape Palmas	1868
Montserrado	
Charity Hall	–
Church Aid Society of Trinity Church	–
Ladies Benevolent Society	1836
Ladies Dorcas Society of the Methodist Episcopal Chruch	1844
Union Sisters of Charity Society	1833
Sinoe	
Benevolent Society of Greenville	1854
Ladies Benevolent Practical Society of Greenville	–

Sources: *Liberia Herald*; and Minutes of the House of Representatives and Minutes of the Senate, Archives of the Liberian Government, Monrovia, Liberia.

Dorcas Society were organized in other settlements as the work of the group spread.[41]

Church-related benevolence tended to help mainly the churches' less fortunate adherents. Nonsectarian benevolent societies also served the poor. The Ladies Benevolent Society expressly carried forth their program without regard to religious affiliation. Membership was open to all with good moral character and the ability to be useful. The distribution of its charities gave no special preference because of religious tenets or connections.[42] As time passed, benevolence became an important social value among settlers. Everyone felt the pressure to publicly conform to the *standard*.

Poverty was an embarrassment to the Liberian settlers. So was the widespread illiteracy among adults as well as children. There were few qualified teachers in the settlements, but the settlers organized schools to teach basic literacy to children. The Lancasterian system of education was used in Liberia to offset the disadvantages of a high student-teacher ratio. The system was particularly effective for teaching reading. The instructor would select a few advanced students, called monitors, to learn a given lesson, and they in turn would teach the lesson to ten other students.[43] The demands of citizenship weighed heavily on adult settlers with little or no educational background. A number of literacy associations organized by both males and females were popular (see table 12).

Groups like the Ladies Liberia Literary Institute, organized in 1848, had weekly meetings, at which members read alternately from books on a wide range of subjects and answered questions from the audience.[44] Oratory

Table 12. Literary Societies in Nineteenth-Century Liberia

County	Founding Date
Grand Bassa	
Female Literary Institute of Edina	1881
Young Men's Literary Association of Buchanan	1856
Montserrado	
Liberia Lyceum	1847
Literary and Social Club of Monrovia	1852
Monrovia Athaeneum	1864
Monrovia Ladies Literary Institute	1848
Sinoe	
Ladies Literary Institute of Greenville	1856

Sources: *Liberia Herald*; and Minutes of the House of Representatives and Minutes of the Senate, Archives of the Liberian Government, Monrovia, Liberia.

and debate also were encouraged by the literacy associations. During the 1847 meeting of the Liberia Lyceum the question of whether women should have the same political rights as men stimulated a lively discussion.[45] President Joseph Jenkins Roberts announced the free distribution of books and tracts to the citizens of the republic in 1855; his goal was to have at least one volume and several pamphlets in the home of every family.[46] A bill to provide for a public library was considered by the legislature in 1849. The government did not have the necessary funds then; however, in 1864 a private association opened a public reading room in Monrovia. The Monrovia Athaeneum made available a number of literary journals, such as *Harper's* and the *Edinburgh*.[47] The attention to intellectual pursuits had positive effects, ranging from the publication of poetry by Mrs. R. H. Gibson, of Monrovia, in 1855 to general advances in literacy by native-born settler youth.[48]

The variety of Liberian settlers' shared experiences tended to foster a strong sense of brotherhood. This feeling was further reinforced by bonds of racial unity, which gave many settlers motivation to survive and succeed. Fraternal orders drew on the strength of settler brotherhood and ultimately

Table 13. Fraternal Orders in Nineteenth-Century Liberia

Order	Founding Date
Grand United Order of Odd Fellows	1888
Independent Order of Good Templars	–
Independent Order of the Sons of Ham	1849
King Solomon's Tabernacle of Maryland County	1874
Masonic Grand Lodge of Liberia	1851
Sisters of the Mysterious Ten	–
United Brethren Society	–
United Brothers of Friendship	–

Sources: *Liberia Herald*; and Minutes of the House of Representatives and Minutes of the Senate, Archives of the Liberian Government, Monrovia, Liberia.

Figure 5. Masonic Temple, West Benson Street, Monrovia, Liberia

institutionalized it. They stressed conformity and upheld the moral values deemed essential for the advancement of Liberian society. The fraternal orders blended secret rituals with occasional, flamboyant public ceremonies, and their activities became very popular among settlers. Several different orders were formed in Liberia, but none was more prominent than Freemasonry (see table 13).

Settler interest in fraternal organizations paralleled the interest in similar organizations among Afro-Americans in the United States. Undoubtedly many settlers were already initiated Prince Hall Masons when they came to Liberia.[49] The first independent Masonic Order of Liberia was formed in 1851. Several leading settlers met in convention and established the Independent Restoration Grand Lodge. Joseph Jenkins Roberts was installed as the first Grand Master. The conveners believed that they had full right and authority to act, noting that American Masons had established the precedent when they broke away from the original English Grand Lodge after the American Revolution.[50] Settler association through the order was a direct means of transmitting the accepted societal values of Christian propriety, which included good moral character and a charitable nature. It also was clearly a politicized institution serving the needs of the settler elite in much the same way that the Poro society functioned within African society. The secrecy that shrouded the Masons probably both lent additional legitimacy to the highly placed elites and gave them a safe forum to discuss differences of opinion.

Four lodges were established under warrants from the Restoration Grand Lodge, each in a different settlement: the Grand Tyler Lodge, the St. John's Lodge No. 3, the St. Paul's Lodge No. 2, and the Oriental Lodge No. 1.[51] Installment of officers, celebration of Masonic feast days, and the laying of foundations for new buildings were all occasions for elaborate Masonic programs. When a new Grand Master was chosen by the order in 1868, the activities inspired a graphic description: "On this occasion, the order had a public procession. Arrayed in official robes, with the divers paraphernalia, the members marched, with lively music, from their hall to Trinity Church, where the Hon. and Reverend John Seys, D.D., the American Minister, delivered an address, which was at once graphic, eloquent, full of information, and replete with the spirit of benevolence and charity."[52] Five years later the cornerstone for a new market house was laid in Monrovia with Masonic honors. In 1875 the Masons celebrated the anniversary of Saint John the Evangelist, a major feast day for Freemasonry. A public program was held at the Presbyterian Church in Monrovia that included singing, prayers, and a speech by H. D. Brown on the "Use and Abuse of Freemasonry."[53]

Settler associations also extended into the practical realm of economic self-help. In 1837 a meeting was held in Monrovia to consider ways of advancing agriculture. The result was the formation of the Liberia Agricultural Society. The founders resolved that their object was to join together and pursue vigorously the cultivation of sugar cane. Membership was based on a contribution of no more than five hundred dollars and no less than ten dollars to a special fund to support activities of the society.[54] Artisans also found advantages to collective action as a way of bettering their economic opportunities. The leading artisans of Monrovia formed the Union Mechanics' Association in 1859. Three years later there were forty-one active members, including the printer of the *Liberia Herald*, G. Killian. The association purchased a house and lot in Monrovia from the Episcopal Church for the sum of six hundred thirty dollars. In 1862 the Union Mechanics' Association petitioned the legislature for a charter, which was granted the following year.[55] Other economic associations sprang up in other settlements. The Young Men's Prudential Association of Cape Palmas, the Young Men's Mercantile Association of Bexley, and the United Daughters of Economy Society were just a few of the more active ones.[56]

The government also found ways of supporting the developing settler standard. It chartered associations to ensure legal protections necessary for growth. The charter privileges enabled associations to hold title deeds to land in the same manner as individuals. Some issues affecting the standard were of such importance that government regulations eventually covered many of them. Legal protection to the integrity of the family was one case in point. All divorces required the approval of the legislature. The chairman of the

Liberian Senate Committee on Petitions expressed the reasoning of the government in 1864: "We are not disposed to open the gates of Divorce too wide, lest too many might attempt to pass, nevertheless Your Committee is of the opinion that to close it entirely we thereby open another gate of a far more serious nature, that is, murder and suicide."[57] The dilemma of the legislature was resolved by the passage of an Act Relating to Divorces in 1873. The act required that divorces be granted by the judge of the Court of Quarter Sessions and Common Pleas in each county, but only on the grounds of proven infidelity. The offense could be on the part of either husband or wife, but it had to be established upon the oath of good and substantial evidence or by the confession of one of the parties.[58]

Legal redress was even available to engaged parties. In the December term of the 1887 Court of Quarter Sessions and Common Pleas, Sarah Irons brought an action of damage against James M. Outland for breach of promise. The case gives insight into the economic significance of marriage for social mobility among settlers. James Outland defended himself against the charge. He stated that Sarah Irons had refused to marry him by saying that she could not and would not live in a thatched house. Outland produced a love letter from her as evidence: ". . . I love you sincerely from my heart and the Lord knows it, and would desire to follow thee where thou goest, but in the present condition of your house, without some preparation, it would be unwise for me to leave a snug brick house to go into a open thatch one, what good would it be to me, or even what pleasure and advantage would it be to you to have me sick with a heavy cold or consumption soon after our marriage?"[59] James Outland also pointed out to the court that Sarah Irons had dismissed him of his marriage promise, telling him that they were both out of their own "circles" and that thereafter she desired nothing of him other than common politeness as a townsman.[60] The jury decided unanimously in Outland's favor.

The settler standard that gave Liberia its characteristic style developed from an institutional base. Originating within the family, the ideals of Christianity, western education, and social upliftment flourished among the settlers. A network of associations constantly reinforced the principles of the standard by both example and rhetoric. Thus private and public policy combined to give the settlements the "air of society" that Charles W. Thomas described in the 1850s. Few settlers attained the status of a Joseph Jenkins Roberts. But even families like the Skipwiths, on the edge of disaster, supported the principles that embraced the settler standard. Some may argue that all this was really more style than substance. After all, societal ideals often vary considerably from social realities. The best way to evaluate the functional aspects of the settler standard is to examine the many forces in Liberia that placed the ideals of the settlers under stress.

4/Settler Standards under Pressure: Ideals Confronting Reality

I look forward to the day when Civilization and Christianity shall be disseminated throughout the Continent of Africa, and the Sons and Daughters of this now benighted land, "shall own Jesus Christ as Lord to the honor and glory of God." . . . And who more capable to act as instruments to bring about the great change of morals, then those who sprang from African stock!

—Daniel Bashiel Warner,
December 31, 1850

Notwithstanding our doubts on the subject, the people [Recaptured Africans] are here; and we are bound by every humane, as well as christian motive, money or no money to help us, to do by these our brethren in misfortune, the best we can. The dilemma is already upon us; we must educate, enlighten, and christianize these masses, or they will in time bury us and our children in a grave as full of darkness and uncertainty of the future as that in which their fathers are fallen.

—Editor, *Liberian Christian Advocate*,
January 1861

The cultural accent in the settler enclaves was unmistakably American. The settlers viewed their own life style as progressive and worthy of African emulation. Thus they were reluctant to compromise on the question of cultural orientation. When, for example, Edward Wilmot Blyden described the settler goal as assimilation with Africans to effect "an improved and powerful class," he was not suggesting an equal exchange.[1] The settler intention was always to convince Africans to give up their traditional beliefs and values in favor of "Civilization and Christianity." Despite the settlers' distinct cultural posture, however, the realities of life in nineteenth-century West Africa made compromise and adaptation impossible to avoid completely. The settler standard became more of an ideal than an accurate expression of Afro-American life in Liberia.

The Slave and Rum Trade

The sale of African slaves to Portuguese, Brazilian, and Spanish traders was an aspect of Liberian life that Afro-Americans found particularly abhorrent. The colonization movement was supposed to help to suppress the slave trade, yet the traffic in human beings went on in spite of the settler presence. In the 1820s Jehudi Ashmun complained that slavers had contracts for over eight hundred men from within eight miles of Monrovia. He was shocked to learn that more than half of the number were for purchase by two *American* traders.[2] Ashmun responded by organizing settler raids on several slave stations in the immediate vicinity of Monrovia.

Each of the society's agents made attempts to stop the slave trade during his tenure. Such measures, however, were rarely effective given the limited resources and manpower at the agents' disposal. Settler attacks against slavers also alienated those Africans economically tied to the traffic, sometimes with disastrous results. In 1834 a settler enclave was built on land provided by Chief Bob Gray, of the Bassa people. The settlement, called Port Cresson, had been founded by individuals committed to Quaker peace principles.[3] The small, defenseless community was attacked by two of Bob Gray's rivals, kings Joe and Peter Harris. Twenty settlers were killed during the raid. The settlement was destroyed, and the survivors fled to Monrovia. Settler opinion held that the French slaver Theodore Canot was the main instigator behind the outrage. They believed that Canot intended to reestablish the slave trade at the mouth of the St. John's River after driving the Port Cresson people away.[4]

Battling the evils of slaving unified the settler community. The struggle became justification for recommending the expansion of settler political jurisdiction. Government leadership argued to both Americans and Europeans that settler control over a continuous stretch of coastline was the only sure means of suppressing the slave trade.[5] While a clear consensus existed with regard to the slave trade, the settler community was sharply divided over a related trading item. A protracted debate ensued concerning the propriety of selling and using rum and other spirituous liquors.

The American Colonization Society officials had reservations about the introduction of spirituous liquors to their colony. The board of managers passed a resolution expressing their displeasure on April 30, 1833. They vowed to use all their influence to discourage and diminish the evil and to allow no spirituous liquors to be introduced by the board or its managers, except when they were needed for medical purposes.[6] The commonwealth legislature, in turn, tried to pass a law prohibiting the importation of "all and every kind, species, or quantity of ardent spirits into the commonwealth of Liberia." The motion failed to carry, despite numerous petitions from settlers

Table 14. Temperance Societies in Nineteenth-Century Liberia

Order	Location
Anti-Tobacco Society	Monrovia
Grand United Order of the Daughters of Temperance	Monrovia
Philanthropic Order of the Sons of Temperance	–
Rising Star Union Daughters of Temperance	–
Rose of Sharon Union Daughters of Temperance	Monrovia

Sources: *Liberia Herald*; and Minutes of the Senate, Archives of the Liberian Government, Monrovia, Liberia.

supporting the prohibition. The legislature finally settled on a direct taxation of the rum trade. They ordered that "merchants or others who may retail in ardent spirits, shall pay previous to their doing so, the sum of twenty-five dollars per year."[7]

In 1846 Joseph Jenkins Roberts was still trying to convince the legislature to pass a law that would totally ban the rum trade. He acknowledged that there were differing opinions about such legislation. "We are told that the unrestrained use of intoxicating drinks is a moral evil that should be corrected only by moral suasion, and not by legislative authority." Roberts nevertheless put the full weight of his influence behind prohibition. "For my own part, I am decidedly of the opinion that tipling shops, in any community, are public nuisances, and should be deemed so by law . . . . I am persuaded, gentlemen—that you will do all in your power to suppress this unrighteous traffic."[8] The legislature failed to be moved by Roberts's appeal. They merely decided to require a special license for selling ardent spirits that carried a five-hundred-dollar fee.

Reaction to the special license generated petitions from affected traders. The legislature received a petition from twenty-four Monrovians calling for a repeal of the license tax. The editors of *Liberia Herald* noted that "judging from the way it was received, we are quite sure that the prayer of the petitioners will avail nothing."[9] The editors' statement may well have expressed their hope rather than their confidence. The substantial commercial advantages to the rum trade made it an attractive business for many settlers. Moreover, many persons not actually engaged in the trade enjoyed the use of rum even when it was not medically prescribed. To combat these tendencies, settler leadership established a number of temperance societies, whose primary goal was to secure individual pledges to temperance (see table 14).

As in the United States, the Methodist Church spearheaded the temperance movement in Liberia.[10] The first settler temperance society was organized by the Methodist Episcopal Church of Monrovia. John Seys served as president; D. W. Whitehurst, vice president; Nathaniel H. Elebeck, secretary; and James Brown, treasurer.[11] The society held quarterly meetings and welcomed the general public to attend. The Methodist Episcopal Church also tried to discourage the use of tobacco, in part because it was thought to increase the desire for spirituous liquors. An anti-tobacco society was formed in 1839. This crusade, however, was not an immediate success. One year later a Monrovian wrote to the *Liberia Herald* demanding to know what had become of the organization. "The practice of using tobacco, which the society aims at putting down, by arguments founded on reason and good sense, is gaining ground fearfully."[12]

The temperance movement fared somewhat better than the anti-tobacco campaign. Temperance societies were active throughout the nineteenth century. Community leaders spoke out in favor of abstaining from alcohol. Edward Blyden publicly denounced intemperance as an evil afflicting the institution of the family.[13] Yet neither organizations, speeches, nor newspaper editorials could effect a legal prohibition against the rum trade. All that the agitation accomplished was a rise in the license fee from twenty-five dollars to two hundred.[14] The economic incentive to the rum trade was obvious. In addition, the temperance movement had a feature that hampered its efforts. In 1901 the *Liberian Recorder* evaluated the drive against spirituous liquors as follows: "We fear . . . that the association of temperance with secrecy has greatly cramped it, especially in this community. We remember persons who were kept out of the Sons of Temperance, once a flourishing society in this community, who would have proven useful members."[15]

Africans, Missionaries, and Integration

Suppression of the slave trade and related activities were only part of the mission of Afro-American colonization. Various Protestant denominations sent missionaries to Liberia to establish missions among both settler and African populations. The settler leadership was willing to allow missionaries to assume a large responsibility for converting Africans to Christianity because the leadership's own resources for such activities were marginal at best. The Methodists and the Baptists were the first to send ordained missionaries to Liberia. They were followed by Presbyterian, Episcopalian, and Lutheran missionaries.[16] Liberia was fertile ground for American foreign-mission activity.

The actual impact of missionary work in Liberia was disappointing to its supporters. Most Euro-American missionaries died in the land of their labors, often before they could accomplish much. In 1853 the General Conference of the Methodist Episcopal Church sent out its own observer, Bishop Scott, to report personally on the condition of its missionary program in Liberia. The bishop was impressed with the Christian appearance of the settlers, noting that the Sabbath was observed with strictness and that all the churches were crowded with orderly worshipers. He was, however, far less impressed with the effect of the missions among the Africans. He reported that his inquiries had produced discouraging responses and he feared that the General Conference would be disappointed. The bishop qualified his judgment by saying that "these results were not due to any want of faithfulness on the part of the missionaries . . . but are the result of the peculiar condition of the native population."[17]

Thus despite the efforts of many different Protestant denominations, the impact of mission work in Liberia was never great during the nineteenth century.[18] The high mortality of missionaries, especially Euro-Americans, along with the limited monetary means provided from America, reduced the effectiveness of missionary work among Africans. In the 1843 census the colony could report the conversion of only three hundred fifty-three Africans to Christianity. The number of active churchgoers, even among the settlers, was far from universal. Less than half of the total settler population in 1843 were communicants of either the Baptist, the Methodist, or the Presbyterian church (see table 15).

The Afro-American settlers did not leave the task of converting Africans to Christianity solely to missionaries. Many settlers adopted Africans, particularly young children, and used the family structure as the means of socializing them to settler culture. In cases where the association of Africans with settler families resulted in the assumption of the settler life style, the achievement was noted in the press. When Lewis Tulliver died, on April 11, 1840, the Methodist newspaper, *Africa's Luminary*, published an obituary. The newspaper noted that Tulliver was a "native youth" raised by settlers and converted to Christianity while in the family of Stern Tulliver, a settler living then in Upper Caldwell.[19] A year later the paper announced the passing of another African long associated with the Afro-American settlements. Eliza Jones, adopted as a child by the Reverend Anthony D. Williams and later married to a settler man, became a member of the Methodist Episcopal Church before her death.[20] In 1841 the paper provided its readers with a biographical sketch of a converted African woman, Betty Preston, who was also a member of the Methodist Episcopal Church. The account stated that "old mammy Betty preferred civilized habits to those of her country people, could never be induced to quit the cape and retire with her tribe, but remained among the settlers."[21]

The government soon found it necessary to establish official guidelines for the integration of Africans into the settler community. The legislature passed "an act to regulate the residence of Native Africans within the Republic." The first section of the act required that all Africans resident within the bounds of the several counties of the republic wear clothes and that a fine be imposed for violations. The second stipulation was that no African

Table 15. Christian Church Affiliations in Liberia, 1843

Denomination	Communicants			Total
	African	*American*	*Recaptured African*	
Baptist	60	431	63	554
Methodist	293	564	49	906
Presbyterian	0	20	4	24
Total	353	1,015	116	1,484

Source: U.S., Congress, Senate, *U.S. Navy Department, tables showing the number of Emigrants and recaptured Africans sent to the colony of Liberia by the government of the United States . . . together with a census of the colony and a report of its commerce, &c. September, 1843: Senate Document No. 150,* 28th Cong., 2d sess., 1845.

youth under the age of eighteen years could live with a settler family unless he was bound for a specified term of years by his apprentice contract.[22] The apprentice system was a legal means of regulating the adoption of individuals—usually children—by settler families. Contracts were drawn up detailing the obligations of the apprentice, as well as the responsibilities of the master or mistress.

Prudence Spendlove was apprenticed to F.L. Sheridan on December 4, 1839. The contract bound Prudence, an eight-year-old orphan, to "faithfully serve her said mistress, keep her secrets and obey her lawful commands. She shall do no hurt to her said mistress nor suffer it to be done by others, but shall forthwith give notice thereof to her said Mistress to the utmost of her power. She shall not embezzle nor waste the goods of her said Mistress nor lend them out without her consent. She shall not play cards or dice or indulge in any other species of gambling. She shall not frequent taverns or Tipling houses. . . . "[23] F. L. Sheridan's responsibilities were also outlined in the apprentice contract. She was to instruct her apprentice in sewing and to provide her with food, apparel, and lodging. She also was obligated to teach her apprentice reading, writing, and arithmetic. When Prudence became eighteen years of age, she was to receive twelve dollars from her mistress and to have the right to marry.[24] This arrangement in general applied to all apprentice relationships.

The apprentice system was administered through the courts in an effort to limit abuses and protect the rights of both apprentice and master. The Commonwealth Court heard many cases like that of Harrison Boyd versus John Clark in 1840. The mother of apprentice Harrison Boyd charged that her son's master had ill-treated him. The court decided that the apprentice should be returned to Clark, that Clark should be reprimanded and told not to abuse Boyd in like manner again, and that Clark should bear the cost of the trial.[25] When possible, the courts assigned guardians to protect the interests of apprentices. In the November 1839 session of the Commonwealth

Court, guardian D. B. Brown applied to the court to have apprentice Daniel Hunt taken away from Wily Brown. D. B. Brown argued that Wily Brown was a felon and therefore was not fit to keep an apprentice. The court decided in favor of the guardian's petition.[26]

In 1838, sixty apprentices were assigned to masters by the Commonwealth Court. Slightly more than half—thirty-two—were Africans, while the rest had settler backgrounds. Twenty-seven had court-appointed guardians. It has been suggested that the apprentice system in Liberia was not only a means of training and acculturation but at times a form of domestic slavery.[27] The available data for 1838 do not indicate the level of activity necessary to encourage widespread abuse. In that year fifteen of the apprentices were between the ages of five and ten, and twenty-eight were between eleven and twenty-one (the ages of the remaining seventeen are unknown). Thirty-six apprentices were assigned one to a master, and only three masters had more than two apprentices. The point at which the system underwent unusual strain was when it was called upon to absorb the thousands of recaptured Africans introduced into the settlements after 1840. It was only then that the Liberian courts were no longer able to effectively regulate the apprentice system. The integration of recaptured Africans was more threatening to the settlers than the presence of neighboring African people. In fact, the arrival of thousands of recaptured Africans almost altered the very nature of settler society.

Recaptured Africans

The rescue, or liberation, of Africans from the slave trade was linked to the American Colonization Society's plan to establish a colony in Africa. The necessary funds to attempt the founding of such a colony had come from the U.S. government. From 1820 to 1843, two hundred eighty-seven recaptured Africans were sent to Liberia by the U.S. Navy. This number, however, represented only 6 percent of the immigrants for the period.[28] During these years the recaptured Africans present no unusual problems; they generally identified with the Afro-American settlers and integrated well into the settler social environment.

The settlement of New Georgia, near the left bank of the Stockton River, attracted many recaptured Africans. By 1834 it was a breadbasket community for Monrovia, supplying foodstuffs cultivated by recaptured African farmers. Beyond the fact that mostly recaptured Africans lived there, New Georgia was not unlike the other settlements. The settlement had two main streets intersected by several crossroads. Most of the houses were of one story and wood-framed, and like the houses in other settlements, they were raised two or three feet from the ground, atop pillars of wood or brick.[29] An 1840 visitor to New Georgia found the community upholding the settler standard: ". . . they called themselves *Americans*; and from the little civilization they have acquired, feel greatly superior to the natives around them; they have the same privileges as the emigrants; have a vote at the elections; each man has his musket, and is enrolled in the militia. Their women, instead of being nearly naked, as all the native African women are, we found dressed in the same modest manner as our own emigrants; all take great pride in imitating the custom and manners of those who are more civilized, having furniture in their houses, and many comforts they never dreamt of in their own country."[30]

The New Georgia settlement had both a Baptist and a Presbyterian church, as well as a common school—all of which served to encourage identification with the settler standard. In 1839, however, the annual report of the Liberia Mission of the Methodist Episcopal Church indicated that the assimilation process was not without some failures. In referring to the recaptured Africans of New Georgia, the reported noted that "a small decrease has occurred in the society, owing to the instability of the men, some of whom, not walking circumspectly nor amending when admonished, had to be put away from us."[31] This suggested the fundamental issue that faced the recaptured Africans: association with the settler community required that they maintain a social and cultural distance from the surrounding African people. The following case is typical for the years before 1840: When asked whether he wanted to return to his people, one recaptured African said, "No, if I go back to my country, they make me slave—I am here free—no one dare trouble me. I got my land—my wife—my children learn book—all free—I am here a *white man*."[32]

The situation for recaptured Africans began to change markedly in 1846. In that year the slave ship *Pons* was captured by the American Naval Squadron, and its cargo of seven hundred fifty-six slaves was brought to Liberia. Fourteen years later the number of recaptured Africans entering the society increased dramatically. In one year nearly five thousand recaptured Africans arrived (see table 16). The recaptive population had suddenly jumped from 6 percent of the total population to a number threatening to surpass the Afro-American settler population in 1860. Unlike the indigenous Africans, these recaptured slaves were introduced directly into the settler communities; and their incorporation was an immediate problem of extraordinary dimensions. President Stephen A. Benson reacted on behalf of the settlers with an appeal to the American Colonization Society for assistance. "For humanity's sake, relieve us! and the poor unfortunate creatures cast among us, as soon as possible."[33] The settler press also reacted. They too were shocked by "the suddenness of an avalanche" and concerned about the impact on settler

Table 16. Recaptured Africans Received in Liberia During the Nineteenth Century

Date of Arrival	Ship	Origin	Number of Africans Landed
1846	*Pons*	off Kabenda	756
August 21, 1860	*Storm King*	off Congo River	616
August 22, 1860	*Erie*	off Congo River	867
September 1, 1860	*South Shore*	Key West, Florida	218
September 3, 1860	*Star of the Union*	Key West, Florida	338
October 14, 1860	*Cora*	off Congo River	694
October 27, 1860	*Bonito*	off Congo River	734
1860	*Castilian*	Key West, Florida	233
1860	*Niagara*	Key West, Florida	200
1860	*Nightingale*	off Kabenda	801
Total			5,457

Source: Warren S. Howard, *American Slavers and the Federal Law, 1837-1862* (Berkeley and Los Angeles, 1963); U.S., National Archives, Microcopy 169, "Despatches from United States Consuls in Monrovia, 1852-1906"; Journal of John Moore McCalla, 1860, West Virginia and Regional History Collection, West Virginia University Library, Morgantown, W.Va.; and U.S., Congress, House, Executive Documents, *Report of John Seys, 1856-1863: House Executive Document No. 28*, 37th Cong., 3d sess., 1863.

standards. "What shall we, what *can* we do with such an appalling amount of heathenism, superstition, and barbarity all at once?"[34]

Who were these people that frightened the settlers so? Dr. John Moore McCalla kept a diary of his journey aboard the clipper ship *Star of the Union*, carrying three-hundred eighty-three recaptured Africans to Monrovia. McCalla had been appointed special agent of the American Colonization Society and was responsible for delivering the Africans to the U.S. Agent in Monrovia, John Seys. His recorded memoirs include descriptions of the people placed in his care.

The American Colonization Society chartered the *Star of the Union* in New York City for a voyage from Key West, Florida, to Liberia. On June 23, 1860, the ship left New York City for Key West with McCalla on board. The trip took just about three weeks and was generally uneventful, except that McCalla suffered often from seasickness. At Key West the U.S. government had erected a number of long houses and sheds near the ocean. These facilities were used to shelter the recaptured Africans brought there by the American Naval Squadron. McCalla was surprised to find a town of some three thousand inhabitants with comfortable homes, several large stores, churches, and a fort.[35] A U.S. marshal turned over three hundred eighty-three recaptured Africans to McCalla and the *Star of the Union* set sail for Liberia on July 19, 1860. Of the Africans on board, there were two hundred eighty-five males and ninety-eight females. McCalla believed that they were mainly from Whydah and mentioned that there was "a princess among them to whom they show particular respect. The Princess has a more haughty bearing than the others."[36] The voyage took more than a month, and during that time McCalla made daily entries in his journal.

On July 24 McCalla recorded the death of an old African woman, who was then wrapped in white muslin cloth with pieces of coal added for weight and dropped over the leeward side of the bow.[37] This burial-at-sea ceremony was repeated many times. Forty-five Africans died before the *Star of the Union* reached West Africa. McCalla observed the behavior of the recaptives, most of which he did not understand and considered savage.[38] Despite his negative attitudes, on several occasions McCalla described in detail activities of Africans that he witnessed. He was struck by the scarification of an African woman and the technique of a "charm doctor" administering to a sick person.[39]

The recaptured Africans on the *Star of the Union* continued traditional cultural practices. The voyage, however, introduced many Africans to aspects of Western cultural patterns. Marriages were performed joining African couples in Christian ritual. The first mate married twenty-four couples on August 5. He explained the nature of the ceremony through an interpreter and told them to live together in the future "forsaking all others.'[40] Monogamy would be further stressed by the settlers in Liberia. Several African children were given Christian names during baptismal ceremonies. When an African woman gave birth to a son, McCalla wrote, it was proposed to name the boy Buchanan McLain.[41] Thus even before the *Star of the Union* landed in Monrovia on September 3, 1860, the recaptured Africans were exposed to social patterns that would be emphasized in their new home.

The arrival of hundreds of recaptured Africans like those from the *Star of the Union* caught the settlers unprepared to manage their support and integration. The Liberian government was willing to accept recaptured Africans brought to the country by the U.S. Navy, but only if financial help was also forthcoming. They requested that the United States pay into the Liberia treasury "the same sum per capita, which the Hon. Secretary of the Interior of the United States had contracted to pay the American Colonization Society for the recaptives from Key West . . . ."[42] The U.S. agent for liberated Africans maintained a temporary facility to receive the recaptives landed in Monrovia. The Liberian government, however, insisted that as soon as it was practicable the recaptives were to be distributed among the different counties and not allowed to concentrate in one place. Towards that end, the government established a committee of leading citizens to work with John Seys in organizing the placement of the recaptives among settler farmers and householders. Agent Seys agreed to the basic plan and established his own policy for carrying it out. He paid upriver farmers fifty cents for every African taken and Monrovians, twenty-five cents. He also supplied the necessary clothing and bedding.[43]

The U.S. agent recognized that the responsibility was tremendous and that despite his close supervision, the distribution of recaptured Africans might create hardships for the Liberians and abuses to the recaptives. In a letter to the U.S. secretary of the navy, Seys cautioned that "it is to be feared that, however wisely they may be distributed, and however ample the sum I give *per capita* to those who take them, the larger portion of the people of Liberia cannot furnish in advance the food and clothing for such large addition to their households . . . ."[44]

At first recaptured Africans were placed with settlers through the apprentice system. When the slave ship *Pons* landed in 1846, most of its passengers were taken in by settler families as apprentices. Joseph J. Roberts recommended that "suitable persons be appointed to the general guardianship of those apprentices, whose duty it shall be to see them at stated times, to inquire respecting their treatment, and to see that the provisions of the act concerning apprentices are fully carried out in regard to them, and report their doing semi-annually to the Probate Court."[45] Later, when hundreds more arrived, family placements were not sufficient to absorb the additions. In 1860 the Monrovia commercial firm of Payne, Yates, and Company asked for and received ten recaptives to work at their sawmill at Junk. Settlements away from Monrovia began to accept within their communities recaptives who were not apprentices. When the ship *Cora* arrived on October 14, 1860, two hundred twenty-two recaptives were received by the upriver settlement of Careysburg.[46]

The missionary stations in Liberia offered to receive recaptives. The Lutheran missionary station at Muhlenberg, near the rapids of the St. Paul River, became known for the large number of recaptured Africans it served. The Reverend Alfred F. Russell, an Episcopalian minister in the St. Paul River area, reported that there were one thousand two hundred recaptured Africans in his district alone. He stated that "more attended services than can find room in the church and houses occupied for worship."[47] The Presbyterian mission at Harrisburg ran a boys' boarding school that had in attendance "eleven Congo boys, and three Congo girls, three boys and two girls from the Golahs, an aboriginal tribe now included in Liberia, and one boy from the Veys."[48]

Unattached recaptives sometimes created problems that troubled the settlers. President Stephen Benson made reference to the situation in a letter to the secretary of the American Colonization Society. He stated that "complaints and memorials are being constantly received . . . from various sections of the Republic, from county and town meetings, respecting the damages they are daily sustaining from the depredations of those Congoes and other recaptives from Whydah."[49] Although the nature of the alleged "depredations" and their reason were not clear, it cannot be denied that not all recaptives found life among the Afro-American settlers desirable. The essence of uncertainty comes through in a ditty sung among the recaptured Africans:

> Thus far we've haply come:
> But here we cannot stay
> Soon we must go again
> Tell which way,
> Tell which way,
> Nor can we tell which way.
>
> Perhaps to a slaver sold,
> Perhaps it is not so;
> Do not know,
> Do not know,
> Because we do not know.
>
> Here food and drink we find,
> And pity, too, is shown;
> Is not known,
> Is not known,
> The future is not known.[50]

Some recaptives left the settlements attempting to return to their ethnic homelands. In one day John Seys saw twenty-five recaptured Africans apprehended while trying to leave the jurisdiction of the Liberian government. One man hung himself in "a fit of despondency."[51] J. W. Lugenbeel, medical officer for the American Colonization Society, also recognized the runaway problem but saw it as a temporary reaction: "most of those who ran away during the first few months after their arrival, returned to their homes, being convinced that they could fare much better in the colonial settlements than in the bush."[52] The *Liberia Herald* agreed with Lugenbeel's assessment: "They seem perfectly satisfied with their circumstances; and we find no great difficulty in accustoming them to our habits."[53]

The vast influx of recaptives into Liberia in 1860 led to the spread of settlements similar to New Georgia. Apparently not all such settlements were approved. In 1864 the citizens of Bassa County suggested to the legislature several measures that would have abolished all Congo towns not established by the government.[54] One month after the petitions reached the legislature, the body considered a bill to prevent runaway Congoes from leaving one county for another. The bill was passed as An Act to prevent recaptured Africans from leaving one County and settling in another without consent of Government or the County where such settlement is proposed.[55] The availability of land provided recaptives an alternative to the apprentice system. The legislators refused to grant a petition by a group of citizens from Montserrado County that would regulate the activities of recaptives more closely. They reasoned that to pass such an act would be unconstitutional, "as no such law can be passed to effect the aborigines of this Country without effecting the Americo-Liberians, since we are but one people."[56] The lawmakers further explained that in their opinion the existing statutes on apprenticeship were sufficient for the needs of every citizen and that a new law might indirectly sanction servitude. Finally, mention was made by the legislators of a danger inherent in such a bill. The act "would not only compel the *natives* to *serve us*, but also our own sons and daughters, if otherwise, then it would be slavery to all intents and purposes."[57]

The Liberian government was cautious with regard to the possible implications of servitude in the apprentice system. There was always a realization, nevertheless, that the recaptured Africans represented both a resource of manpower that could benefit the republic and a potentially potent political force. For the rest of the century recaptured Africans—or Congoes, as they came to be called locally—played a vital role in Liberian affairs. This was especially true as settler communities were formed beyond the coastal enclaves. Recaptured Africans, who at first seemed to present a major threat to the settler standard, became in time a key factor in settler expansion on the frontier. Frontier expansion, particularly along the St. Paul River, presented a more intense challenge to the conservative settler standard that flourished on the coast. The upriver settlements were the first, tentative probes by the settlers into the matrix of African life in Liberia.

5/The St. Paul River Settlements

By Deed, this purchase includes generally all the lands
bounded North by the St. Paul's and West by the Stockton,
such expressly excepted as are or may be at the time of
forming and extending on it the Colonial Settlement,
occupied by and necessary to the subsistence and comfort
of the Natives of the Country, it being no part of the intention of this purchase to deprive these people of a single
real advantage; but on the contrary to improve them and
advance their happiness, by carrying christianity and civilization to the doors of their Cabins.

> —From the first deed for land
> along the St. Paul River,
> negotiated by Jehudi Ashmun in 1825

The American Colonization Society constantly pressured the settlers in
Liberia to become self-sufficient in agriculture. This mandate motivated
inland expansion of the Afro-American settler society. Rivers that drained
into the Atlantic Ocean offered the easiest access to the interior. The alluvial
flood plains provided fertile land that was ideal for agricultural settlements.
Advocates of inland expansion also considered it a positive step towards the
goal of amalgamation with the African people of Liberia. They argued that it
could have the salutary effect of radiating the influences of "Christianity and
Civilization" throughout the country. Although the influences were expected
to move in one direction, the upriver settlements in fact became the focus
of an exchange between two cultural orientations. It was there that a unique-
ly Liberian personality developed blending both settler standards and local
African standards to create the "river man." This was the Liberian who
adapted to the environment by combining American social values with African patterns of life. In the years after 1850 there developed in the upriver
settlements an alternative settler standard, which competed with the more
conservative standard of coastal settlers.

Patterns of Settlement along the St. Paul River

The first Afro-Americans to live in the vicinity of the St. Paul River came
there before 1847. Jehudi Ashmun was the first agent of the American

73

Colonization Society to become interested in the land bordering on the St. Paul River as a site where new immigrants could settle.[1] His interest was in establishing the first purely agricultural settlement. Ashmun used the arrival of immigrants on the brig *Hunter* on March 13, 1825, as an excuse to seek new territory away from Monrovia. He secured the land after some delay and a general palaver with several African headmen. The ceded land became the first St. Paul River settlement. Ashmun selected a few families to lay the foundations for the new site, which he named Caldwell, in honor of the first secretary of the American Colonization Society. The land was first occupied on November 14, 1825. Jehudi Ashmun led the first group personally and recorded the event while "seated on a Bamboo pallet, in a solitary native Cabin, on the margin of the St. Paul's."[2]

As more settlers came to Caldwell, Ashmun issued private instructions on exactly how land was to be distributed among the families. His instructions covered other details as well. He required that the fronts of all dwelling houses be placed on a line ten feet from the south line of Water Street, which ran parallel to the St. Paul River. Every settler was called upon to clear the land in front of his lot to the bank of the river; only shade trees designated by the settlement steward were left. Ashmun also prohibited the use of thatch for the roofing of buildings and declared that he expected no settler to leave Caldwell for the purpose of trading.[3] These initial guidelines were followed by detailed regulations concerning governance and settler responsibilities. The regulations called for the election of various settlement officers such as steward, magistrate, constable, health officer, and head farmer.[4] Every male settler above the age of sixteen was required to enroll in the militia and perform public labor as directed by the head farmer and steward.[5]

Dr. Richard Randall, colonial agent in 1828, visited Caldwell three years after its founding. He was pleased with the community's progress and impressed that "most settlers had good houses, and all of them have flourishing plantations of rice, cassada [sic], plantains, and potatoes, with many other fruits, and vegetables."[6] Thus Caldwell, with river transportation to the coast, was becoming a breadbasket community for Monrovia, like the recaptured African settlement of New Georgia. Dr. Randall recognized that none of the Caldwell people were as prosperous as the Monrovians, who had the advantage of commercial opportunities. He believed, nevertheless, that their future was bright because their lands were ideal for the cultivation of sugar and cotton.[7] Such optimism no doubt influenced the decision to establish a second river settlement in 1828.

Millsburg was established by a small company of volunteers some twenty miles upriver, near the limit of tidal navigation. As time passed, both Caldwell and Millsburg became places of active internal trade. By 1830 a

Table 17. Settlements Adjacent to the St. Paul River

Settlement	Founding Date
Left bank	
Bensonville	—
Caldwell	1825
Careysburg	1859
Crozierville	1865[a]
Harrisburg	—
Louisiana	1843[a]
White Plains	—
Right bank	
Arthington	1869
Brewerville	1879
Kentucky (Clay Ashland)	1847
Millsburg	1828
Virginia	1846[a]

Sources: *Liberia Herald*; Jehudi Ashmun Papers, 1826-28, and Minutes of the House of Representatives and of the Senate—all in Archives of the Liberian Government, Monrovia, Liberia.
[a]This date is approximate.

road was opened from Millsburg to the indigenous commercial center at Bopolu—an accomplishment that stimulated trade between settlers and Africans.[8] There were those, however, who considered trade as a short-sighted alternative to agriculture. Dr. J. W. Anderson complained that although the soil was fertile, the majority of the river settlers depended on trade for their support. Anderson acknowledged that there was good business for those who had the proper articles of trade (that is, tobacco, cloth, rum, and so on), but he maintained that "there are many who would do much better if they would turn their attention to the cultivation of their little farms."[9] What Anderson failed to fully understand was that profitable farming required a dependable labor source, as well as crops that were valuable to the international market. The local settler population was too small to provide the sole consumer market. Both the labor source and cash crops capable of making agriculture pay developed through a trial-and-error process.

After the establishment of Millsburg in 1828, the land on both banks of the St. Paul River was taken up by other settlers. One new community after another was formed by newcomers (see table 17 and map 4). The method of settlement tended to foster a distinctive character to the upriver settlements. Each settlement was organized first by an original pioneer company led by individuals whose family names are still generally associated with the particular community they helped to build.

J. D. Simpson was sent to Liberia by the colonization auxiliaries of New York and Kentucky in 1847. He was responsible for finding a location

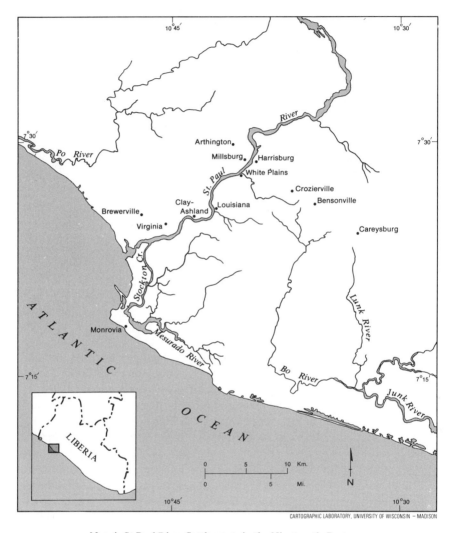

Map 4. St Paul River Settlements in the Nineteenth Century

suitable for settling by freed Afro-Americans from both states. Simpson traveled up the St. Paul River and decided on this area for the proposed settlement. After returning to America, Simpson led a company of emigrants to Liberia in 1853. The Colemans, Ricks, Ashes, Lomaxes, and Houstons were among the families that established Clay Ashland on the right bank of the St. Paul River.[10] One lifelong resident of the community recalled being told that "some came here, some went to Caldwell. You know they went all about to farm. But the first man that jumped off the boat, they tell me, in

Clay Ashland, was named Houston—Augustus Houston. He was on a boat and he sprung off and said, 'Well, I'm free!' "[11]

In 1869 immigrants from North Carolina, South Carolina, and Georgia came to Liberia on the ship *Golconda*. They settled in an area three miles northwest of Millsburg that they called Arthington. The leader of the group was Alonzo Hoggard. A separate group from Virginia, led by John Butler Munden, came on the same ship. This company was composed of artisans noted in America for making shingles. In 1870 they founded Brewerville to the rear of the Virginia settlement, on the right bank of the river.[12] More companies arrived in 1870 and 1871—led by John Roulhac and Jefferson Bracewell—and settled in Arthington.

Family relations were just as important to the upriver settlers as they were to the coastal people. The experiences of the Richards family of Clay Ashland were representative of the experiences of many upriver families. The family now spans five generations, and over one hundred fifty persons have descended from its founding ancestor, Othello Richards (see table 18).[13]

The Richards Family of Clay Ashland

Othello Richards was emancipated by his owner, Mrs. S. P. Taylor, of Lexington, Virginia, in 1850. Othello was literate and an active Methodist preacher. After his emancipation, Othello purchased the freedom of his wife, Mary, and their six children. The Richards family was among the thirty-seven emigrants from Virginia that joined a company on board the *Liberia Packet*.[14] The vessel left Baltimore, Maryland, on July 4, 1850, on her eighth voyage to Liberia. A case of smallpox immediately broke out among the crew, forcing the captain to order a stop at Hampton Roads, Virginia, where the entire company was vaccinated as a precaution against the further spread of the disease. By July 24 the *Liberia Packet* finally set sail for Liberia with "all on board in good health and spirits."[15] Othello Richards, upon reaching Liberia, decided against remaining in Monrovia; he choose instead to establish his home upriver in the settlement of Clay Ashland.

Othello Richards gained a reputation for piety among his neighbors in Clay Ashland that led to his appointment as a supervisor of the Clay Ashland circuit of the Liberia Methodist Conference in 1864.[16] His affiliation with the Methodist Church in Liberia began when the St. Peter's Methodist Church was built in Clay Ashland. Subsequent generations of the Richards family retained loyalty to Methodism.[17] Othello was a deeply religious man and also a firm believer in the importance of labor. Economic opportunity in agriculture was the foundation for the Richards family's stability.

Table 18. The Richards Family Genealogy

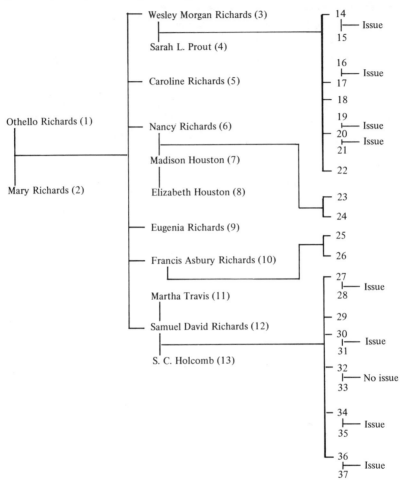

See appendix B for Richards family names through three generations.

An Act Pertaining to Bounty Land was passed by the Liberian Legislature on January 9, 1857 (see appendix C).[18] In 1869 President James Spriggs Payne used his authority under this act to grant Othello Richards forty-five acres of land at Kings Governors in the settlement of Louisiana.[19] The act enabled the Liberian government to reward citizens who performed military service to the republic by giving them land once the service was certified. Bounty land was only one means of acquiring real estate for upriver settlers like Othello. All newcomers were entitled to draw a town lot and ample farmland (up to ten acres) and to receive a certificate from the government. "If, within two years from that date, two acres of land on the plantation shall have been brought under cultivation, the town lot cleared and inclosed, a legal house built, the said certificate may be exchanged for title deeds of such lands, to be held, thereafter in *fee simple.*"[20]

The government also offered the sale of public lands to settlers who wished to make further investments in property. A land commissioner was appointed for each county by the president. The commissioner was responsible for regulating and effecting the sale of public lands. The Act Regulating the Sale of Public Lands established minimum prices: " . . . land lying on the margin of rivers, shall be one dollar an acre, and those lying in the interior of the lands on the river fifty cents. Town lots each shall be thirty dollars, except marshy, rocky and barren lots and plots of land which may be sold to the highest bidder."[21] Property transference of real estate occurred in other ways than through government programs. Individuals sold land outright in fee simple to other persons. On occasion, land was sold out of an estate in order to pay the outstanding debts of the deceased (see appendixes D and E).[22] Some settlers issued mortgage deeds for their land to secure cash, while in other instances land was sold by order of the Court of Quarter Sessions and Common Pleas as part of litigation settlements.

Although the ground rules for property transfers were explicit in the law, the actual transactions often involved conflicts and disputes. Surveying was seldom very accurate, since few individuals had the necessary training to do it correctly. In 1856 the *Liberia Herald* reported that the government was obliged to order new surveys of land in the St. Paul River area so as to "render every part and particle of land drawn, sold or taken up, to be easily designated."[23] The situation did not improve with time, however. The surveying difficulties were complicated by inefficient record-keeping. As late as 1892 the attorney general of Liberia spoke out candidly on the problem: "It has happened that owing to carelessness, or worse, one lot of land has been proved in account to have been deeded to three different numbers. In consequence of such and singular errors, persons frequently settle on, improve and take steps to acquire title to lands supposed to be vacant only to find out that they have laboured in vain and that they have improved the property of others."[24]

The attorney general was hinting at the possibility of criminal fraud in the deeding of titles. Charges of land fraud had been made by other public officials even earlier. The superintendent of Maryland County, J. T. Gibson, said in 1872 that "for the last 6 or 8 years it has been custom or practice of our Land Commissioners to take advantage of the ambiguity or malconstruction of the law defining and regulating their duties and prerogatives and making the office one of mere individual speculation, to the great detriment of Government, and injury to the public interest."[25] He went further and described how the abuses developed. Private understandings, according to Gibson, were worked out between individuals to outbid all others at public land auctions conducted by the land commissioner. Once the bid was won, regardless of the final price, the bidder refused to pay and instead secured the land at government price in a private sale after ninety days. The land commissioner was paid a fee for cooperating in the private sale and not penalizing the bidder for his original forfeiture.[26]

Fraud in the deeding of titles could sometimes be traced to politics. Land ownership was a basic requirement for the franchise privilege. In 1855 the Court of Quarter Sessions and Common Pleas convicted forty-one persons for voting on "false or spurious deeds."[27] As land in the St. Paul River area became more valuable economically, the possibility of fraud also increased. When sugar-cane cultivation flourished, the price of land in the settlements along the river became exorbitant. This tendency accounts, in part, for the success of early upriver settlers, who by virtue of their time of arrival secured the choice land bordering the river. Not only was the soil rich, but the cost of overland transportation to markets on the coast was greatly reduced.

The Richards Family and Conflict Resolution

In the 1880s two of the sons of Othello Richards, Samuel David and Wesley Morgan, became embroiled in a dispute over land that both claimed was given to them by their father. The dispute reached the Montserrado Court of Quarter Sessions and Common Pleas in 1887. Samuel David Richards filed a complaint against his brother's widow, Sarah Richards; and Samuel T. Prout was also named as a defendant in the complaint, since he was the executor of Wesley Morgan's estate.

The complaint detailed the nature of the dispute from the point of view of Samuel David Richards. He claimed that his father had verbally distributed his property among his children. He declared that after his father's death in 1873 all of the children agreed to their share of his property but that Wesley Morgan then violated the agreement. Wesley Morgan "notwithstanding the remonstrances of [Samuel David] and other members of the family would persist and did persist in building his house on a portion of ten acres of the original homestead that had been allotted to Samuel David."[28] After building his home on the disputed property, Wesley Morgan willed to his wife and children one and one-half acres of Samuel David's original ten acres, on which he had "unlawfully" built his house. He also willed to his family twenty-two acres of farmland on Kings Governors plot, although allegedly he was only entitled to fifteen and two-thirds acres there.

Sarah Richards and Samuel T. Prout responded to the complaint on December 11, 1887. The defendants claimed that Othello Richards had made no lawful will during his lifetime. They asserted that after the death of Othello in 1873, Wesley Morgan took up the land and built his house without any formal objections from Samuel David Richards. They also pointed out that when Wesley Morgan's will was probated in 1882, Samuel David Richards failed to challenge its provisions, although he was aware of the probate proceedings.[29] After lengthy testimony from many witnesses, the court reached a decision on September 26, 1887.

Judge C. A. Pitman made a reference to a number of key issues in the suit when he made his ruling. He noted that Othello Richards died intestate and that no documentary evidence had been presented to the court to support the claim that the disputed land belonged to Samuel David Richards. The judge stressed Samuel David Richards's delay in bringing legal action until after his brother had died. " . . . the Court says that by his said act of agreement . . . the Plaintiff cannot now claim interference of Equity—He is estopped."[30] Finally, Judge Pitman cited a legal technicality. Samuel David Richards had alleged that his brother attempted to defraud the heirs of his sister Nancy and his brother Francis Asbury, as well as himself. The court pointed out that after naming these individuals, "the plaintiff has neglected to join them in this suit . . . which neglect is fatal in a case of Equity."[31] In conclusion, the court ruled that the plaintiff's bill in equity be dismissed and that Samuel David Richards pay all court costs involved.

Critical to the court's decision was that Samuel David Richards had brought suit after the death of his brother and thus had delayed legal action too long to be credible.[32] It is interesting that part of the delay was caused by an extralegal proceeding that was described in the testimony of the case. Madison Houston (husband of Nancy Richards) testified that an effort had been made to settle the dispute locally in Clay Ashland; the Methodist neighbors of the Richards family had tried to resolve the conflict by conducting a church trial on the matter. Samuel T. Prout offered Samuel David Richards one hundred fifty dollars for the disputed property in the Clay Ashland Methodist church. Madison Houston's description of the trial deserves lengthy quotation:

> Mrs. Sarah Richards and Miss Addicate Holcomb [sister of Samuel David Richards's wife] had had a fuss. Miss Addicate Holcomb said Mrs. Richards struck her and then sued Mrs. Richards. After she sued Mrs. Richards the church took Miss Holcomb up for sueing Mrs. Richards; it was on a Sunday when they all came to church. Mr. Prout came with her—after they all commenced to talk the Preacher in charge wanted Miss Holcomb to beg Mrs. Richards pardon for sueing her, and wanted Sister Richards to acknowledge her wrong for striking her and they all come together and make the matter up. Sister Richards was willing to beg pardon and compromise but Sister Holcomb would not come to any compromise at all. She said Sister Richards had been telling lies on her and

Figure 6. Settler Home in Bensonville (now Bentol), Liberia

troubling her long enough, and she would not shake hands with her to save her life. The preacher in charge told her to sit down and behave herself then Mr. Prout asked to make a few remarks and he got up and said he had heard right smart talk about how that young lady had been treating his sister before and he said I see it today . . . Mr. Richards started to say something and then everybody began to talk and the whole church got to talking and I told the Preacher in charge why not put them out doors—you have enough Stewards here; the Preacher in charge worried with them awhile and got them straight and then Mr. Prout offered Mr. Richards $150 for the land where his sister's house was at, then Mr. Richards said no I won't sell you the land because thats my birth place.[33]

The church trial failed to resolve the conflict between the members of the Richards family; however, local-level mediation within the upriver settlements was an important mechanism.

Upriver Settlement Institutions

Each upriver settlement had various means for resolving community conflicts while at the same time encouraging unity. Institutions other than the church wielded considerable influence over individuals in the community. Upriver settlers used town meetings as a forum for discussing problems of general concern. Resolutions and petitions expressing majority opinion on a given issue resulted from town meetings. Usually the petitions were printed and

Figure 7. Settler Home in Crozierville, Liberia

posted in the community; some were sent to Monrovia for the attention of either the legislature or the president.

Town meetings occasionally became the means for organizing economic associations. In 1866 the citizens of Caldwell held a town meeting and drew up a plan for the creation of a settlement association. A petition was sent by the group to the legislature requesting a charter for the Union Agricultural and Live Stock Society of Caldwell.[34] The citizens of Brewerville called a town meeting in 1892 to discuss the closing of an important school in their settlement. One hundred nine persons from Brewerville called on the legislature to appropriate funds to keep the Garnet Memorial School open.[35] Town meetings sometimes generated petitions expressing a settlement position in conflict with neighboring communities.

Sixty-three citizens of Virginia held a town meeting on August 27, 1885. They sent a petition directly to the president expressing their objection to a boundary line separating their settlement from Brewerville:

> We your humble petitioners having learned that the Legislature at its last Session passed an Act to have the line run or surveyed between Virginia and Brewerville and in accordance with said act the government has proceeded to cause Mr. Anderson to commence said line without notifying the authorities of this settlement the time, place nor direction said Line would run; and to our regret he has commenced the said to be line, at a place within the jurisdiction of Virginia, and if allowed to continue will be greatly detrimental to our interest.[36]

The petition went on to list ten specific facts to support their contention. The president was reminded that the sons of the Virginia settlement "have been ever ready and are still ready to face her [the Republic's] enemies upon all occasions when called upon, and her many battlefields will always tell her sons have been second to none."[37] The president responded to the Virginia petition by suggesting the appointment of two commissioners to represent the interests of both settlements and a surveyor to correct any errors in the boundary line.[38]

The most important role of town meetings was political. It was through town meetings that upriver settlers made their contribution to both local and national politics. The *Liberia Herald* published a letter from a settler in Clay Ashland in 1852 describing a town meeting in Clay Ashland that produced a call for a national convention to select a slate of candidates to stand for national election. The correspondent carefully recounted the proceedings of September 10, 1852: Debrick Simpson was called to chair the meeting, and George M. Moore was elected secretary. D. T. Harris stated the purpose of the meeting and offered a preamble and several resolutions for approval by the body. He called for consideration of "the appointment of delegates, by an equal ratio of representation, throughout the Republic, to meet in convention at Monrovia . . . then and there to make a national ticket of the most available men for the Presidency and Vice Presidency."[39] Harris's proposal specifically suggested that the appointment of delegates to represent the different counties and settlements be based on the ratio of one delegate to every ten voters. The proposal included a list of principles that the delegates would be called upon to endorse. The final resolution declared that it was not advisable to allow any indigenous Africans to participate in the national balloting.[40]

All the resolutions were adopted with only slight amendments. Several prominent men made speeches supporting the resolutions. After the speeches, a committee was appointed to nominate the Clay Ashland delegates to the proposed convention. H. W. Erskine, A. B. Hooper, R. McMurtry, and James Capps were nominated and elected unanimously. Before the meeting was finally adjourned, a vigilance committee was appointed to keep the community informed of later developments. One month later, the citizens of Virginia held their own town meeting to endorse the Clay Ashland platform and elect their delegates.

Town meetings were also used to present partisan views shared by only a segment of the settlement community. Several citizens of Clay Ashland held a town meeting to protest the election procedure in their settlement during the 1875 presidential election. The protest, addressed to the secretary of state, declared that the Clay Ashland returns were invalid because "we believe and have good cause to believe that aborigines of the County who are

Table 19. Militia Companies in Nineteenth-Century Liberia

Company	Manpower strength
Barclay's Guard	55
Benson Volunteers	45
Company "C"	45
Company "G"	46
Coopers Invincibles	44
Marshall Volunteers	50
Montserrado Regulars	–
New Georgia Dragon Bloods	–
Newport Volunteers	–
Robertsport Guard	–
Sherman's Cadets	–
Williams Guards	42

Sources: State Department Correspondence, Foreign and Local, 1886-1906; Minutes of the Senate, January 11, 1872, Archives of the Liberian Government, Monrovia, Liberia.

wholly unqualified to vote at such elections, were illegally allowed to vote at the Polls in said Township, to the great injury of your lawful constituents and in violation of the laws of this Republic; and we beg your Honourable Bodies to inquire into these facts believing there is sufficient evidence to prove the allegations herein made."[41]

Town meetings were called periodically within each settlement, while church meetings were held each Sunday and often during the week as well. The fraternal organizations that began in Monrovia spread upriver. Clay Ashland, for example, was the center of Masonic activities in the St. Paul River area after the St. Paul's Lodge No. 2 was established there. Members from neighboring settlements traveled to Clay Ashland to attend Masonic meetings. Those living on the left bank were obliged to cross the river by canoe. Other upriver settlements had chapters of different fraternal orders, and they too held meetings and organized activities. Taken together, these institutions were all vehicles for community interaction and solidarity.

The organization of volunteer militia companies was of special significance for upriver settler unity. The militia's primary purpose was to provide a defense apparatus for the frontier settlements. The Liberian legislature passed an Act to Regulate the Militia, which set up the rules for the Republic's primary defense institution. The act required that "every able bodied male citizen . . . between the ages of 16 and 50 . . . shall be enrolled in the Militia; and that every male citizen between the ages aforesaid; shall be considered 'able bodied' unless he shall produce to the Commander of the Regiment a certificate from a Physician of his inability."[42] The commander in chief of the militia was authorized by the act to grant charters to any body of men as a volunteer company providing that a roll of forty rank-and-file members were presented. Rules were outlined in detail specifying pay scales

Figure 8. Dedication Ceremony for New Baptist Church Building in Clay-Ashland, Liberia, 1975.

by rank, chain of command, discipline procedures, and uniform responsibilities for all ranks.

The settlements in the St. Paul River area organized volunteer companies (see table 19). These volunteer companies not only mobilized settler manpower but also provided a means of integrating Africans who lived within the settler jurisdiction. In 1885 the president's secretary wrote to the captain of the Virginia militia on that subject: "I write by direction of His Excellency the President to direct that in enrolling the names of Native youth to perform Military duty, you will do so impartially, that is, you will enroll *all* who are of the proper age (16 years) and who are sufficiently advanced in civilization to perform such duties."[43]

Volunteer companies mustered on a regular basis for parades. The *Liberia Herald* often published announcements for the assembly of militia troops.[44] Regular militia meetings were held to organize activities and handle administrative details. In 1845 the top militia officers were called together by the president to make arrangements for a public celebration of the December 1822 Battle of Fort Hill.[45] The meeting produced several resolutions regarding the proposed celebration, including that "any and all mercantile operations (desist) on that day."[46] The organization of volunteer companies accomplished more than protection of the outlying settlements from attack. The militia was a significant means for supporting settler values, developing local leadership, and linking individuals to a structure that was ultimately controlled by the president in his position as commander in chief of the militia.

For families like the Richardses life in the upriver settlements involved many different kinds of associations. Religion, politics, and defense all were common interests that facilitated the development of strong relationships outside the family structure. In small communities, resolution of interpersonal conflict became an important function of community associations. Internal unity remained vital to settler communities on the fringe of a potentially hostile environment that the settlers were only slowly able to understand. Leadership developed as trade and agriculture began to offer the foundation for upriver economic viability. The emergence of the St. Paul River area as a competing central place to Monrovia was in large part a response to external influences on settler society in Liberia.

Part Three/Overview

As the Afro-American settlers struggled to build the kind of society that they hoped would endure, many external factors affected their progress. The relationships the settlers had with their African neighbors, as well as with foreigners, had a direct bearing on the economic situation. It must be understood that in reality these factors were never separate. Coherent discussion and analysis, however, requires some dilineation, at the cost of chronological order. Liberian settler society did not exist in a vacuum. An overview of the external factors should help to explain why survival was such a remarkable feature of the Afro-American experience in nineteenth-century Liberia.

6/Africans and Settlers

I do not mean to insult the Americans, or to do anything
to create a war—all of my people and myself are under their
laws; but the Americans have bad men as constables; they
come out here, take our women, sleep with them, and persuade them off, and when we attempt to put a stop to it,
then they go to you with falsehoods trying to set up war.
Now what advantages is it for us to fight war with you,
when all our salt, tobacco, cloth, powder, guns and every-
thing comes from the Americans? My father Farquaquae
never fought your people and he was much stronger and
more able than I am, then where could I get this notion to
do such?

> —Dwallah Zeppie to President
> Hiliary Richard Wright Johnson, August 1, 1887,
> Executive Mansion Journal of H.R.W. Johnson,
> 1885-88

The first violent confrontation between Afro-American settlers and Africans
occurred during the now legendary Battle of Fort Hill on December 1,
1822. Tradition maintains that the first settlers in Monrovia were outnum-
bered and on the verge of being overwhelmed by the attacking Africans. At
that crucial moment a settler woman, Matilda Newport, fired a cannon with
her pipe. The blast is said to have killed and wounded many of the attackers,
causing the rest to retreat in disarray. This early victory against great odds
has become an important element in the settler ethos. It marks the triumph
of "civilization over barbarism; of enlightenment over gross ignorance; and
of Christianity over paganism."[1] Unfortunately this emphasis on the Fort Hill
encounter tends to obscure the varied aspects of African-settler relations during the nineteenth century. Conflicts were frequent, but the motives were
often more complicated than simply a struggle between civilization and barbarism. Africans were never unified in opposition to the presence of Afro-
American settlers. As immigration increased and new settlements were
formed, settler attitudes towards their African neighbors also became dif-
ferentiable.[2]

Settler curiosity about the Liberian hinterland and its inhabitants was initially stimulated by the prospect of trade. African traders carrying their pro-

ducts for sale in Monrovia and other settler enclaves also brought stories about life in the interior. Enterprising settlers involved in the "native trade" made cautious attempts to explore the hinterland for themselves. Ruben Dongey was one of the first settler traders to venture far upcountry. In 1828 he described a journey that he and three others took to Bopolu in order to initiate direct trade links with the powerful chief Sao Boso.[3] The only route to Bopolu then was a circuitous one, taking travelers over both land and water. Dongey's description of Bopolu was consistent with its prominence as the central place of interior trade. "The town contains more than 1000 houses, and is well fortified with a barricade, and 8,000 men armed with muskets, can be brought to its defence."[4]

Ruben Dongey reported that Sao Boso was anxious to open a direct path to the Afro-American settlements for purposes of trade. He also described the St. Paul River and declared that it was navigable to within twenty-five miles of Bopolu. This information prompted the colonial agent, Richard Randall, to speculate that by means of the St. Paul River "we may divert to this place [Monrovia], much of the gold and ivory, which is now carried to Sierra Leone, on the North and Cape Coast to the South."[5] In later years the establishment of settler communities along the St. Paul River represented a direct thrust into the existing economic and political patterns of western Liberia.

The death of Sao Boso in 1836 plunged the western hinterland into a long period of political turmoil. An intense struggle for the control of trade commenced as different chiefs competed for expanded authority. This turmoil quickly involved the settlers as well. An African attack on the settler community at Millsburg in 1839 was one consequence of the troubled times. Getumbe (Gatoombay), an interior chief and ally of the Condo Confederation, led an assault on the vulnerable settlement. The incident was not particularly serious; in fact the Millsburg militia was able to repel the attack with no loss of life among their number. The Liberian government, however, responded to what they considered an "outrage" by organizing a punitive military expedition to Getumbe's town, Suehn.[6] The swift and effective action of the settlers increased the prestige of the colony among the coastal Dei people. In the wake of the Getumbe expedition, the Dei (who were trying to retain their precarious position as commercial middlemen at the coast) identified more closely with the settlers.

Other raids and threats kept the interior situation unsettled until the 1860s. In that decade Momolu Sao, the son of Sao Boso, gained firm control over Bopolu. The upriver settlements along the St. Paul River had expanded considerably. The community of White Plains became the key depot for trade items moving down from the interior because of its strategic location on the left bank of the river at the head of the rapids. From White Plains canoes and packet boats carried goods up and down the St. Paul to Monrovia. In 1860 the Reverend C. C. Hoffman, a missionary living beside the river, described Saturday as market day, when up to sixty canoes would take produce to market at Monrovia.[7] Four years earlier the *Liberia Herald* had announced the launching of the first packet boat, the *Helena Augusta*, plying the waters between Millsburg and Monrovia.[8]

The stability occasioned by the rise of Momolu Sao helped the upriver settlers to establish themselves in the area. His death in 1871, however, created an atmosphere of political and economic uncertainty once again. The renewed difficulties adversely affected upriver settlers, as they did Africans. The fortunes of Africans and settlers were increasingly interconnected, despite the strong tendency towards isolationism among the settlers.

Dwallah Zeppie and Upriver Conflict

In 1885 the settlers of Clay Ashland addressed a long petition to President Hiliary R. W. Johnson about the worsening situation in their vicinity since the death of Momolu Sao. The Clay Ashlanders declared that the Gola and Bopolu countries were filled with tribal and domestic feuds and petty wars. The conflicts had produced an unprecedented season of scarcity and depression. Just when better times seemed to be approaching, the same old wars had started up again with greater intensity. Africans employed by settler farmers were leaving their labors without notice to defend their homes and support their chiefs. The petitioners stated that the best solution to the continuing wars would be to occupy the Bopolu area with an Afro-American settlement and annex the surrounding territories. They realized that the president might not be willing to take such a radical step, but at least, they said, the native authority commissioner should be given real power to summons and bring to account the "refractory chiefs."[9] Johnson agreed to order the secretary of the interior and the native authority commissioner to meet with two representatives from Clay Ashland to discuss the problem.[10] The cautious approach to the situation that Johnson adopted became characteristic of the chief executive's policy—a policy that underwent a major test two years later.

In July 1887 a relatively minor incident led to a serious confrontation between the upriver settlers and a Gola chief, Dwallah Zeppie. The justice of the peace for Arthington had issued writs for the arrest of two Africans on formal charges made by an African named Gouh living in Arthington. In the first writ Basse, a Gola man, was charged with unlawfully detaining Gouh's wife and refusing to return her. The second writ charged Basse and Walbor, another Gola man, with default of a thirty-three-dollar debt to Gouh.[11] When

John Walkup, the constable for Arthington, attempted to arrest the men, he and his party of deputies were seized and held by Dwallah Zeppie.

Conflicting accounts of the incident quickly began to filter back to Monrovia. Arthington justice Bracewell asked the president for authorization to mount a party to rescue the men and requested the immediate delivery of a dozen guns and ammunition to protect the settlement.[12] At the same time, the native authority commissioner, Thomas Mitchell, wrote the president from Millsburg giving his version of the incident: He believed that the problem could be traced to Constable Walkup, who had attacked a town controlled by Zeppie.[13]

Johnson considered the situation carefully before acting. He took the position that settler authority and laws had to be respected by Africans. With this in mind, he ordered Mitchell to demand the immediate release of the constable and his people. Meanwhile he wrote to Justice Bracewell and appealed for calm. He explained his decision to let Mitchell handle the problem. "I think the best course is first to endeavour to get the men back as quietly as possible, as resorting to force precipitately might endanger their lives. Should Mr. Mitchell fail, then other steps will have to be taken."[14] In order that his decision would be more acceptable to the nervous people of Arthington, Johnson informed Bracewell, the comptroller would send "by Mr. Moore some guns and ammunition for the protection of your settlement."[15]

The Arthington settlers continued to press for an immediate military response to the incident even while Mitchell was trying to secure the release of the captured men. A town meeting was called to discuss the situation, and seventy-seven citizens signed a petition that was carried to Monrovia by an appointed committee of three settlement leaders. The petition accused Dwallah Zeppie of attacking a "country town" in Arthington and carrying away people and property. When the constable, two other settlers, and eight Africans attempted to carry out the writ, the petition continued, Zeppie seized the men, confining the settlers for five days and still holding the Africans. The petition ended with an appeal for action: "Now Mr. President, these men are our citizens, they pay tax annually to government as citizens of our townships, therefore we hope that some immediate steps will be taken for the delivery of our captured native citizens and to bring Dwallah Zeppie and his subjects to justice, unless this may embolden him to commit other depredations worse than this."[16]

Neighboring settlements learned of the events as rumors began to spread, despite Johnson's desire that the matter be handled quietly. The citizens of Clay Ashland addressed the president on the subject as early as July 16. They indicated not only that Dwallah Zeppie had seized men from Arthington but also that they believed he intended to attack Clay Ashland and kidnap William David Coleman, a prominent settler of the community.[17]

The upriver settlers saw the situation simply as an outrage committed against them by a "refractory chief." There was, however, another side to the story, which Thomas Mitchell brought to the attention of President Johnson. Mitchell found resolution of the problem difficult precisely because the issues were not cut and dried. He managed to secure the release of three of the captives and expected Zeppie to return the remaining men shortly. He informed the president that the constable had been accused by the Golas of stealing one of Zeppie's women and refusing to return her and that this initial action caused Zeppie to seize the constable and his men. Mitchell admitted that he did not know how truthful the charge was and expressed frustration in his position: "I am put to my wits end sometimes as to how and what to do, there being such a strong current of opposition to my efforts; after all it is *hard, very hard* indeed for one to do anything in Liberia—so many want to be pleased, and if not, then we are misrepresented."[18]

Dwallah Zeppie had established relations with the settler government in Monrovia through earlier negotiated treaties of friendship. He was thus able to present his side of the controversy to President Johnson in a petition prepared and presented by an attorney in Monrovia. Zeppie assured the president of his continued respect and loyalty to the Liberian government and appealed for a redress of the injuries he had sustained. He charged that a Mandinka man, Saine, was attempting to control the Gola country and intended to bring war against Zeppie. According to Zeppie, Saine, hoped to drive Zeppie and his people from their own country and deprive them of trade opportunities. Zeppie added that Saine had told him that the Liberian government and people were prepared to support his design. In conclusion, Zeppie asked the president to restrain from interfering should it become necessary for the Gola people to defend their rights. "Your petitioner . . . to show that he wants peace is willing to resort to due course of law to meet the desired end; and would do so could he effectually execute it within the region, but he fears that the law would not have its effect in this particular—therefore he prays to be left untramelled to the result of the defensive position."[19]

Dwallah Zeppie's petition suggested several aspects of the conflict. There was apparently a major struggle for control of trade between the Gola and Mandinka people of western Liberia. What was not quite clear was the way in which the upriver settlers were involved. To what extent could settler authority be effective in reaching a solution? Mitchell's actions provide insights into these questions.

Following his orders from President Johnson, Mitchell sent two messengers to Zeppie; on August 1, 1887, they returned to report on their mission. The messengers succeeded in getting Zeppie to release some of the men he held, and they convinced him to return the rest in a few days. Zeppie again expressed his respect for the Liberian government and declared that he had no desire to fight the Americans. He explained his action against the constable by saying that he had received bad treatment from the settlers of Arthington in the past. They, including constable John Walkup, had taken Gola women and put them in "half-towns"[20] within Arthington and had refused to give them up when he demanded their return.[21]

When the captured men returned to Arthington, their accounts of being stripped, whipped, and placed in stocks further enflamed emotions among the settlers. They described personal humiliations graphically and said that Dwallah Zeppie had vowed to drive all the Americans back to the Cape and take over their coffee farms.[22] More town meetings were then held, and new petitions were sent to Monrovia demanding retribution. This time direct charges of malfeasance were made by the settlers against the native authority commissioner in order to encourage the president to act himself: ". . . we are afraid that if this matter is left to the Commissioner we will be in a worse condition with this man, than we ever were. Zeppie must be told that he was wrong and this will be hard for the Commissioner to do. . . . We feel assured that you are doing all you can to have the matter put to rest, but we do think some one else could effect it much quicker and with more satisfaction than the Commissioner."[23]

The conflicting reports that reached Monrovia gave Johnson no easy means of determining the true facts of the case, so he decided to call all the key persons involved in the controversy to Monrovia for direct discussions.[24] Although the precise details of the Monrovia talks are not known, Johnson subsequently deputized a three-man commission to resolve the dispute on the spot. Apparently Thomas Mitchell managed to retain the confidence of the president, for along with J. S. Washington and Cornelius Miller, he was selected as a member of the commission.[25] In November 1887 the commission reported on its work. The report assured the president that calm had once again been restored to the area and that free access to trade by all the different groups was now guaranteed. The confident tone of the commission's report was to be premature. Three days after it was submitted Thomas A. Sims, superintendent of Careysbury District, on the opposite side of the St. Paul River, wrote Johnson sending alarming news.

The superintendent informed the president that the Golas had spread the war across the river into Kpelle country and that hostilities were now in the vicinity of Careysburg. He stressed the negative effects of the trouble for the entire area: "The natives around Careysburg are deserting their towns and farms and fleeing in towards the river for security; even the natives employed on our farms are leaving. We are already feeling the bad effects of it."[26] The communication ended with an appeal for arms to defend Careysburg District in the event the Golas tried to attack the settlement. President Johnson immediately dispatched twenty muskets and twenty-five kegs of powder to Careysburg, to be used only if it were unavoidable.[27]

The reports of war on the right bank of the St. Paul River proved to be exaggerated. Superintendent Sims admitted as much in a letter to Johnson. Sims attributed the safety of Careysburg to the prompt arrival of weapons and ammunition from Monrovia. He nevertheless advised the president that conditions upriver were still volatile: "All that section of the Pessy [Kpelle] country between us and the Gollahs have already been broken up; the people have all fled from their homes, thereby destroying their substance. The whole country is in great confusion, especially among the Pessy and us. The war has not befallen any particular town, yet the fact of its being in the Country has been so well established, that the natives have fled as it were, from their homes and all their rice and other effects have been greatly destroyed. The evil effect of this war has done as much damage as if it had already been fought."[28] Sims reinforced the picture of eminent danger by mentioning that the settlers had agreed in a town meeting to post a continuous guard and to place Careysburg under martial law. In closing, the superintendent implored the president to issue orders for two or three military companies to assist the upriver settlers in ending, once and for all, the disturbances in the area.[29]

No further evidence remains to indicate what response—if any—was made by Johnson to Sims's request for a military solution. But by April 1890 the president received word from upriver settlements concerning a renewed outbreak of war. Reports of African towns being attacked and burned came from many different sources. African men, women, and children fleeing their homes to seek refuge in settler towns and mission stations testified to the spreading violence.[30] Johnson could no longer justify caution; he sent specific orders to the commander of the militia's First Regiment, Colonel James D. Jones, authorizing an immediate military expedition to capture a number of rebellious chiefs, including Dwallah Zeppie. He ordered Colonel Jones to destroy the towns of all chiefs who eluded capture and to demolish all barricades obstructing roads.[31] The expeditionary force organized by Colonel Jones was of regimental strength. It comprised four companies of armed men and over two hundred camp baggage carriers recruited from among the Kru, Bassa, and Vai peoples.[32] The exact number of weapons in the regiment is not known, but Colonel Jones complained that five thousand rounds of small-arms ammunition were defective, although he was confident that there was enough to accomplish the mission.[33] One field cannon was also included, which necessarily slowed down the progress of the march.[34]

Colonel Jones's force reached Dwallah Zeppie's town by May 24, 1890. They succeeded in capturing Zeppie alive with the help of other Gola chiefs, like Zolu Duma. The colonel then sent messengers out to call in all the neighboring chiefs for a full investigation of the war.[35] At that time Jones informed the president of an alleged attack on the Gola town of Jolla Mina by Africans organized and led by Thomas Mitchell and two other settlers.

The colonel recommended that Mitchell be arrested and the charges investigated by the president himself.[36] The following day, however, Jones wrote to Johnson again that the real aggressors were three settlers from Arthington and not Mitchell.[37]

President Johnson sent Colonel Jones new instructions on June 6, 1890. He stated that "the Government considers Zeppy, alias Zwie, the principal aggressor in this war, and charges him with murder; and to meet the ends of justice, and to restore the country to peace and quiet, I have directed a Court Martial be held, over which you will preside for the trial of the aforesaid Zeppy."[38] Despite the capture and trial of Zeppie, the disorders continued. The Mandinka chief Samoro pressed an attack deep into Gola country. Some settlers also acted independently of the militia to exploit the situation. I. J. Saunders, of Brewerville, became the subject of sharp criticism from the appointed commissioners trying to end the hostilities: "I am to earnestly beg Your Excellency to bring to bear immediately the strong arm of executive or judicial intervention, and cause the arrest and detention of Mr. Saunders, in the same manner as native intruders are dealt with. This will put an end to these trifling men, who will commit any wrong upon the natives, for the sole purpose of obtaining without remuneration laborers and women for their idle convenience. The speedy arrest and punishment of one or two of these lawless characters will restore confidence and enable Your Commissioners to arrive at the desired end with safety."[39]

The Gola-Mandinka-settler conflict between 1887 and 1891 suggests fuller consideration of several significant points. Although the confrontation took place upriver, President Johnson played a central role from his residence in Monrovia. Johnson followed a conservative policy by electing to use his options cautiously. He deftly manipulated his authority over appointed officials and the militia to control the scale of events upriver. Ultimately, his power to authorize the deployment of the militia proved to be a strong factor in keeping the upriver settlers from taking independent actions. The upriver settlers had concrete reasons for desiring an aggressive policy when conflicts developed with or between Africans. Stability was their lifeblood. Not only was the lucrative trade disrupted by wars—even when the settlers were not directly involved—but the agricultural needs of settlers were jeopardized as well. African laborers on settler farms had become essential to the settler upriver economy. The upriver settlers had also come to depend on neighboring African rice cultivators for that important staple. These economic ties to Africans were strained considerably when wars broke out. As the citizens of Clay Ashland had seen it in 1885, for example, refractory chiefs had to be stopped from "lying waste some of the fairest sections of this country, and ruthlessly destroying next year's rice crop on which the entire Americo-Liberian population subsists—either that or India rice at 500% dearer than it can be raised on the spot by the natives."[40] Thus in the eyes of the upriver settlers, a conservative policy by the president only tended to prolong the period of economic hardship brought on by instability. They saw immediate military reactions to disturbances as the shortest possible route to the return of stability and prosperity.

The Dwallah Zeppie episode reflected much more than tension and conflict; it indicated the extent to which the affairs of Africans and settlers in the St. Paul River area were inextricably linked. On the coast, African-settler relations were made difficult by the Liberian government's anti-slave-trade campaigns and general economic activity, which were inimical to the trade interests of coastal people like the Bassa, Kru, and Glebo (see chapter 7). By contrast, the upriver settlers could ill afford to constantly alienate the African population around their small settlements. The reality of living in the interior, away from the immediate protection and influence of Monrovia, encouraged settlers to reach out to their African neighbors. They did so by creating and maintaining channels of communication and interaction. The settler modus operandi for formal political relations was through treaties of friendship with local chiefs. Such alliances—fragile and temporary as they often were—provided an initial atmosphere of political tolerance, which made more enduring relations between settlers and Africans possible. Such formal agreements were validated by African chiefs in the traditional manner of offering children as wards in settler households and women as wives to settler men. Subsequently their subjects endeavored to do likewise.

The settlers readily accepted African children into their households. Not only did this fostering practice provide convenient domestic labor, it provided a channel through which the influences of "Christianity and Civilization" could be spread among the young and impressionable. Families sheltering African children had to live up to the expectations of both their settler neighbors and the relatives of their wards. In 1892 one settler discovered how difficult that responsibility could become. For eight years T. W. Smith raised a young girl entrusted to his care by a Kpelle chief. Suddenly, and without warning, she left his household and married. Smith found the girl and "at once arranged that she be sent to her people, fearing that in the event he went into the Interior that he would be held responsible if anything should happen to her." Meanwhile rumors spread among other settlers—who were unaware of his actions—that Smith had murdered his ward. He was charged with that crime and was almost convicted before he managed "after great trouble and expense [to produce] her before the Court of Quarter Sessions."[41]

Most relations between settlers and wards did not end in the confusion that Smith experienced. Genuine bonds of affection found tangible expression in the provisions of many settler wills. Catherine L. Mills, of Arthington, requested that upon her death ten acres of land be given to "George Mills (a Pessa man raised by us) and his son George . . . to be used and enjoyed by them during the term of their natural lives."[42] Samuel R. Hoggard, also of Arthington, gave twenty-five acres to "a native boy I raised by name of Kinsley who shall hold the same as long as he cultivates it."[43] Samuel C. Coker, of Bensonville, gave generous grants of land to three of his wards, provided " . . . they all remain with my wife or among the civilized elements. . . . Aborigines are supposed to wander among the natives of their Tribe. Therefore should this occur then they shall forfeit all that have been bequeath unto them. . . ."[44] Samson Lambirth, of the Louisiana settlement, apparently held great confidence in his ward, who carried his surname. In 1881 Lambirth made a statement to that effect in his will: "I request that after my death, Grando Lambirth will act as Head Man, and keep up the town to the best of his ability, and understanding that the said Grando Lambirth is also to take care of my wife and daughter the said Cahn."[45]

While the practice of wardship was analogous to the established concept of apprenticeship and could be justified by the principles of the settler standard, the sexual liaisons implicit in African offers of women to settler men was quite a different matter. This intimate channel of interaction, once begun, continued as a locally accepted custom of informal polygamy in the upriver settlements. Settler men, both married and single, had sexual relationships outside the bonds of lawful, Christian marriage. Outside wives and childred created significant kinship ties between Africans and settlers. Sexual liaisons of this nature had repercussions on the settler family and strained the ideal of Christian monogamy, however. In 1893, for instance, Patsey Gordon, of Caldwell, filed for divorce from her husband, Alfred J. Gordon, charging that in 1887 he had deserted her to live in adultery with Guarnyer Baebo, a Vai woman, thus contravening his marital obligations.[46] Five years earlier the Liberian legislature had moved to recognize the obvious consequence of informal polygamy by passing an act providing uniform procedures to legitimate children born outside of lawful wedlock.[47] The act recognized in law an existing social practice. It protected the settler-family structure by establishing the means for incorporating outside children. The emerging social variant nevertheless was still grounds for domestic discord, as in the Gordon case.

The impact of the interaction described here persisted over many generations. Warren L. d'Azevedo has documented the effects of Gola contact with the settlers and argues that the relationships formed became "an intricate network of latent commitments and obligations between various levels of Liberian [settler] and tribal culture. . . . thousands of Gola members of interior chiefdoms carry the names of Liberian families who raised them or who patronized one of their ancestors, while many others carry names of the Liberian patron of a female ancestress who passed his name on to certain favored children of his "country wife."[48] Settler residence in the St. Paul River area had lead to an intimate level of interdependence with the neighboring African population. That interdependence could be strained—and it often was—by misunderstandings or short-sighted excesses by individuals. Behind all of this, however, was a growing struggle for power on the part of the settlers. They saw their future tied to their ability to manipulate the environment. To that end, the upriver settlers needed a firm economic base. In the latter part of the nineteenth century the upriver settlements became a central place as their cash-crop economy developed and their trade connections increased. Economic growth enabled upriver settlers even to compete for preeminence with Monrovia. The interconnection between economic developments and central-place competition placed additional pressure on the settler society from external sources.

7/Economic Realities and the International Dimension

We have frequently noticed how rapidly the quantity of sugar manufactured on the St. Paul's is on the increase. No calculation can now be made as to the probable quantity which will be produced this season. When you enter the St. Paul's you can discover in every direction large cane fields; and persons who formerly prosecuted other avenues of employment, are now employed in cutting land to plant sugar cane. If seed can be procured—which is somewhat doubtful, it is supposed, that there will be nearly fifty new farms of sugar cane before the end of the present year.

—Liberia Herald, April 17, 1854

Liberia, unlike Sierra Leone, was founded without an explicit commercial motive.[1] Although the American Colonization Society did not expect to receive financial gain from its enterprise, it anticipated settler economic self-sufficiency. The society's managers endorsed agriculture because they believed that Afro-Americans were unsuited for occupations other than tilling the soil. The managers not only harbored racist stereotypes about the ability of the settlers but also romanticized the virtues of agrarian society in Jeffersonian fashion. And yet despite the efforts of the society, commerce was the first sector of the economy to flourish in Liberia. Jehudi Ashmun informed the society of this trend shortly after his arrival in Monrovia: "The two great interests of the colony, its *agriculture* and *trade*, have advanced through the year with a sure and regular, if not rapid progress. Though to foster and extend the first of these has been a primary object of the managers and their colonial agent, yet truth demands the avowal that to the latter is the colony principally indebted for its unexampled prosperity. Nor can we reasonably expect that this order of things will be speedily reversed."[2]

The need for a strong economic base capable of generating sufficient revenue to maintain a government treasury became imperative once the settlers declared their independence from the American Colonization Society. The new Liberian government was no longer able to depend on continuous financial support from America and therefore faced an uncertain future. A

102

measure of security was provided by the initial success of the commercial entrepreneurs, but they were not without competition from outsiders, most notably British subjects from Sierra Leone. The struggle for control of both the coastal trade and the more extensive mercantile trade linked to foreign markets was intense during the early years of settlement.[3] The commercial competition on the coast eventually placed the republic in a perilously dangerous fiscal condition.

The Economic Motive for Settler Independence

The fateful decision to sever formal ties with the American Colonization Society was as much economic as political. The Afro-American settlers, as wards of a private organization, found themselves without the rights and privileges inherent within the principles of sovereignty. This was especially damaging as far as the commercial trade was concerned. The settlers claimed control over the Liberian coastline from Monrovia to Cape Palmas, but foreign governments refused to consider their claims as constituting sovereignty. Thus British traders, many of whom had factories along the coast older than the Afro-American settlements, refused to stop trading with Africans simply because Liberians now claimed exclusive rights in the area. The British government backed the traders on this issue. Joseph Jenkins Roberts understood what was at stake when he addressed the legislative council at its last meeting before independence: "A majority of the people . . . has decided in the affirmative [for independence] ; which opinion is sustained by the unanimous vote of the Board of Directors of the American Colonization Society. In their opinion it is the only course that will, or can, relieve us from the embarrassments we labor under with respect to the encroachments of foreigners; and the objections by Great Britian in regard to our sovereignty."[4]

Once independence was achieved, the government immediately tried to ensure Liberian control of the coastal trade. An Act Regulating Navigation, Commerce and Revenue was passed in 1849. It was based on earlier, but ineffectual colonial ordinances and included a port-of-entry policy.[5] The port-of-entry policy represented an overt attempt by the Liberians to establish monopolistic control over coastal trade. Under the original guidelines of the policy, all foreign traders were required to conduct their business at only six designated ports of entry. Each approved port also was the location of settler enclaves. There the foreigners were supposed to accept local Liberian merchants as intermediaries for the sale of their cargoes and to pay into the Liberian treasury a substantial customs duty on their merchandise.[6] England had acknowledged Liberia's sovereign right to make laws applicable to all persons within her jurisdiction by signing a treaty of commerce and friendship with Liberia in 1848. British traders, however, were never willing to concede Liberian sovereignty when it interfered with the conduct of their business.

The British commerical firm of Laurie, Hamilton and Company tried to dissuade the British government from recognizing Liberian independence and sovereignty by writing to Lord Palmerston of the British Foreign Office.[7] At that time the British Foreign Office saw advantages to the existence of a Liberian republic. If British traders insisted on pursuing commerce along the Liberian coast, they could now appeal directly to the Liberians for redress of any grievances that might grow out of their activities. Thus the appeal of Laurie, Hamilton and Company was ignored by Palmerston. The company, nevertheless, continued to write the Foreign Office once the port-of-entry policy began to have adverse effects on its operations.

In 1849, Laurie, Hamilton and Company once again communicated with Lord Palmerston. They expressed objections to the territorial rights claimed by the Liberians and, in particular, their right to impose trade duties on British subjects. They reminded Palmerston of the longevity of their established trading stations at Trade Town, Settra Krow, Nanna Krow, Grand Bootan, and Sangwin and expressed fears that all might be lost because of the Liberian laws. They also informed Palmerston that their chief trader, Captain David Murray, was being accused of landing within Liberian jurisdiction without paying customs duties.[8] Palmerston answered, after some delay, simply reminding the company that the sovereignty of the Republic of Liberia was recognized by England.[9] The company, undaunted by the unsympathic response of the Foreign Office, continued to write long, detailed letters to Palmerston as new developments unfolded on the Liberian coast. The obviously monopolistic strategy of the Liberians was especially galling from their point of view: "It is surely most tyrannical and unjust, and at variance with the ordinary principles of trade, that business with the Natives should be carried on through the medium of land, and houses made by foreigners, should be all declared void—A more exclusive system could not well be devised."[10] Laurie, Hamilton and Company invoked the spirit of international mercantile rivalry by warning that should they and other British traders be driven from the Liberian coast, American traders were ready to fill the void.[11]

British Consul Augustus W. Hanson

The British government not only avoided an immediate confrontation over the complaints of her traders but in fact took steps to assist the infant republic directly. Joseph Jenkins Roberts made an official visit to England in 1848 as the first president of Liberia. He negotiated the terms of the treaty of commerce and friendship and secured the schooner *Lark* as a gift from the British government. The *Lark* became Liberia's first coast-guard vessel and enabled the government to keep a token vigilance against slave traders and other violators of her commercial laws.[12] The British Foreign Office authorized the appointment of a consul to Liberia in 1850. In Liberia's efforts to establish international respect for her sovereignty, the arrival of Augustus W. Hanson in Monrovia on November 11, 1850, represented a substantial victory.[13]

Several large manufacturing firms in England viewed Liberia as a potential supplier of raw cotton. President Roberts took advantage of the opportunity to court this interest. He hoped to indicate Liberia's desire to have solid economic ties with England despite the unpleasant difficulties with certain of her traders. Roberts assured Palmerston that there were many settlers with years of experience in the cultivation of cotton.[14] By 1852 the chamber of commerce of Manchester, England, had shipped five roller gins to Liberia as an inducement for settlers to begin cotton cultivation. Consul Hanson presented the machines to the Liberian president on behalf of the manufacturers, expressing the hope that attention would be devoted to cotton.[15]

The continued support of the British government was very important to Liberia, especially since the institution of slavery prevented the American government from officially recognizing Liberia's independence. President Roberts tried to be cooperative with Hanson, expressing his willingness to suggest a modification of the port-of-entry policy when the legislature convened in 1850.[16] On the recommendation of the president, the legislature passed a compromise amendment to the Act regulating Navigation, Commerce and Revenue on December 30, 1850. The amendment specified that all foreigners trading "at points of the coast other than the ports of entry must furnish the Collector of the Port with a written declaration of his intentions, containing the names of places he intends to trade at."[17] The modification of the port-of-entry policy was the main consular achievement of Augustus W. Hanson. Unfortunately, his fall from grace was rapid and had negative effects on Liberian-British relations.

On the surface, Hanson's appointment as consul to Liberia had appeared a perfect choice. He was a British subject of African descent and became the first person of color to represent the British government anywhere in the world.[18] Hanson became deeply involved in the affairs of settler society once he arrived in Monrovia. It is possible that he believed his "affinity" would allow him to function less as a foreigner and more as a social equal to the Afro-Americans. Although officially prohibited from engaging in mercantile pursuits while serving as consul, it seems likely that he found the temptations of trade irresistible.[19] It was not long before his experiences in Monrovia motivated Hanson to write a confidential letter to a friend in England describing Liberia in very unflattering terms. Hanson characterized Liberian society as being morally and socially degraded. "The prevailing principal [sic] in every dealing of man with his fellow man here, especially with foreigners, chiefly perhaps with an Englishman, seems to be to get every thing, if possible, and give nothing in return."[20] Much to the embarrassment of Hanson, his letter was intercepted and published anonymously in the *Liberia Herald.*[21]

President Roberts met the Liberian legislature in joint session on December 23, 1851, to discuss the offensive letter. By that time Hanson had been identified as the real author. A resolution was passed at the meeting calling upon the British government to remove him as consul.[22] Hanson's position in Monrovia quickly became intolerable. The hostility of the Monrovians prevented him from receiving any services or local supplies. He began to feel that he and his family were in danger of physical violence.[23] Before the year was over, Augustus Hanson fled Liberia and returned to England. John N. Lewis expressed the attitude of the Liberian government in a private letter to William McLain, of the American Colonization Society:

> Now, the fact is, that Mr. Hanson has not been molested—we did not know until today, that he had been insulted, or that he thought he had been—Hanson you know was born at Cape Coast of African parents, and we thought he would more likely side with us than with the low bred whitemen—we honor him for attending to his duties; but we never supposed that he would so forget his race, as to try to injure them without a provocation. In a few words, at this present time, we are surrounded with difficulties: and some plan must be adopted to insure a true representation of matters at the Court of St. James.[24]

The difficulties that Lewis alluded to involved more than Consul Hanson. On November 5, 1851, the Bassa Cove settlement was attacked by Kru-speaking people from Trade Town and New Cess. In the wake of the assault, William Lawrence was accused of instigating the hostilities.[25] Lawrence was a liberated African from Freetown living in Trade Town as a representative of British trading interests there. The charge carried the implication that the British traders were trying to encourage African rebellion against Liberian authority in order to force British intervention, which might lead to British rule. This suspicion was greatly increased among the settlers by Consul Hanson's decision to visit Trade Town just days before the attack on Bassa Cove occurred.[26] The British presence offered Africans an alternative to acquiescing to Liberian control. King Bowyah, of Trade Town, tried to exploit that alternative in a letter that he sent to Consul Hanson prior to the Bassa Cove incident:

I hear that you are Head man for Englishmen, now mine, be English country, not the American . . . . For as the American try to join with Jim Flaw, on making war for me. For the purpose of taking away my Country from me, but we settled it without them. I write this to let you know that this Country is not belong to Americans, and I will not sell it. I have this Country from my Fore Father, and when I die, I wish to left to my sons. I want all English to come here and make trade with my people. Please Sir try all the best to do for me and my Country.[27]

The situation became so dangerous to Liberia's sovereignty and to control of the African population within her boundaries that President Roberts was forced to go to Freetown to consult with the Sierra Leone governor, and then to England, where he explained the circumstances personally.[28] Roberts's meeting with the officials of the British Foreign Office produced a compromise and the beginning of a long period of controversy over Liberia's territorial claims. The territory adjacent to the Sierra Leone colony remained in dispute throughout the nineteenth century. Roberts agreed to drop the prosecution of William Lawrence by the Liberian courts if the British government issued a stern warning to him about his future conduct. He also accepted a plan to appoint commissioners to examine Liberia's title deeds with respect to the western boundary limits of the republic.[29]

British Traders and the Liberian Boundary Question

Following the Hanson affair and the resultant strain of relations with England, the Liberian government once again attempted to strictly enforce its restrictions on foreign traders. In 1860 the Liberian Court of Quarter Sessions and Common Pleas issued statements of libel against John Harris, the British owner of the schooners *Emily* and *Phoebe*, for violating the republic's law regulating navigation, commerce, and revenue. The Liberians seized both vessels and charged Harris with landing goods in the vicinity of Solyma in the Gallinas territory without first entering the regular port of entry, thereby denying Liberia her just duties.[30] The action produced the predictable appeal by Harris for assistance from the British Foreign Office. This time the British authorities responded because the seizure had taken place in an area where Liberian claims of sovereignty were still controversial. The British cruiser *Torch* was ordered to call at Monrovia to demand the release of the vessels. Once in Monrovia, Commander Smith, of the *Torch*, rejected the statements of libel; took control of the two vessels; and demanded that the Liberians pay an indemnification at the rate of fifteen pounds sterling per day for nineteen days.[31] The Liberian secretary of state, John N. Lewis, faced an ultimatum without any means of resisting it. He informed Commander Smith that "the case will be regularly tried notwithstanding you may arrest them from this Government by superior force."[32] Commander Smith did exactly that.

The Liberian interest in the Gallinas territory was an outgrowth of the founding of Robertsport, Grand Cape Mount, in 1855. The Liberians promised suppression of the slave trade and the introduction of legitimate commerce to secure deeds of cession from the local chiefs of Gallinas for the sum of five thousand dollars.[33] The British assessment of the Liberian case for territorial expansion was summed up by Commander Smith in a report to the governor of Sierra Leone. Smith conducted a personal investigation of the situation in the Gallinas and concluded that a settlement of the boundary question must be made before British merchants defended themselves with arms against the Liberians. It was his opinion that the Liberians had taken possession of Cape Mount by force and against the will of the Africans, who considered it British. This view was no doubt reinforced by the British traders residing in the Gallinas. Finally, Smith charged that the Liberians brought a petty chief to Monrovia, bribed him, and used his consent as proof that they had brought the Gallinas.[34] The Sierra Leone colony shared the views of Commander Smith, although the colony's views were motivated by the commercial interests of the business community and not by any special political issue. In 1862 the Sierra Leone council chamber recommended that Liberia not be allowed to possess territory north of the River Gallinas, since it would threaten the commercial interests of Sierra Leone.[35]

The bilateral commission to which President Roberts had agreed in London finally met for a week of discussions at Monrovia in April 1863.[36] The British commissioners were anxious to check carefully the actual treaties and deeds of cession that the Liberians claimed gave them sovereignty over the region between Cape Mount and Sherbro Island. The Liberian commissioners were led by President Roberts's successor, Stephen Allen Benson. They were willing to produce the documents in question, but they also pressed for an immediate decision on the boundary line that would separate Liberian and British territories. At the end of the week's sessions no concrete conclusions had been reached other than the acknowledgment that certain inconsistencies existed in the Manna and Solyma deeds. The British commissioners avoided making any potentially binding agreements, noting that "the President evidently intended and nearly succeeded, in getting us to admit the Liberian boundary claims without making inquiry on the subject."[37]

The failure of the bilateral commission to resolve the dispute occasioned a flurry of diplomatic dispatches from the Liberian government to the British Foreign Office. Edward Wilmot Blyden presented the Liberian case. He eloquently evoked the principles of the Liberian standard. Blyden pointed out that the Liberian settlers' relation with the Africans, unlike that of Europeans and Africans, was not merely a commercial relation but rather a fraternal association between "kith and kin." At the time of Blyden's writing the American Civil War was in progress. He carefully linked the events of that war to Liberia's territorial claims. This approach added urgency to his argument and showed the practical application of ideological assumptions:

> Liberia is the only portion of Africa which her civilized descendants, returning from a painful exile of centuries, occupy; the only spot on this vast continent, the inheritance of the children of Ham, where any portion of the race can be said to hold an intelligent rule. To this bright spot thoughtful Africans everywhere are looking with the deepest interest. We may reasonably expect that after the war in the United States there will be an immigration of large numbers of blacks from the Western Hemisphere into this Republic; and it is very much deplored that our territory, already very limited, a mere speck on the Continent of our fathers, should be further circumscribed and that, too, after we have exerted ourselves to enlarge our borders by fair purchase and honourable treaty stipulations, preparatory to the influx of our worn-out and downtrodden brethren from abroad.[38]

Thus from the Liberian perspective, suppression of the slave trade, the Christianizing and civilizing mission, and the continued immigration of Afro-Americans all supported her territorial claims.

The boundary dispute was not resolved for many years, the eloquence of Blyden's arguments notwithstanding. The British government saw no advantage to reopening discussions on the question and therefore choose to ignore the Liberian request for immediate and favorable action.[39] In 1868 the Liberians precipitated renewed attention to the subject by threatening to move against Sierra Leone traders operating in the disputed Mannah River district. Several liberated Africans from Freetown had established trading stations at Salijah, in the Manna country, and carried on trade in the area on behalf of the British Company of African Merchants. Tensions began to rise when one of the traders, Isaac T. Pratt, visited Robertsport and was arrested and imprisoned by the collector of customs for violating the Liberian port-of-entry policy. This action was followed by the decision of Abraham Blackford, superintendent of Robertsport, to dispatch thirty armed men to Salijah with orders to seize the property of Pratt and his fellow traders.[40] The seizure of British property at Salijah was not immediately accomplished, but rumors persisted that the Liberians were preparing to mount a major assault during the next dry season. Meanwhile, the Sierra Leone traders, through George M. Macaulay, the principal agent of the Company of African Merchants, appealed to the governor of Sierra Leone for protection. The basis for their appeal was the belief that the Liberians had no jurisdiction in the Manna

River country and that the local chief, Prince Mannah, denied ever alienating his territory to them.[41]

The situation reached the point of confrontation in 1869, when the Liberians finally carried out their threats. On March 2 a Liberian expeditionary force of three hundred men led by Colonel Robert A. Sherman entered the Manna River and seized the schooner *Elizabeth*, which belonged to the Company of African Merchants.[42] Five Sierra Leone traders were arrested, brought to Monrovia, and charged with inciting Africans to oppose the Liberian government, as well as with the usual customs law violation.[43] Sentiments against Sierra Leoneans were running high in Monrovia in 1869, as the following excerpt from an editorial in a Monrovian newspaper makes clear: "It is a lamentable fact that 'these Sierra Leone people,' as they are called, are taking almost entire charge of the trade of Liberia. They pay no taxes, serve on no juries, and do no military duty. And though some of them take the oath of allegiance, yet, when they are tired with trade here, or fail to have secured a goodly sum, they return to Sierra Leone and are British subjects again."[44]

The trial of the traders began on June 17, 1869. The prosecutor, W. M. Davis, reminded the jury that the defendants could not enjoy any special immunities because of their claim to be British subjects. In fact he declared that the Liberian government was not impressed by the supposed power of Her Majesty's government because it "has ever been roaring like a lion and we have not seen what it has done."[45] Two days later the jury returned an unanimous guilty verdict against all the defendants that carried a fine of five hundred dollars.[46] George Macaulay secured a bond in Monrovia and agreed to pay the fine in full within thirty days. He then returned to Freetown and presented an affidavit of the incident directly to the Sierra Leone governor.[47]

The governor decided against initiating a response himself and instead sent a confidential dispatch to London recommending action. He suggested that a force be sent to Monrovia sufficient to make the Liberians submit to British demands in the case. The governor not only discussed whether Liberia had the right to seize British property in the Manna River district but also stated what he felt was the real motive for Liberia's actions: "It is proper for me to state that it was the popular belief that these seizures here made on the eve, or during the Presidential election, just concluded, with a view to making political capital, and at the same time providing pecuniary means of rewarding supporters."[48] Orders based on the report of the Sierra Leone governor were sent to the British Naval Squadron on the west coast of Africa. The H.M.S. *Sirius* arrived at Monrovia on September 10, 1869. The man-of-war brought J. J. Kendall, administrator-in-chief of the British West African Settlements, and was accompanied by another warship, the H.M.S. *Peterel*. Kendall delivered an ultimatum to Liberian president James Spriggs-Payne, ordering him to release the schooner *Elizabeth* and accept an indemnification charge of £3,701 9s. 11d. within four hours or face the humiliation of "compulsory obedience" to the demands of Her Majesty's government.[49]

The Liberians were no better prepared to challenge the second ultimatum than they were the first. Their president was forced to submit to the unavoidable, but he tried to use the capitulation as the vehicle for a new diplomatic approach to the boundary impasse. Payne asked the British government to consent to submit the entire boundary dispute to a third party for arbitration.[50] The British, however, were primarily interested in receiving full payment of the indemnification. The Liberians could not raise the full amount at once, so the British accepted several five-hundred-pound bonds, to be paid over a period of time. The first installment of the bond included marketable goods like palm oil and camwood, as well as coins and bills of exchange. The goods were sold in Freetown, but the bills of exchange, drawn from Liverpool and New York banks, were all returned uncollected.[51] As a result, the first installment was less than the required five hundred pounds, and Liberia's prospects of meeting the future deadlines were bleak.

In the midst of the fiscal crisis brought on by the English bond obligation Liberia held a presidential election. It was won by a prosperous merchant, Edward James Roye. The ill-fated Roye administration inherited the English debt and sought a major foreign loan to pay it.[52] What followed was a government crisis over the terms of the negotiated loan and a coup d'état. The loan controversy was one of the immediate causes of the overthrow of Roye's government, but other internal cleavages had become salient also. Cash-crop agriculture in the St. Paul River area had begun to rival coastal commerce. In fact, upriver planters were challenging the political preeminence of coastal entrepreneurs precisely because their economic needs were different.

Agricultural Development in the St. Paul River Area

Agriculture in the upriver settlements developed slowly as circumstances emerged that were favorable to large-scale activities. It was necessary to clear the land at the same time that public buildings and individual homesteads were being built. Experimentation with different crops was a trial-and-error procedure that was necessarily expensive, and the results were not always favorable. In the case of cotton cultivation, when actual experimental efforts proved disappointing, even the encouragement of British mercantile companies could not induce upriver farmers to emphasize the crop.[53] Information about crops and farming techniques was shared by farmers through agricultural societies. These economic associations aided individual farmers in their search for crops suitable to the soil and climate.[54] Once particular crops were identified, it was necessary to have a labor force sufficient to meet the requirements of intensive cultivation. Although many settler families were quite large, they could not provide the labor necessary to produce a large agricultural surplus. Finally, export markets had to be available to absorb most of the surplus, since the domestic market was too limited to provide substantial profits. Thus the development of upriver agriculture was a gradual process.[55]

The first crop to generate enthusiasm among upriver farmers was sugar cane. As early as 1842 there were reports of some upriver farmers having good luck raising sugar cane. The *Liberia Herald* mentioned that a number of farmers had managed to grow enough sugar cane for their own purposes and even had reserved enough cane for the next planting season. The newspaper declared that the sugar produced by the farmers was of good quality and singled out a pair of sugar growers for special mention. The Reverend Wilson, of the Methodist Episcopal Mission at White Plains, and Cyrus Willis, of Millsburg, were ready to make four thousand and one thousand pounds of sugar, respectively. All of this was anticipated despite only "an inefficient temporary affair of a mill which they borrowed . . . ."[56] Such positive reports encouraged some settlers to invest in sugar mills. By 1857 John B. Jordan, owner of the Bellevue Farm, St. Paul River, was able not only to announce his purchase of a steam sugar mill but also to declare "that he will be prepared, in a short while to serve the Public, upon the delivery of the Cane, at his Mill door for a Toll of one fourth of the net yield."[57]

During the ten-year period after 1842 those upriver farmers who devoted sizable acreage to sugar cane found the investment beginning to pay off. Abraham Blackledge, of Caldwell, wrote in 1851 of his progress in sugar making. "I have already made five thousand seven hundred pounds; and of that quantity, I have sold four thousand pounds. My prospects this year will be of making ten thousand pounds of sugar and between eight and nine hundred gallons of syrup."[58] Blackledge, along with A. B. Hooper, of Clay Ashland, was among the most successful growers of sugar cane in the 1850s.[59] The extensive cultivation of sugar cane created a secondary industry upriver. Charles Cooper, also a successful cane grower, reportedly discovered local wood and vines suitable for the construction of barrels and hogsheads for shipping sugar cane.[60]

The editors of the *Liberia Herald* reported on the progress of sugar cultivation in 1863. W. S. Anderson, a prosperous upriver farmer, provided detailed information in answer to a questionnaire sent to him by the editors. Anderson began by stating that there were two steam mills in operation, rated at twelve and six horsepower. Seven other sugar mills depended on oxen or human labor for power. He noted further that the settlers had built one water-powered mill as well. The steam mills were capable of processing from one to one and a half acres of cane per day, while the smaller units processed approximately one fourth of an acre daily.[61] In response to the question of how much sugar syrup could be made, Anderson's report indicated the extent to which the farmers sought to understand the science behind sugar cultivation as the best means of increasing their yields: " . . . I can say, that, as a general thing, we do not receive over fifteen hundred pounds to the acre. It has long since been scientifically ascertained that during the rapid vegetation of cane, the saccharine matter is re-absorbed from the cells almost as rapidly as it is deposited in them, and is employed in affording materials for the formation of its new parts. To cut, then, during such time, must be extremely prejudicial to the interest of the planter."[62]

Anderson also offered some revealing estimates on the export volume of sugar cane. He stated that in the year 1863, fifty thousand pounds of sugar had been shipped to the United States; two thousand pounds had gone to neighboring British settlements; and twenty thousand pounds had been purchased by the several settler enclaves along the coast. Anderson noted that even allowing for the amount used locally in the St. Paul River area, a quantity of sugar would be available for shipment.

The level of production that Anderson described indicates the presence of a large labor force. Anderson stated that on his own farm he employed seventy-five workers during harvest time. When the harvest was over, he released thirty; he retained the rest to care for other crops, such as corn, potatoes, and cassava. Farmers like Anderson secured a large portion of their labor force from the sudden—and from their point of view, fortuitous—arrival of recaptured Africans in 1860. Unlike the local African population, recaptured Africans proved to be a dependable labor source year-round. Anderson acknowledged their contribution to his own agricultural success: "Allow me to digress a little and speak a word for the recent laborers thrown into our midst [the Congoes from U.S. cruisers]. My entire farming operations are carried on with them and some few Golahs. My steam mill has for engineer a Vey boy. My sugar maker, cooper, and fireman are Congoes . . . . My cooper is far in advance of many Americo-Liberians, who style themselves such; and likewise my sugarmaker."[63] Thus a combination of circumstances made possible the rise of successful sugar-cane growers, who built large plantations and attained the status of planters. Like the coastal commercial entrepreneurs, however, only relatively few upriver farmers were able to secure the means to become planters. The scale of operations for most sugar cultivators remained modest throughout the nineteenth century.

The smaller sugar cultivators could not hope to produce sugar in sufficient quantity for overseas export. The production of rum, earmarked for the domestic market, was for them the most attractive alternative. The manufacture of local rum by upriver settlers accounts in part for the failure of the Liberian legislature to pass laws outlawing the rum trade in the country. Rum, unlike sugar, could be made cheaply by an uncomplicated method. Liberian rum, locally called cane juice, continues to be made by the same, time-honored method of the nineteenth century:

1. The cane is cut and allowed to sit for two weeks to sour.
2. The sour cane is placed in a mill for grinding.
3. The ground cane is placed in drums and allowed to ferment (from four to five days).
4. The fermented cane is passed through a still, where the juice is boiled. The heat produces the rum, which has an alcoholic content of about 50 percent.[64]

The manufacture of cane juice, which was at variance with the settler standard, was commonly undertaken by small upriver farmers. One upriver farmer made a point of stressing that at least one sugar cultivator did not succumb to the temptation of making cane juice. "Mr. Jesse Sharp has a splendid crop of cane this year, and what is best of all, he makes no rum. He began here a few years ago with little or nothing, and he is now well off. I tell him God will prosper him just as long as he lets rum alone!"[65]

Only the planting of coffee trees was more popular than sugar cultivation among upriver settlers. The cultivation of coffee required considerable experimentation to develop ideal breeding varieties for the area. Eventually the variety known as Liberica emerged as the distinctive coffee of the country. In 1852 the *Liberia Herald* carried a story about an upriver farmer who had created a nursery and was busy transplanting thousands of coffee plants.[66] Farmers along the St. Paul River increased their planting of coffee when prospects of a strong export market became apparent. At first some farmers tried to sell their coffee overseas through personal contacts. In 1859 Charles Starkes, of the Virginia settlement, had difficulties selling his coffee—which was probably a general problem at the time.[67]

The promotional activities of Edward S. Morris and the quality of Liberica contributed to the development of a reliable export business for coffee grown in Liberia. Morris was a member of the Society of Friends in Philadelphia and had an active interest in encouraging Liberians to raise coffee for sale in the United States.[68] In 1863 he visited Liberia bringing samples of machines he had designed for cleaning and hulling coffee. Morris delivered an address on the subject of coffee cultivation to an audience in Monrovia and then traveled upriver, where he gave a similar talk to the agricultural society in Clay Ashland on February 15, 1863.[69] Liberian coffee gained swift acceptance in the world market because of its quality and because of Morris's promotional campaign in the United States and Europe.[70]

The pace of cultivation picked up rapidly once an export market opened for Liberian coffee. Even mission stations in the interior became sites for

Table 20. Coffee and Sugar-Cane Cultivation in St. Paul River Settlements, 1843

Settlement	Acres of Cane	Coffee Trees
Harrisburg	2.0	500
Kentucky (Clay Ashland)	33.0	14,000
Louisiana	39.0	–
Millsburg	a	–
Virginia	5.5	17,000
White Plains	27.0	–
Total	209.0	32,800

Source: Adapted from *African Repository* 39, no. 10 (October 1863).
NOTE: At Caldwell, as at Millsburg and throughout Monrovia, are small parcels of coffee
  trees and patches of sugar cane not included above.
aNumerous small parcels of cane from .25 to 1.75 acres each.

raising coffee to support religious programs. The *Missionary Advocate* reported in 1863 that the Methodist mission at White Plains had a coffee
plantation run by John Robinson, a recaptured African from the slave ship
Pons.[71] The planting of coffee trees in the St. Paul River region had advanced
beyond the number of acres devoted to sugar cultivation by the time of the
Missionary Advocate story (see table 20). Reverend William C. Burke, of Clay
Ashland, remarked that "the planting of coffee is now receiving attention
from every farmer in Liberia. I regret, and it seems to be the regret of almost
every farmer, that they did not attend to planting coffee many years ago."[72]
In the 1870s coffee cultivation still was thriving in Liberia. The dispatches of
U.S. consuls resident in Monrovia included frequent comments on the status
of the product.[73]

International Competition and Agricultural Decline

The extensive cultivation of sugar cane and coffee notwithstanding, by the
close of the nineteenth century both export products already were falling
into decline. Locally, the labor requirements for plantation agriculture often
were adversely affected by the circumstances of settler-African relations
described in chapter 6. The upriver planters, unable to use coercive methods,
continually were plagued by sporadic losses in their labor force for reasons
beyond their control.[74] International competition from other sugar and
coffee producers drove the price of the Liberian products down during the
1880s and 1890s. The disruption of the southern sugarcane market during
the American Civil War cause an increase in the demand for Liberian sugar.
After the war was over, however, there was very little encouragement for the
export of Liberian sugar to the United States.[75] Cuba, using slave labor,
emerged as the dominant sugar producer in the latter half of the nineteenth
century. By 1877, 82 percent of all Cuban sugar was going to the United

States.[76] The price of Liberian coffee, meanwhile, began to steadily decline in the face of competition from other world coffee producers, most notably Brazil. In 1897 the *Liberian Recorder* described the bleak outlook:

> The November coffee future on the coffee exchange yesterday at 5.15 cents a pound, was the lowest price on record since the exchange was established. The previous lowest price was 5.20, fifteen years ago. The decline in November was immediately due to the sending out of notices of delivery to the extent of several thousand bags. While the November future brook 25 points, the others further show an average decline of only 5 points. The cause of the weakness is the expectation of a heavy Brazilian crop, estimated at 9,000,000 bags, following a crop of 8,900,000 bags in 1896, and an enormous visible worlds supply of 5,900,000 bags, the largest ever known.[77]

Before the economic decline delivered a near-fatal blow to settler agriculture, the St. Paul River settlements parlayed their period of prosperity into political gains that had a significant impact on the republic. The 1859 elections in Liberia resulted in the reelection of Stephen Allen Benson as president. Joseph Jenkins Roberts, then acting as British consul following the removal of Augustus Hanson, made a remark about the election results, which he considered most noteworthy: "The newly elected Legislature is composed chiefly of men, who, for the first time, are assuming the duties of legislation. They are mostly from rural districts, and profess to be particularly interested in the promotion of agriculture; and are supposed to be liberal in respect to foreign commerce."[78] The new legislators reflected the upsurge of agricultural activities that by 1864 saw 46,649 coffee trees planted in the upriver settlements and 682 acres devoted to sugar cultivation. Large planters and small farmers alike believed that their continued prosperity depended on the further advancement of agriculture. They became convinced that their way of life was the only appropriate direction for the republic to move. As a Clay Ashland correspondent to the *Liberia Herald* put it in 1852: "Let the Government encourage the farming interest of the country and the recurrence of panic stricken, death like times such as that now sit upon Monrovia will be seldom."[79] The Clay Ashland correspondent criticized those in Monrovia who continued to desire foreign produce at enormous prices when the upriver farmers were capable of supplying cassava, rice, greens, fish, and fowl for the entire country. As time passed, the upriver settlers began to challenge Monrovia's position as the central place of the republic.

The first overt challenge came in the form of a controversy over the site of Liberia's first college. The legislature passed an act establishing Liberia College and incorporating its board of trustees on December 24, 1851. The legislature approved a site of one hundred acres in Clay Ashland for the

Figure 9. Stephen Allen Benson, c. 1850

college that was considered to be "fine agricultural rolling farm land."[80] The difficulty began when the appointed members of the board of trustees, mainly prominent Monrovians, ordered the college to be built in the vicinity of the capital. The people of Clay Ashland responded by pressing a case of injunction in the courts, hoping to prevent the college from being built anywhere but in their settlement.[81] The case had overtones that went beyond the legal technicalities argued in court.

The location of the college would affect the focus of the curriculum. Up-river settlers, in supporting the Clay Ashland site, were anxious to see the college develop a strong agricultural emphasis. The attorney representing the board of trustees, however, accused them of more sinister motives: "In the present instance she [rumor] assures us that this action is entirely for political affect [sic] —that certain parties have whispered their intention of doing all in their power to unite and array the citizens of the upriver settlements 'in one solid phalanx' against the political preferences of the citizens of Monrovia; and by that means will be able to control all county elections: and that this action, is one step in that direction."[82] The court sided with the plaintiffs and issued the injunction, which temporarily delayed construction of the college. The trustees, however, eventually succeeded in their original intent. In 1860 the legislature amended the act establishing Liberia College to give the trustees authorization to build the college near Monrovia.[83] One citizen voiced his concern over the outcome of the controversy:

"Without expressing an opinion upon the *law* of the case, I think a mistake has been made in placing the institution here. The expenses of living, the temptations to students, and the strong tendency to centralization here, are all against its location in Monrovia. But this belongs to others to judge and determine.[84]

The St. Paul River settlers, having failed to win the college issue, continued to try to have other important settler institutions transferred from Monrovia to their region. Beginning in 1862, legislators from upriver settlements offered bills designed to authorize the removal of the seat of government from Monrovia.[85] The following year a petition was presented to the legislature requesting the removal of the Court of Quarter Sessions and Common Pleas for Montserrado County to Clay Ashland.[86] President Benson gave one of the arguments in favor of the trend during his annual message to the legislature in 1863. He stated that over the years the government had been under excessive strain caused by the "mischievously if not feloniously exerted influence of a few individuals over the uninformed and unstable portions of the community, for the purpose of forcibly controlling and directing those whom the people have elected and appointed . . . ."[87] The movement to support the transfer of government institutions upriver received a major setback in 1871, however, as a direct result of the political crisis in that year.

The Roye Episode

The 1870 election of Edward James Roye as the fifth president of Liberia marked a brief but important victory for those in the republic opposed to the conservative leadership that previously had dominated settler political affairs. The national leadership among the settlers came from the early, free Afro-American immigrants and their descendants.[88] This leadership coalesced into the Republican Party, or True Liberian Party. It represented the interests of successful, commercially oriented settlers and became identified with conservative politics. Moreover, the Republicans appeared to support caste distinctions, for many of the same individuals, usually light-skinned mulattoes, continually secured appointments to high political office.[89] Rather than a clique based solely on color, the Republicans probably represented a close-knit political aristocracy in small, enclave communities, where it was difficult for others to match their influence. Thus drawing on their early entry into Liberian politics and the substantial financial resources at their disposal, the Republicans had been able to put their candidates into national office. By extension, they also were able to dominate the politics of all the settlements at the local level. This in no way meant that differing political sentiments did not exist. The settler ideals, however, in the abstract implied that a unani-

Figure 10. Edward James Roye, c. 1850

mity of opinion prevailed with regard to national goals. The Republicans exploited this mythical concensus by stressing its importance to continued settler survival against external enemies. Factionalism in any form was considered by the Republicans as a divisive tendency. Yet despite the Republican platitudes of unity, party politics persisted in Liberia. Factionalism was intense in the early 1870s, in part because the stakes had become fairly high.

The Whig Party was responsible for the election of Roye over his incumbent Republican opponent, James Spriggs Payne. The Whigs were an opposition party organized in Clay Ashland in 1860.[90] Unlike the Republicans, the Whigs depended on support from the more recent Afro-American immigrants and the enfranchised recaptured Africans. Thus they symbolized a liberal, if not radical, party that embraced the common people in a direct, political sense. Their political strength was concentrated in the rapidly developing upriver settlements.[91] The Whig victory that elevated Roye to the presidency coincided with a peak in upriver economic prosperity. The election was very close and hotly contested. The Republicans even proposed an amendment to the constitution that would lengthen the term of office for all elected officials prior to Roye's surprising win. The move was conceived as a tactic to sustain Republican political strength in the face of growing Whig popularity; ironically, Roye would later be bitterly criticized for employing the same tactic. The settlers chose Roye over Spriggs-Payne, thereby creating a volatile political situation.

Roye alluded to the tense climate during his inaugural address, declaring, "I do not expect immunity from the criticisms of our opponents, nor do I ask for it; but I shall endeavour so to act for the good of the people that while allowing our opponents . . . the utmost latitude in their criticisms of the administration . . . they shall not be able to shake our stability by their votes."[92] What followed his initial triumph, however, proved more than Roye or his supporters could have anticipated from their opposition. The troubles, which reached crisis proportions just one year after Roye took office, revolved around the interlocking issues of a foreign loan and Roye's attempt to remain in office for four years rather than the customary two-year term.

Roye's decision to seek a foreign loan came only after the British government refused to release Liberia from its bond obligation that grew out of the "seizure" of the schooner *Elizabeth*. A loan of one hundred thousand pounds was negotiated through a British banking firm in 1871. The loan, intended to pay off the British obligation and help finance government development projects, had the prior approval of the Liberian legislature.[93] The Republicans attacked Roye on the specific terms of the loan agreement. The British financiers required a 30-percent discount on the principal as a service charge for what they considered to be a high-risk loan. A 7-percent annual interest rate was imposed, and the loan was to be repaid over a fifteen-year period. Thus Liberia could expect to actually receive less than half of the total amount of the loan.[94] Once the details of the financial agreement reached Liberia, rumors circulated that Roye and his associates had retained large sums of the loan for their own personal aggrandizement.

The controversy over the foreign loan reached fever pitch when Roye announced his intention to remain in office beyond the traditional two-year term and to prohibit the biennial elections scheduled for May 1871.[95] Opposition became so intense that Roye tried to organize a force of men from the St. Paul River settlements to march on Monrovia and protect him and his government. One eyewitness was later to testify: "I learned that Mr. Johnson [Roye's attorney general] had passed down to Monrovia that morning, and was to return that morning to make a statement of what the president wanted with the men they wanted to come down as guard. When Mr. Johnson returned to Caldwell he met those Congoes and some Americans. Mr. Clark said that Mr. Johnson said that they wanted to get a number of men so that when called on they would be ready to come down, and protect the Government."[96] The upriver force was not organized quickly enough to save Roye. On October 21, 1871, his opposition rallied in the streets of Monrovia. They were armed, and they demanded the resignation of the president. The precise sequence of events that followed during the next few days has been obscured by conflicting eyewitness reports. The results were nevertheless profound and decisive. Roye was deposed, and he eventually died in Monrovia.[97] The opposition issued a manifesto declaring that a provisional government would hold power until the legislature could be convened.[98]

The internal reactions to the political upheaval were divided, as might be expected. Reverend Alexander Crummell, whose own son was imprisoned during the period of reprisals that followed the coup, saw the whole affair as a triumph for the reactionary elements in the country. "It is an uprising of a whole class of persons, who are opposed to culture, improvement, and native elevation. These men have now at last made a deed set against civilization, enlightenment and mission."[99] Whether or not Crummell's remarks were accurate, stability returned to Liberia when the settlers called upon the venerable Joseph Jenkins Roberts to lead the country once again. By February 1872 his new government was well in control and receiving resolutions of support from throughout the republic.[100]

The Roye episode was a tragic result of the convergence of many different forces impinging on Liberian settler society. In a narrow sense, much of the blame can be attributed to Roye's own ill-timed attempt to remain in office without the endorsement of the people through the electoral process. It should be remembered, however, that the rise of the St. Paul River settlements allowed Roye to assume that his gamble for continued political power could succeed. The foreign-loan incident made clear the extent to which international relations were becoming evermore dangerous to Liberia. Once European governments began to actively pursue colonization in West Africa in the 1880s, Liberia's sovereignty became more precarious. As the settlers faced the last quarter of the century, aware that dangers threatened them from every side, they searched for ways to fortify their Promised Land.

8/Afro-American Immigration and the Atlantic Community

Liberia and Hayti are as yet the only countries to which colonists of African descent from here could go with certainty of being received and adopted as citizens; and I regret to say such persons contemplating colonization do not seem so willing to migrate to those countries as to some others, nor so willing as I think their interest demands. I believe, however, opinion among them in this respect is improving, and that ere long there will be an augmented and considerable migration to both these countries from the United States.

—Abraham Lincoln,
Second Annual Message to Congress, December 1, 1862

Liberia remained a fragile settler society throughout the nineteenth century. The central purpose of the republic seemed to become less attainable to the settlers as the years passed, despite the sacrifices of life and labor. Sustained by the concept of Negro nationality, the settlers tried to prepare a place in Africa for their racial brethren in America. Yet as they struggled to maintain familiar institutions and acquire territory, the anticipated mass exodus of the Afro-American population to Liberia never quite materialized. By the 1890s even the unflagging Edward Blyden had succumbed to pessimism on this most vital issue. "We are keeping these lands, we say, for our brethren in America. But they are not willing to come, and they will not be ready to come for the next hundred years."[1] The failure to attract and sustain high levels of Afro-American immigration during the nineteenth century denied Liberia the infusion of human resources so critical to any settler society.[2] The reasons lie in the course of American history during and after the Civil War. After 1860, Afro-American immigration seemed a likely consequence of the war; but Liberia was only one of several Atlantic communities hoping to receive the potential manpower from America.

The Republican Party, which achieved national power when Abraham Lincoln was elected president in 1860, was a fusion party of diverse political partners. A small but vocal antislavery faction had joined with northern capitalists supporting high protective tariffs, Free Soilers demanding homesteads in the West free from the competition of slave labor, and former Whig partisans seeking the political kingdom. Their party platform reflected all the diversity of factional interests. At the helm of the Republican coalition stood a shrewd but nationally obscure politician from the state of Illinois. In the words of historian T. Harry Williams, "no polygot army of an ancient emperor ever exhibited more variety than did the Republican Party in 1860."[3]

Opposition to the planter aristocracy of the slaveholding South represented the only common bond holding the Republicans together as a party. And yet all Republicans were not of the same mind even on this issue. The radical, antislavery faction called for the immediate end to slavery in America. The party, however, had not nominated a genuine abolitionist to run for the presidency. Abraham Lincoln defined his opposition much more narrowly than did the radicals. He was willing to accept the presence of slavery where it already existed; he desired only to prevent its spread into new areas of the nation. He was also a committed adherent to the philosophy of colonization—supporting gradual emancipation linked to an established program of deportation.[4]

Despite Lincoln's less than radical position on slavery, the South perceived his election as a clear and present danger to its most controversial institution. During the interval between the presidential election of 1860 and Lincoln's inauguration in March 1861, seven states of the lower South seceded from the Union. In this worsening period of national disintegration, Lincoln tried desperately to turn the tide of mounting crisis set in motion by his election victory. He took the occasion of his inaugural address to send a conciliatory message to the South by explicitly reiterating his position on slavery. "I have no purpose, directly or indirectly, to interfere with the institution of slavery in the States where it exists. I believe I have no lawful right to do so, and I have no inclination to do so."[5] In selecting government officials for his administration, Lincoln tried to demonstrate constraint to reassure the South. He purposely kept recognized Radicals out of his Cabinet, save Salmon P. Chase, who became secretary of the treasury. Border-state conservatives with solid southern connections, such as Edward Bates and Montgomery Blair, won Cabinet-level appointments. Lincoln even selected loyal Democrats to visible government posts. Yet none of these gestures avoided the fateful attack on Fort Sumter that signaled the start of America's bitter internecine conflict.

Once begun, the Civil War forced Lincoln to face up to the policy question raised by the growing number of slaves—or in the military language of the Union Army, "contraband"—captured during the initial months of warfare. In December 1861 he proposed to Congress that these slaves and any others that might subsequently follow be freed and that funds be appropriated to provide for their colonization outside of the United States. Although Lincoln did not then specify a particular place for this colonization, Liberia was easily the most obvious choice, especially since Lincoln used the same opportunity to propose diplomatic recognition of the independence and sovereignty of Haiti and Liberia.[6] The U.S. agent for liberated Africans in Monrovia, John Seys, asserted in response to Lincoln's publicized proposal that "if this be the home, the only safe home for the recaptured Congo, how much more for the Americo-Africans!" Seys described Liberia as ideally suited for this role. "There is room enough on these shores and in the rich interior country for all you may send."[7]

If Lincoln left the destination of his proposed colonization plan vague, he was careful to insist from the start that any Afro-American emigration under federal auspices had to be voluntary. With this stipulation in mind, Lincoln invited a delegation of Afro-Americans to the White House on August 14, 1862, to hear his ideas firsthand. Although Lincoln mentioned Liberia in favorable terms, he pointed out that there was little interest among northern Afro-Americans to emigrate there, and he chose to promote Central America as a location superior to Liberia. Lincoln emphasized Central America's proximity to the United States, its abundance of natural resources, and "especially . . . the similarity of climate with your native land—thus being suited to your physical condition."[8] By the time Lincoln addressed this delegation, activity already underway brought both the West Indies and Central America to the fore in administration discussions about Afro-American colonization.

Lincoln's use of the term "colony" caused uneasiness within his Cabinet. Attorney General Edward Bates supported the idea of Afro-American deportation but saw a serious legal problem with colonization. He argued that a colony implied a dependency on the mother country and the right of the colonists to protection by the same. In contrast, emigrants would be incorporated as individuals into the body politic of the host country. "They may still have sympathies of their former country, but have no right to its powers for protection, except upon grounds of international comity, and of treaty stipulations, made in their favor."[9] The distinction that Bates drew between colonist and emigrant was more than just a legal fine point. Lincoln advocated colonization, while all the possible host countries, including Liberia, were only interested in emigration. The reasons for Lincoln's position became clear in his overtures to the British regarding their West Indian colonies.

The British colonies in the West Indies had been active in developing emigration programs to meet the labor needs of planters from as early as 1831, when Her Majesty's government outlawed slavery in all her overseas possessions.[10] These colonies secured labor through emigration from India, China, and West Africa. On July 5, 1862, Lieutenant Governor Edward Eyre, of Jamaica, outlined in a letter to the Colonial Office the specific reasons why Afro-American immigrants to his colony were more desirable than immigrants from other sources. He noted that "recent events in America" made it probable that large numbers of Afro-Americans would be removed from that country with the aid of Lincoln's government. Eyre suggested that the Afro-Americans were "of industrious habits, and superior as a class than the present peasantry of the West Indian islands." He also pointed out that because of a general depression in the prices of tropical produce, most planters could no longer afford to pay the cost of bringing laborers from India and China. Finally, Eyre reminded the Colonial Office that the prosperity of Jamaica depended on increasing the population of the country and at the least expense.[11]

One month earlier the British charge d'affaires in Washington, D.C., had informed the British foreign secretary that the Danish government was making arrangements to transfer Afro-American contraband to St. Croix.[12] As news of the Danish activity spread, other British colonies followed Eyre's lead and sent appeals to the Colonial Office for help in attracting labor from America. The pressure on the Colonial Office prompted the Duke of Newcastle to check with the foreign secretary in August to determine whether "the matter might not properly be made the subject of a communication to the Government of the United States." He did not comment on the advantages of Afro-American emigration to the West Indies, which he considered all too obvious. He did, however, mention the possibility that political difficulties between England and America might interfere with such a scheme. Would emigration tend to make likely a controversy between England and the Confederate States? What consequences would be likely if an emigrant ship bound for the British West Indies were stopped on the high seas by a Confederate ship and the passengers were declared fugitive slaves from the South? Having said this, however, the Duke of Newcastle still argued that "he would strongly urge that no unsubstantial apprehension should be allowed to prevent Great Britain from availing itself of what appears to him as an advantage not only substantial, but capable, under circumstances easily conceivable, of assuming immense importance." He ended his communication by detailing a plan of operation should the foreign secretary see no reason to object. Agents would be sent to the United States at the expense of the colonies to charter ships to convey the emigrants provided by the United States government. Male emigrants would be required to sign three-year contracts for labor at wages currently paid to other emigrants going to the colonies. At least one third of the emigrants on each ship should be females, and all children should be sent with their parents. No persons sick, of old age, or unfit for field labor should be included.[13] On August 19, 1862, Earl Russell responded to the Duke of Newcastle that he approved of the proposal so long as "the ports selected for the embarkation of the negroes were in the Northern states, Massachusetts, New York or Pennsylvania." He also added that the emigration must not encourage slaves in the southern states to run away, that those who came must do so voluntarily, and that the emigration offer must also be open to France as well as Great Britain.[14]

By the end of August 1862 machinery had been set in motion to bring Afro-Americans to the British West Indies. Agents representing different colonies were on their way to Washington. The following month, however, Earl Russell began to receive a number of disturbing cables from his charge d'affaires in the American capital. William Stuart wrote on September 4 that in a private meeting with the American secretary of state, William H. Seward, he had learned that Seward was personally opposed to Afro-American emigration. Seward considered it impractical and expressed doubts about the eventual success of similar schemes being considered with the Danish government and several Central American republics. Stuart recommended that Great Britain avoid making any formal commitments until the "events more clearly show the disposition of the negroes themselves, and the future policy of the United States in regard to them."[15] Eleven days later, Minister Stuart again addressed Earl Russell. This time he reported that the Central American republics of Guatemala and San Salvador had protested against the introduction of Afro-American colonists into their countries. Stuart also stated that Seward believed that if Afro-American emigration was to occur, the British West Indies were "far better adapted than any other destination for negro emigrants." Stuart ended by informing Earl Russell that he had spoken with the French minister in Washington, who thought the time was not ripe for either France or Britain to get too deeply involved in emigration schemes.[16] On September 28 Stuart notified Earl Russell that the U.S. government was ready to conclude a convention with Great Britain "for the purpose of enabling Her Majesty's government to transport from this country such of the negroes who have lately been, or who may become, emancipated, as may be willing to emigrate to Her Majesty's West Indian or other tropical possessions." Stuart cautioned the Earl that such a treaty was probably an attempt to connect Great Britain with "the Government of the United States in a common act of hostility against the so-styled Confederate States."[17]

Stuart's recommendations to avoid a formal agreement on emigration through a convention because it was potentially politically embarrassing won the acceptance of both Earl Russell and the Duke of Newcastle. Agents already in America or on their way from the West Indies were instructed to "govern themselves implicitly by Mr. Stuart's direction." Circular dispatches were sent to the governors of Jamaica, British Guiana, and Trinidad making these instructions explicit.[18] At first the advocates of emigration in the West Indies were not aware of the reason behind Stuart's sudden prominence in the matter. Governor Eyre, of Jamaica, continued to send reports of favorable interest in the emigration possibility. On October 24 he informed the Duke of Newcastle that the British colony of Honduras had passed an act to encourage the immigration of agricultural and other laborers. This information followed shortly behind a cable informing the duke of a public meeting in Kingston called to promote the immigration of black and colored persons from the United States into Jamaica.[19] It was not until October 31 that the Duke of Newcastle finally told Governor Eyre that the British government did not think it probable that Afro-Americans would emigrate and that moreover there were "serious difficulties in the way of any arrangement to which the British government could be a party."[20] The next month saw a flurry of dispatches in which an attempt was made to stop all diplomatic activity begun in August.

Despite the official caution of London resulting from the advice of William Stuart, proposals in support of Afro-American emigration continued to come from the islands and other British possessions. On November 18 the manager of the British Honduras Company wrote to the Colonial Office on behalf of American labor emigration. He declared that the company's hope of planting cotton seed and cutting sugar cane then growing depended on obtaining laborers from the United States, since laborers they had expected from China were not available.[21] Earl Russell decided to delay any further consideration of the matter until he received an opinion from Lord Lyons, the British minister to the United States. He finally received that communication on December 26, 1862. Lord Lyons had met personally with Seward and related his impressions of their discussions. Lyons endorsed the view that it was not then convenient to establish a formal agreement with the United States. He added additional reasons for his position. Lyons concluded that Lincoln's own Cabinet was divided on the question of removing Afro-Americans. Although Lincoln supported separation, many of his closest advisors opposed it. "There existed in many quarters a strong opposition to sending away the coloured people at all, and, in some quarters a special dislike to transferring them to British or French Colonies. It is asked whether it was wise to deprive the country of so much muscle and sinew; whether it was prudent to add to the strength of nations which might not be always friends of the United States."[22] The minister was as pessimistic as Stuart had been in earlier communications. The Duke of Newcastle, under pressure from the colonies, suggested a compromise when he was told of the minister's response. The duke proposed "that private persons should be permitted by the American Government to obtain in the United States negro emigrants, and to enter into contracts with them for three years in the British West Indies, and under such superintendence by paid Agents appointed by each or all of the Colonies as may be sufficient to prevent abuse."[23] To this, Earl

Russell voiced no objection, but clearly the signing of a formal convention was now a dead issue with the British government.

The turn of events described thus far was crucial in determining the fate of Lincoln's colonization scheme. The factors involved were a complex blend of domestic and international politics. Liberia's hopes for mass immigration from America were exceptionally high during the years of the Civil War. Lincoln believed that Afro-American deportation was the only long-term solution to the race problem in America. As chief executive of the Union at a time of national crisis, he held extraordinary powers to act on his convictions. Yet ironically, the very circumstances that offered this unique situation worked to frustrate the hidden agenda of the president and to deny Liberia her much-anticipated immigration.

At home, Lincoln initially projected his national policy as one mandated solely to preserve the Union. He publicly denied any plans to interfere with the institution of slavery. This approach was calculated to retain the loyalty of the border states, to deny the Confederacy an emotional focus for their cause, and to help to shore up the unity of the North. While this tactic had its domestic imperative, it raised serious problems on the international front. Great Britain, for example, was troubled by Lincoln's failure to identify slavery as a significant issue in the conflict between North and South. The British press interpreted this as a lack of commitment to abolition. Once war broke out and the question of slavery was still unclear as an issue, the liberal British press argued that economic self-interest should be used as the best index for deciding which side the British people should support.

The British government adopted a neutral posture at the outset of the American conflict. The need to protect British commerce created the dilemma of "reconciling sentiments of humanity long preached by Great Britain, with her commercial interests and her certainty that a new State was being born."[24] Lord Lyons saw Secretary of State William H. Seward as the real power in Lincoln's administration, which caused Lyons much concern. Lyons believed that Seward might try to instigate a foreign war with England as a means of unifying America. He therefore recommended that England and France adopt identical policies towards America that would make it impossible for the United States to dare to try a foreign war.[25] These attitudes partially explain the British government's reluctance and ultimate refusal to enter into any formal treaty arrangement with Lincoln's government on Afro-American emigration to the West Indies.

As the fighting dragged on, months turning into years of bloody battles, Lincoln could not continue to avoid the slavery issue. The contraband problem and the independent actions of his field generals forced him to make policy explicit in this area. Specifically, colonization became a crucial component of his domestic strategy for winning the war. In order to publicly broach the subject of emancipation, which Lincoln increasingly saw as an effective war measure, he tried to couch it in terms that would soften the impact of the decision. He advocated gradual emancipation with compensation to the slaveholders and then called for a federal program of colonization to remove the freedmen from the country. Before making a major appeal for public support of colonization, Lincoln first had to achieve consensus within his own Cabinet—a task that required consummate political skill and genuine luck. Lincoln was up to the political challenge, but luck eluded him in this instance.

The men in Lincoln's Cabinet were of diverse opinion on the question of colonization. Attorney General Edward Bates, Postmaster General Montgomery Blair, and Secretary of the Interior Caleb B. Smith all supported colonization. But William H. Seward considered it an impractical alternative. As secretary of state, he certainly represented a major impediment to any successful colonization program, although he dutifully made foreign inquiries for Lincoln. Edwin M. Stanton opposed colonization for reasons that were purely expedient. As secretary of war, he had to consider the future military and labor needs of the Union. Salmon P. Chase, secretary of the treasury, was in the abolitionist camp and had long opposed colonization schemes. When he read of Lincoln's talk with the Afro-American delegation, Chase confined his reaction to an indignant entry in his diary. "How much better would be a manly protest against prejudice against color!—and a wise effort to give freedmen homes in America!"[26] Even among the Cabinet supporters of colonization there were important differences of opinion. Bates argued for compulsory deportation, believing that Afro-Americans would not leave the country voluntarily.[27] Lincoln, however, vetoed any measures that would force Afro-Americans to leave against their will. Although Lincoln was unable to unite his Cabinet behind an aggressive colonization program, nevertheless he did pursue two separate ventures—the Chiriqui program in Central America and the Ile A'Vache program in Haiti.

Both projects were proposed to Lincoln by business speculators with political influence. Lincoln reasoned that if Afro-Americans were removed, European immigration to the United States would accelerate in the absence of significant labor competition.[28] He also recognized the political advantages of countering the growing British influence in the Caribbean by establishing an American colony in the region. This viewpoint was reinforced by tangible military and economic advantages in the Western Hemisphere. When Secretary of the Interior Smith introduced the Chiriqui project proposal to the Cabinet on September 26, 1862, he linked naval coal needs with the transfer of Afro-Americans to Chiriqui. Although Welles, Chase, and Stanton were unconvinced, Smith and the president pressed for approval.[29] In the end, however, Lincoln was forced to abandon the Chiriqui project when both

Guatemala and San Salvador issued strong protests against it. Latin America perceived colonization sponsored by the United States government as an only slightly disguised excuse for territorial aggrandizement. In the light of the long-held notions of Manifest Destiny in the United States, this fear certainly was not unfounded. For just as the Union cause needed the diplomatic support of Europe, it was important for Lincoln's administration to prevent Latin American countries from recognizing the Confederacy.[30] Lincoln quietly dropped the matter, however regretfully.

As late as December 1862 Lincoln still hoped for a successful colonization program. With the British initiative all but over and the Chiriqui project undermined, Liberia and Haiti remained as the two countries willing to accept Afro-American immigration. In his second annual message to Congress, Lincoln expressed regret that Afro-Americans still seemed disinclined to emigrate to either place. He believed, however, that "opinion among them in this respect is improving, and that ere long there will be an augmented and considerable migration to both these countries from the United States."[31] With this faith, Lincoln opted to pursue the Haitian alternative.

The plan to colonize Afro-Americans in Haiti was the brainchild of one Bernard Kock (although Haiti had indicated an interest in attracting Afro-Americans much earlier).[32] In August 1862 he obtained a twenty-year lease to land on the island of A'Vache from President Fabre Geffrard of Haiti. He envisioned establishing a large cotton plantation there using Afro-Americans as the labor force. Kock then left Haiti for Washington, where he lobbied administration officials on behalf of his scheme. He sought a government contract to take contraband slaves to Haiti. After months of frustrating delays, Kock finally gained an audience with Lincoln. The president, known to favor colonization, had grown wary of the opportunistic "jobbers" then flooding Washington with grand designs for colonization that tended to be blatantly exploitative. Kock, however, managed to overcome the president's apprehensions of his motives and left the meeting with Lincoln's promise to "send for the contract the following day, examine it again, and do [Kock] justice."[33]

Confident that he had the president's support, Kock immediately went to New York City to raise capital to finance his project. A group of New York speculators—Paul S. Forbes, L. W. Jerome, and C. H. Tuckerman—agreed to invest seventy thousand dollars in exchange for a half-interest in the enterprise.[34] In the meantime new obstacles to the execution of the government contract surfaced in Washington. Although the president still favored the project, many other administration officials were unhappy over Kock's "personal connection" with it. In order to expedite bureaucratic approval, Kock transferred his government contract and land lease in Haiti to his New York partners, retaining his half-interest in the enterprise. Apparently the maneuver worked, for by April 1863 Kock and the first contingent of Afro-Americans sailed for Ile A'Vache. Disease, local administrative conflicts, and the dissatisfaction of the colonists all converged to destroy the project shortly after it was begun. By February 1864 Lincoln was compelled to order the secretary of war to dispatch a transport to Ile A'Vache and "bring back to this country such of the colonists there as desire to return."[35] Virtually all who survived returned.

Even if events in Haiti had been otherwise, circumstances in America had already changed so drastically that overseas colonization was no longer realistic—especially on a strictly voluntary basis. Afro-Americans had some reason to feel optimistic about their future in America. Abolitionist forces in the country continued to press for unconditional emancipation. Slaves liberated by the Union army in Port Royal, South Carolina, during the first year of the war were being prepared for freedom by northern schoolteachers and missionaries.[36] In the summer of 1862 Lincoln found it necessary to permit the recruitment of Afro-Americans into the Union army—a policy encouraged by his field generals in the face of recent military reversals.[37] At the same time, Union policy towards the subject of general emancipation began to take a definite shape. In April 1862 Congress passed an act abolishing slavery in the District of Columbia. This was followed two months later by an executive order abolishing slavery in the federal territories of the West. By September Lincoln announced a preliminary proclamation, in which he held out for the last time the possibility of compensated emancipation and renewed his support of voluntary colonization. It is not hard to understand Lincoln's meaning when he later described the situation he faced after the Confederacy ignored his preliminary proclamation: "I was, in my best judgment, driven to the alternative of either surrendering the Union, and with it, the Constitution, or of laying strong hand upon the colored element. . . . I . . . confess that events have controlled me."[38] On January 1, 1863, seeing no recourse, Lincoln issued his Emancipation Proclamation. Although Lincoln insisted that his action was simply a necessary war measure, the document, once promulgated, brought emancipation to the forefront as the primary objective of the Union cause.

The conclusion of the Civil War brought victory to the Union cause and ushered in a period of intense adjustment for Afro-Americans. Once Lincoln made slavery a central war issue, the power of the antislavery faction within his party rose quickly. Determined to transform slaves into freedmen with citizenship rights, that group worked hard to provide constitutional protection for the rights of Afro-Americans. As Reconstruction began, passage of constitutional amendments abolished slavery and extended citizenship and the franchise privilege to Afro-Americans. Suddenly the former bondsmen became a significant political factor in the reconstructed state governments seeking admission back into the Union. Even an acknowledged emigrationist like Martin R. Delany, for example, abandoned the "African dream" to plunge headlong into South Carolina politics.[39]

Annual emigration to Liberia between 1861 and 1900 reflected the developments of both the Civil War and Reconstruction periods in American life. Fewer than two hundred new emigrants left America during the war years. The annual emigration rate accelerated between 1865 and 1868, largely reflecting the domestic uncertainty of the immediate postwar years. Yet the rate never again reached the prewar levels, and after 1868 seldom more than one hundred emigrants left America for Liberia in any single year.[40]

Liberians remained ever hopeful that the downward trend in emigration was only temporary. The course of race relations in America during the last quarter of the century gave them cause to feel optimistic that Afro-Americans would finally be willing to leave the South. As the Reconstruction governments began to collapse in one southern state after another, the social, economic, and political status of Afro-Americans was systematically undermined. The triumph of white supremacy under the banner of returning the South to home rule reduced the Afro-American population to second-class citizenship, enforced by segregation, political disfranchisement, and economic exploitation.[41]

In the midst of this political and social purge, many Afro-Americans sought relief by trying to leave the South. In Chester, South Carolina, during August 1877, for example, Afro-Americans were supposedly "afflicted with Liberia fever. . . ."[42] Such sentiments alarmed Euro-Americans, who feared the loss of cheap labor but were powerless to stop the spread of emigration fever. In the same year the Liberian Exodus Joint Stock and Steamship Company was organized in South Carolina.[43] The company had an ephemeral history, but other emigrationist ventures continually appeared, especially in the 1890s. It was during this decade that several bills were debated in Congress calling for federal assistance to Afro-Americans desirous of emigrating to Africa, the most controversial one being sponsored by Senator Matthew Butler, of South Carolina.[44]

Although the Butler bill never passed—nor did any of the others—the national publicity stimulated the formation of several new emigration companies. The United States and Congo National Emigration Company and the International Migration Society were two of the better-known groups formed in the decade. Bishop Henry McNeal Turner, of the African Methodist Episcopal Church, independently agitated throughout the rural South on behalf of emigration.[45] Despite this activity, vigorous as it often was, the actual results were very disappointing. Fraudulent schemes and mismanagement of funds and facilities combined with widely circulated reports of an unhealthy environment in Africa to discourage most of the potential emigrants. But perhaps most importantly, freedom from southern oppression seemed closer at hand than emigration to Africa. Unfortunately for Liberia, the massive population movement she anticipated became a regional phenomenon rather than an international one. Beginning with the exodus to Kansas and Oklahoma and culminating with massive migration to the urban centers of the North and West, Afro-Americans searched for the Promised Land within the boundaries of the United States.[46] They seemed to believe that racial prejudice was a sectional problem rather than a national one.

The same racial ideology that victimized Afro-Americans in the South became the justification for the European colonial expansion in Africa that challenged Liberian sovereignty. Liberia, already under British pressure because of the 1871 loan, faced threats from the French after the Berlin conference of 1884-85.[47] The increased external pressure stimulated internal opposition to Liberian government authority from Africans within the republic. Wars of pacification drained an already exhausted government treasury and threatened to pave the way for British and/or French annexation of Liberia. Through all of this the post-Roye administration leadership maintained an essentially isolationist posture. Edward Blyden, writing from Sierra Leone in 1894, chastised the Liberian leadership for their short-sighted conservatism. Blyden informed President Joseph J. Cheeseman of his recommendation to former President Spriggs-Payne seventeen years earlier that he grant a thirty-year land concession to a group of English financiers in exchange for their assuming Liberia's 1871 debt. Much to his regret, the government did not adopt the proposal. "More than half the time has now passed away and Liberia would in a few years be coming into possession of an improved and valuable section of country, with the burden of her debt wiped off."[48] Blyden reminded Cheeseman that under Liberia's chosen policy of isolation, the republic had dwindled in population, territory, and influence.[49]

The Liberian leadership did not share Edward Blyden's faith in the potential benefits of foreign agreements. The disastrous loan of 1871 certainly contributed to this feeling. Liberians suspected that the British government had designs on establishing colonial hegemony over Liberia and might use land-concession agreements as the means of gaining such an influence. This suspicion made Blyden's own close ties to the British an issue that called into question his long-claimed desire to work solely for the interest of the Republic of Liberia.[50] Whatever the motives of the enigmatic Blyden, the problems of the republic were real and required concrete solutions. The Liberian government entertained concession proposals by prosperous Afro-Americans as a way of focusing attention on their country. Unlike Europeans, the Liberians felt that Afro-Americans had no desire to undermine the status quo in Liberia and their involvement probably would not prove dangerous to the republic. In 1892 a million-dollar trading company was proposed by a group of Afro-American businessmen from Philadelphia. Five years later another group proposed a concession for the creation of an Afro-American-Liberian Improvement Company. The proposal was submitted to the Liberian legislature for their consideration and approval. In both cases, however, the proposals never matured into concrete projects. The Afro-Americans had the desire to establish commercial links with Liberia but lacked the necessary capital to create such links. They not only wanted special concession privileges but also needed the Liberians to contribute substantial sums to the project.[51]

As the century closed and hopes of large-scale emigration by Afro-Americans or capital investments diminished, Liberia stood in grave financial difficulty, increasingly unable to avoid foreign encroachments. Historians have often characterized Liberian settler society as one frozen in the habits, attitudes, and style of the nineteenth century. The isolation of the settler community that contributed to this impression was fostered by the threatening internal and external environment. The dominant settler response in the nineteenth century was to withdraw and preserve the values and life style that had served them while they created the Republic of Liberia.

9/Liberian Settler Society in World Perspective

Settlements do not cost much, and the prince can found them (and maintain them) at little or no personal expense. He injures only those from whom he takes the land and houses to give to the new inhabitants, and these victims form a tiny minority, and can never do any harm since they remain poor and scattered. All the others are left undisturbed, and so should stay quiet, and as well as this they are frightened to do wrong lest what happened to the dispossessed should happen to them.

—Niccolo Machiavelli, *The Prince*

Liberia has frequently been compared with other countries on the African continent. Traditionally the comparison has emphasized Liberia's (and Ethiopia's) uniqueness in escaping formal European colonialism in the late nineteenth century. More recently, two new comparisons have appeared in the literature, one viewing Liberia as an active instrument of imperialism in its own right, the other drawing crude analogies with the racist minority regime in South Africa.[1] The comparative approach is valuable, although one need not accept these particular models.[2] By paying careful attention to the basis for comparison, comparative data can illuminate and inform an analysis. It is hoped that the following discussion will lead to questions that ultimately can "detect errors or inadequacies in hypothetical explanations which seem unimpeachable if viewed in one single historical or geographical setting" and highlight factors of particular relevance to Liberia.[3]

The nineteenth century was a time of enormous intercontinental population movement. Settler societies—in many cases founded in the previous century—grew rapidly as a direct consequence of immigration from overseas. In this context, the Liberian settler experience can be compared with the settler experiences in South Africa, Australia, and Argentina. All settler societies began with a crucial period of gestation. "Planting the colony" became the euphemism for the often disastrous attempts to establish the first settler enclave. The first settler expeditions to plant a colony like those of the European colonies in North America, usually ended in chaos brought on by the ravages of disease, starvation, attacks by local people, or some

135

combination of all these factors. The board of managers of the American Colonization Society tried to ignore the initial results of their project to settle Afro-Americans in Liberia: "At present we would request our friends not to be discouraged. The Board laments the unfortunate issue of this first effort, but they had no right to calculate upon the absence of those disasters, difficulties, and disappointments, which attend all human affairs, and which are ordered, or permitted, to attend them, for purposes the wisdom and goodness of which, though we may not see, we cannot doubt . . . . To these dispensations of the Almighty we bow in submission and at the same time resolve to go in the path of duty."[4] The religious faith of sponsors was never enough to sustain new settlers in a foreign land. The nature and degree of external support that the settlers received to reinforce their precarious position was far more pertinent.

Can the sponsors in the mother country provide timely supplies, reinforcements of manpower, and military protection? In the case of Liberia, the external support was from the start both thin and irregular. The American Colonization Society was a privately funded organization dependent for most of its resources on public donations and subscriptions. The efforts of the society to raise money were constantly hindered by the controversy that surrounded the interpretation of its motives; as a consequence, the early settlers in Liberia had to endure hardships that might well have been avoided by steady external support. The Dutch colony founded on the South African Cape of Good Hope in 1652 also was backed by a private organization. Unlike the American Colonization Society, however, the Dutch East India Company was a mercantile firm with substantial capital and political influence. From the start, the company was able to give considerable external support to its colony. Its interest in maintaining an enclave on the South African coast, however, was associated with a far-flung, sea-based mercantile enterprise. In fact, the company had an explicit policy of restricting the growth of the Cape settlement in order to protect its Indian Ocean trade monopoly and save administrative costs.[5] Thus for many years the Dutch Cape colony remained little more than a maritime depot for ships rounding the southern extreme of Africa.

Even when governments directly organized the founding of new settler colonies, the results were not necessarily any more dramatic than the limited accomplishments of private organizations. The Spanish crown authorized colonization in Argentina in the sixteenth century as an extension of Spain's South American empire. Starting with settlements in the northwest highlands of the interior, close to the rich mining areas of upper Peru, and eventually extending to the Atlantic Coast, where small urban towns were founded, government support established the Spaniards in Argentina quickly. Yet at the same time, crown restrictions on free trade retarded agricultural development in Argentina until the 1780s. In 1787 the British government ordered the planting of a colony in Australia. The New South Wales settlement was intended to reduce the burgeoning convict population in Britain and also to provide naval stores for British commercial shipping in the Pacific Far East. Despite the active involvement of the British government, the Australian settlement drifted along without any major advance beyond that of small and expensive penal colony for the next forty years. This apparent neglect, which contradicted the initially declared motives of the British government has been explained in a compelling argument by Geoffrey Blainey.[6] Blainey describes the "tyranny of distance" that separated England from her Australian colony. Blainey sees Australia's colonial development profoundly influenced by improvements and breakthroughs in navigation and shipbuilding so that the lifeline to England could become a dependable link. All this took time, but in the interim the Australian colony languished. Blainey's thesis has implications for all settler societies.

Overseas settlers were invariably forced to adapt to new environmental conditions. The concentration of most European settlements in temperate zones speaks to their general inability to cope with tropical disease environments before the twentieth century.[7] High mortality rates and the resultant limitation on settler population growth were common where newcomers were exposed to infectious diseases without natural immunities. Even Afro-Americans, who possessed hereditary immunities unavailable to Europeans, suffered high mortality in Liberia. Each colony faced a different set of environmental conditions, which required special adjustments and influenced the settlement pattern. In Liberia a rocky and uneven coastline posed difficult problems for settlement, while the hinterland contained dense forest, whose development required intensive manpower. In Australia climate was the key environmental factor. Rainfall was extremely unreliable in all areas. The average annual rainfall in the interior, moreover, was dramatically less than that of the coast.[8] Sparse and unreliable rainfall restricted agriculture to limited areas during the early years of settlement in Australia. There were cases where the environmental factors did not pose specific problems for large-scale settlement. European settlers in South Africa discovered that neither climate nor topography restricted their movement; rather the most serious obstacle was the presence of highly organized African societies.[9] The Argentina fertile plain (*pampa*) also was a most hospitable environment for settlement; nevertheless, it was avoided by the early Spaniards, who sought precious metals above all else. It was not until the nineteenth century that settlers took advantage of the temperate climate and productive soil in this vast, open country, particularly in the provinces near Buenos Aires, to raise cattle and cereal grains.[10]

A new settler society implies the formation of a new social order. Social differentiation and then stratification seems to be a function of the need to create and perpetuate an exploitable class of laborers. In many instances the indigenous population falls victim to this process. Spanish colonization in Argentina, undertaken by soldiers, administrators, and aristocrats, began with military campaigns against the Indian population. Although never totally successful, especially with regard to the nomadic and warlike hunters of the *pampa*, the Spaniards were able to subjugate various agrarian peoples surrounding their settlements. In fact the settlers soon came to depend on these *encomienda* Indians for food crops.[11] Before very long, obvious social distinctions became characteristic of settler society in Argentina. The original settlers, or *vecinos*, and their descendants composed the upper class. They were in control of both land and labor. Subsequent Spanish immigrants stood socially between the upper class and the masses of mestizos, mulattoes, and other people of color who performed the manual labor in Spanish settlements and considered themselves above the Indian population in the rural countryside. This pattern of social stratification remained unchanged until the nineteenth century, when large numbers of southern Europeans emigrated to Argentina.

In the Cape colony of South Africa the exploitable class was largely imported during the early years. The Dutch East India Company imported slaves to the Cape colony from other parts of Africa and the Indian Ocean from the time of the first colonial governor, Jan van Riebeeck. Thus as the Dutch employees of the company began to become "free burghers" in increasing numbers, they were able to acquire slaves both from the imported sources and from the Khoi population, which stood vulnerably close at hand. The pattern of relying on non-European manual labor became entrenched. The institution of slavery placed its stamp on the Cape society. The dichotomy between servile worker and free colonist, between black and white, was established at this time.[12] In Australia the penal nature of the British settlement provided a convenient exploitable class within the settler community. It was only after the 1820s that the immigration of free British workmen reached levels large enough to radically alter the composition of the society.[13] The officers of the military garrison were extremely conscious of their social standing. The colony's labor requirements were met by an elaborate assignment system that placed convicts in the employ of free persons. By 1838, 26,000 of the 38,000 convicts were leased to private parties.[14] This convict-leasing system was of a short-term nature, since most convicts could expect eventually to gain their freedom. The key to the long-term labor needs of Australia was the continued immigration of Europeans.

Both status and power were derived from the maintenance of social distinctions in settler societies. Social origin and time of arrival in the colony were important variables in determining status among settlers. In Australia the penal heritage became the focus of conflict during the later years as the social structure polarized between "emancipists" and "exclusives." The emancipists wanted status in Australia to depend on wealth rather than social background. The exclusives struggled to prevent former convicts from attaining social, political, and economic power.[15] Time of arrival was essential in creating social distinctions in Argentina and South Africa. The Dutch settlers at the Cape did not assimilate the settlers who arrived later from England.[16] In Argentina the situation was similar. The descendants of the early *conquistadores* considered their creole status superior to that of the nineteenth-century immigrants from Germany, France, Switzerland, and other European countries. The early free Afro-American immigrants to Liberia used their resources and skills to establish a settler standard. Emancipated slaves and recaptured Africans had little alternative but to follow the standard already in place. By using both an apprenticeship system and a ward system, the settlers ensured for themselves a labor force under conditions they could control.

After the first settler enclaves were planted on the Liberian coast, an effort to expand settlement into the interior began. This movement into the frontier was characterized by a significant modification of the settler standard. Upriver settlers adopted a cultural perspective that blended their American past with their African present. Although in the Liberian case pioneer exploits did not overshadow the dominance of the coastal life style, in other settler societies national myths grew out of romanticizing frontier expansion. The *Voortrekkers* of South Africa and the pastoral shepherds of Australia came to symbolize the ethos of their respective settler societies.

British rule was permanently imposed on the South African Cape colony in 1806. This marked the beginning of the major tensions within the embryonic settler social structure. The British introduced a formal administrative system designed to make the colony pay its own way. The Dutch settlers resented the new system when it became clear that the social order would be affected as well. British religious revivalism, which culminated with the Humanitarian Movement, successfully attacked the slave trade and touched the Cape colony at its most sensitive point of social organization. Governor Caledon's Code of 1809 brought the relations between masters and slaves within the jurisdiction of colonial law. Ordinance 50 of 1828 removed the major mechanism for maintaining the inferior status of nonwhites.[17] The changes in the status of the exploitable class coincided with the arrival of a new wave of immigrants from England in 1820. The five thousand British settlers brought new ideas and attitudes, which were rejected by the Dutch-descendant settlers. The social and economic tensions in the Cape stimulated conservative Dutch settlers (Boers) to seek opportunities to preserve their values and life style outside the control of the British. The South African interior offered the prospect of both free land and freedom from the control of the British colonial administration.[18]

In Australia the key to frontier expansion was a sharp rise in the number of free immigrants. The British government began to use emigration as a means of diminishing a rapidly multipying domestic population. Australia was a popular target for government-encouraged emigration. Over two hundred thousand free immigrants reached Australia with government assistance between 1820 and 1850.[19] The government program was inspired by Gibbon Wakefield's appeals for systematic colonization.[20] Although the goal of providing a uniform land policy never was fully successful, the program increased immigration by propertied people rather than by workers.[21] The economic and social tensions brought about by a sudden increase in free immigration generated an expansion of settlers on the frontier at the same time that pastoral potential on the interior plains was becoming apparent. Experimental sheep-breeding has been conducted as early as 1794 in Australia. It was only in the nineteenth century, however, that land, capital, and manpower came together to make pastoral activities the key to unlocking the frontier, in spite of serious environmental contraints. By 1840 hundreds of squatters occupied the plains with 1,300,000 sheep and nearly 400,000 head of cattle.[22]

Economics was the basic connecting link for settler societies during frontier expansion. The frontier economy was stimulated by and dependent on external market demands for frontier products. Foreign demands for animal hides, meats, and cereal grains encouraged settlers in Argentina to expand their utilization of the *pampa*. The ready market within the English mercantile industry made the wool farming of Australian squatters an alternative to coastal farming. In each case, central places evolved that competed for the power to mediate and hence for the profit from the exchange economy.

Cape Town was the first central place in South African settler history. As the coastal metropolis serving as a provisioning depot for passing ships, Cape Town occupied a strategic position. It was able to hold the position unchallenged until the *Voortrekkers* expanded the frontier eastward and away from the Cape's economic center of gravity. Distance and difficulties of transportation were crucial limiting factors on the power of a central place. As the *Voortrekkers* moved out, Cape authorities took steps to restrain expansion on the frontier line and thereby retain its centrality. Dense settlement around the Cape was more advantageous than a moving frontier both from an economic perspective and from the political point of view of the British government. The persistence of the frontiersmen to move eastward gave coastal areas nearer to the expanding frontier an opportunity to compete with Cape Town for central-place status.[23]

The development of Port Elizabeth and East London was stimulated by their capacity to function as centers of economic exchange for the *Voortrekkers*.[24] Less functionally diverse places developed in the interior, closer to the coastal metropolises. Itinerant traders, or *smous*, moved between these points, bringing a portable market to the moving frontier.[25] Grahamstown emerged in this position vis-à-vis both Port Elizabeth and East London. As the frontier continued to expand, the pattern of competing central places also continued, and Port Natal (Durban) and, finally, Lourenco Marques entered the field.[26]

Settler societies eventually break with the organization or government that spawns them as colonies. Usually the cause of the break is economic, although the timing may differ from one colony to another. In Argentina the *saladero* system enabled the settlers to exploit all parts of the cattle and horses for commercial purposes. The *saladero* commercialized a rudimentary pastoral economy by processing purchased cattle and horses for the export trade.[27] The narrow mercantile policies of the Spanish colonial government placed the Spanish crown at odds with the interests of Argentine settlers. The *saladero* system gave the settlers the capacity to supply a large European market. The cry for free trade rights with the world market soon became translated into demands for political autonomy. Independence from Spain came in 1810, when the *caudillos*, the provincial strong men, provided the leadership necessary for unity.[28]

The discovery of diamonds in South Africa in 1869 marked the beginning of the major transformation of the frontier and the process of settler political consolidation. The attraction of the diamond fields pulled a significant segment of the urban, coastal community into the interior. Men like Cecil Rhodes gained control over the diamond industry by squeezing out the ubiquitous small prospectors. The struggle between the coastal central places accelerated into cut-throat competition for the revenues that accrued from the customs dues collected at the ports on exported diamonds.[29] The discovery of gold in the Witwatersrand area only intensified the turmoil in the interior. These developments made the political climate in South Africa both complex and volatile. The British colonial interest conflicted with the interests of the settlers, now split between the conservative Boers and their equally vocal neighbors in the industrial towns growing up in the interior. The road to open political schism was clear. The spark was the abortive Jamison Raid of 1895; the vehicle was the Anglo-Boer War; and the eventual outcome was political independence from British rule.

By comparison, Liberia's settler society faltered at just the time settler societies in Australia, South Africa, and Argentina experienced significant growth and development. Liberia simply did not experience the high immigration levels that aided these other countries in the nineteenth century. The United States, itself a haven for millions of immigrants, never developed a national policy for Afro-American emigration to Liberia. Efforts to attract immigrants from other African-descent populations, such as from the West Indies, proved only marginally successful. Thus the only effective "push" factor was the Afro-American ideological commitment to racial nationalism.

With regional variations in American race relations, ideological considerations never were strong enough to inspire a massive exodus to Liberia. On the other hand, there were few genuinely compelling "pull" factors associated with Liberia. In fact, persistent rumors of unhealthy climatic conditions mitigated all claims of opportunity in the African Promised Land.

Liberia failed to achieve economic independence during the nineteenth century. The American Colonization Society launched an overseas colony but was able to offer only minimal external support to the settlers once they were in Africa. After 1847 the settlers tried to replace private philanthrophy with more substantial foreign aid from governments. Their overtures, made through negotiated treaties of friendship and commerce, prompted England to give Liberia a few coastal vessels but beyond that little else. The United States refused to even recognize the Republic of Liberia until the Lincoln administration and did not extend foreign aid to the country in the nineteenth century. Unable to get large amounts of capital in any other way, the settlers negotiated their first foreign loan in 1871. When the loan became a political and economic disaster, and when cash-crop agriculture collapsed in the face of international competition, the Republic plunged further into onerous debt obligations that they could not meet. By 1912, repeated defaults on loan repayments culminated with the establishment of an international receivership over all Liberian revenues. Only European rivalries and shrewd Liberian diplomacy prevented outright annexation of the country by England, France, and Germany. In 1927 the Liberian government acquiesced to American pressures and gave Harvey Firestone control over a vast area of the interior for development of a rubber plantation. In exchange for a hundred-year lease to one million acres of land, Liberia received a $5-million loan from the U.S. treasury. Once the agreement was signed, Liberia became a dependent society whose sovereignty was only barely intact.[30] It was not until the administration of William V. S. Tubman in the 1940s and 1950s that the situation was substantially altered.

Under conditions of severe economic hardship the nineteenth-century Liberian settlers could make good their territorial claims only through alliances with African chiefs. The frequency of internal "rebellions" by Africans vividly demonstrated that alliances were poor substitutes for effective government administration. In reality what the settlers chose to view as a nation was in fact two distinct and unequal societies—one settler, the other African. The situation had not changed appreciably when Tubman declared during his first presidential-election campaign that he would "strive with all my might to agglutinate and unify our population."[31] The Tubman National Unification Policy that followed became the first concerted effort to affect national integration in reality as well as in rhetoric. Through all of these difficult and painful circumstances, the settlers and their descendants retained a symbolic faith in the ideals of their predecessors, the original pioneer immigrants. For better or worse, their strongly ideological legacy has remained alive in Liberia to the present time.

Appendix A / Occupational Categories from the 1843 Census of Liberia

Agricultural

Farmer

Appointive

Clerk of court
Collector
Colonial secretary
Governor
Judge of
   the supreme court
Justice of the peace
Overseer
Registrar
Sheriff

Artisans

Baker
Blacksmith
Cabinetmaker
Machinist
Millwright
Nurse
Potter
Printer
Saddler
Sailmaker
Scrivener
Shoemaker
Stonecutter
Stonemason
Tailor
Tinner
Weaver
Wheelwright

Commercial

Factor
Merchant
Trader

Miscellaneous

Blind
Indigent

Professional

Druggist
  (apothecary,
  pharmacist)
Editor
Missionary
Physician
Schoolteacher

Semiskilled

Apprentice
Barber
Barkeeper
Bricklayer
Carpenter
Caulker
Constable
Cooper
Fisherman
Gardener
Hatter (milliner)
Hostler
Housekeeper
Huntsman

Midwife
Nailmaker
Oil miller
Painter
Plasterer
Seaman
Seamstress
Shingle drawer
Spinster
Tanner
Turner
Waiter

Unskilled

Ditcher
Laborer
Laundress
  (washerwoman)
Sawyer
Servant
Whitewasher

Appendix B / Members of the Richards Family as Shown in Table 18

1. Othello Richards
2. Mary Richards
3. Wesley Morgan Richards
4. Sarah L. Prout
5. Caroline Richards
6. Nancy Richards
7. Madison Houston
8. Elizabeth Houston
9. Eugenia Richards
10. Francis Asbury Richards
11. Martha Travis
12. Samuel David Richards
13. S. C. Holcomb
14. R. Van Richards
15. Florence A. Richards
16. _____ Richards
17. Wesley Richards, Jr.
18. Mary Richards
19. Matilda Roberts Howard
20. John Gotlieb Auer Richards
21. Sarah Eloise Richards
22. _____Richards
23. Mary Houston Mullen
24. Jacob Houston
25. Frank Richards
26. Moses Richards
27. Martha Ora Richards
28. Philip Francis Simpson
29. Samuel D. Richards, Jr.
30. Clara Agnes Richards
31. Nathaniel H. B. Cassell
32. Danlet Louise Richards
33. Charles Francis Innes
34. William H. C. Richards
35. Lenora M. Lomax
36. Jessina Ella Richards
37. Daniel H. Scott

Appendix C / Government Grant of Bounty Land

To all to whom these presents shall come, Know ye, that in consideration of Marcus Roberts in the County of Montserrado and the Republic of Liberia, having performed 30 days, military services as a volunteer in the campaign against the Gallinas Tribes under the command of Col. R. A. Sherman in the year of our Lord eighteen hundred and seventy one, and a Bounty certificate having been legally issued for said services, in conformity with the Act of the Legislature, entitled "An Act Pertaining to Bounty Land," approved January 13, 1863, and the right title and interest to and in said certificate having been transferred for a lawful consideration to Thomas Mitchell, Jr. as is evidenced by said certificate, filed in the office of the Commissioner of Public Lands for Montserrado County, in accordance with said Act:—Therefore, I, James S. Payne, President of the Republic of Liberia, for myself, and my successors in office, in pursuance of the Act above cited, have given, granted, and confirmed and by these presents do give grant and confirm unto the said Thomas Mitchell, Jr. his heirs, executors, administrators and assigns, all that lot or parcel of land, situated, lying and being in the settlement of Millsburg—4th Range, County of Montserrado and Republic aforesaid and bearing in the authentic records of said settlement of lot no. one and running S. 66 degrees W 15 chains; then S 33 degrees twenty chains and contains thirty (30) acres of land and no more.

To have and to hold the above granted premises, together with all and singular the buildings, improvements and appurtenances thereof and thereto belonging, to the said Thomas Mitchell, Jr. his heirs, executors, administrators and assigns forever. And I the said James S. Payne for myself and my successors in office, do covenant to and with the said Thomas Mitchell, Jr. his heirs, executors, administrators and assigns, that at an [sic] until the ensealing hereof, I the said James S. Payne by virtue of my office and authority given me by the Act above mentioned, had good right and lawful authority to convey the aforesaid premises in fee simple. And I, the said James S. Payne defend the said Thomas Mitchell, Jr. his heirs, executors, administrators or assigns, against any person or persons claiming any part of the above named premises.

Deed Records, Montserrado County, 1865-69, Archives of the Liberian Government, Monrovia, Liberia.

In witness whereof I, the said James S. Payne, have here-
unto set my hand and caused the seal of the Republic of
Liberia to be affixed this ninth day of August in the year
of our Lord one thousand eight hundred and seventy seven
and of the Republic the thirteenth.

James S. Payne
President

David M. Payne
Land Commissioner, Montserrado County

Appendix D / Title Deed Grant for Completion of Improvement Requirement

Know all men by these presents that I Stephen Allen Benson President of the Republic of Liberia of the one part and Nancy Ash of the County of Montserrado and Republic aforesaid of the other part witnesseth:—That for and in consideration of the said Nancy Ash having made the lawful improvements upon ¼ of an acre of land assigned her agreeable to the regulations of the board of managers of the American Colonization Society established June 26, 1820, I the said Stephen Allen Benson for myself and my successors in office have granted and confirmed and by these presents do give, grant and confirm unto the said Nancy Ash her heirs, Executors, Administrators and assigns forever all that lot or parcel of land situated, lying and being in the town of Clay Ashland and bearing in the authentic records of said Town the number 30 (thirty) and bounded as follows. Commencing at the S. E. Angle of Lot #29:

> Thence running W. 56 degrees S. 8
> Thence running N. 34 degrees W. 5
> Thence running N. 56 degrees E. 8
> Thence running S. 34 degrees E. 5

to the place of commencement and contains ¼ acre of land and no more. To have and to hold the above granted and confirmed premises together with all and singular the buildings and improvements and appurtenances thereof and thereto belonging to the said Nancy Ash her heirs, Executors, Administrators or assigns and I the said Stephen Allen Benson for myself and my successors in office do covenant to and with the said Nancy Ash her heirs, Executors, Administrators and assigns that at and until the ensealing thereof I the said Stephen Allen Benson by virtue of my office had good right and lawful authority to convey the aforesaid premises in fee simple and I the said Stephen Allen Benson will forever warrant and defend the said Nancy Ash her heirs, Executors, Administrators or assigns against any person or persons claiming any part or parcel of the above named premises.

> In witnesseth whereof I the said Stephen Allen Benson hath hereunto set my hand and caused the seal of the Republic to be affixed this 1st day of August A.D. one thousand eight hundred and fifty seven and of the Republic the tenth.
>
> *Stephen A. Benson*
> *President*

Deed Records, Montserrado County, 1865-69, Archives of the Liberian Government, Monrovia, Liberia.

Appendix E / Sale of Land by One Individual to Another

Know all men by these presents, that I Georgiana Elizabeth Moore of the Settlement of Clay Ashland, County of Montserrado and Republic of Liberia party of the first part and Nathaniel A. Doldson of the City of Monrovia, County of Montserrado and Republic of Liberia party of the second part. Witnesseth that for and in consideration of the sum of thirty-five dollars ($35.00) lawful money of this Republic paid me in hand by the said Nathaniel A. Doldson, I the said Georgiana E. Moore have granted bargained, sold and confirmed and by these presents do grant, bargain, sell and confirm unto him the said Nathaniel A. Doldson his heirs, Executors, Administors and assigns forever all that lot or parcel of land lying and being situated in the City of Monrovia, County of Montserrado and Republic and Liberia and bearing in the authentic records of said City the number 404 and being the S.E. half of said lot (404) and containing one Eighth of an acre of land and no more and have the same degrees E. W. N. and S. as all the other town lots have situated in the City of Monrovia.

To have and to hold the above bargained and granted premises together with all the buildings and singular the building and appurtenances thereof and thereto belonging to said Nathaniel A. Doldson his heirs, Executors, Administrators, and assigns. And I the said Georgiana E. Moore do covenant to and with the said Nathaniel A. Doldson his heirs, Executors, Administrators and assigns that at and until the ensealing hereof I had good right and lawful authority by virtue of heirship, the said premises coming to me from my mother Harriet, to sell and convey the aforesaid premises in fee simple. And I the said Georgiana E. Moore, widow of George W. Moore deceased and only living heir of my said mother for myself and my heirs, Executors, Administrators and assigns will forever warrant and defend the said Nathaniel A. Doldson his heirs, Executors, Administrators and assigns against any person or persons claiming any part or parcel of the above named premises.

The word "forever" over the seventh or interlined was done before the ensealing and delivery of these presents.

In witness whereof I the aforesaid Georgiana E. Moore have here unto set my hand and seal this 2nd day of May Anno Domini 1868.

Signed, sealed and delivered
in the presence of
                                                    Georgiana E. Moore

James C. Minor
Richard Pinns

Deed Records, Montserrado County, 1865, Archieves of the Liberian Government, Monrovia, Liberia.

150

Appendix F / Sale of Land Left in an Estate of a Deceased

To all persons to whom these presents shall come, I William C. Burke of the town of Clay Ashland and County of Montserrado Executor of the last will and testament of Matthew Ash, late of the town of Clay Ashland deceased, estate. Whereas the said Matthew Ash, in order to enable his said Executor fully to carry into effect his intention, did by his Last Will and Testament authorize and enpower his said Executor in any manner which he should deem proper to make sale of and, execute deeds, to convey the said Testator's Real Estate. Now therefore, I the said William C. Burke, executor as aforesaid by William D. Coleman, of the Town of Clay Ashland, and County of Montserrado, the receipt whereof is hereby in consideration of the sum of eighty eight dollars ($88.00) to me in hand paid acknowledged, have given, granted, bargained, sold and conveyed and by these presents do give, grant, bargain, sell and convey unto the said W. D. Coleman, his heirs, Executors, Administrators, and assigns, the following described parcel of real estate, which was the property of the said Matthew Ash situated in the town of Clay Ashland and bounded and described as follows to wit, the number twelve (12) commencing at the South Eastern angle of Lot No. eleven (11) and running North 56 degrees East two hundred links, thence east 34 degrees south, one hundred and twenty five links, thence West 34 degrees North one hundred and twenty-five links to place of commencement, and contains one quarter of an acre of land and no more.

To have and to hold the aforegranted premises to him the said W. D. Coleman, his heirs, and assigns to his and their use and forever. And I the said William C. Burke do covenant with the said W.D. Coleman his Heirs, and assigns that I am lawfully the Executor of the Last Will and Testament of the said Matthew Ash and that I have not made any other conveyance on the hereby granted premises since I was appointed Executor, by the said Matthew Ash, and that I have in all respects acted in making this conveyance in pursuance of the authority granted to me in and by the Last Will and Testament of the said Matthew Ash.

In witness whereof I the said William C. Burke hath set by hand and seal this twenty fourth day of January A. D. 1869.

Signed, sealed and delivered in the presence of Isaac James Ash and Preston Freeman
J. Wiles
Registrar

William C. Burke
Executor for Matthew Ash

Deed Records, Montserrado County, 1865-69, Archives of the Liberian Government, Monrovia, Liberia.

Appendix G / Nineteenth-Century Presidents of the Republic of Liberia

Joseph Jenkins Roberts	1848-56
Stephen Allen Benson	1856-64
Daniel Bashiel Warner	1864-68
James Spriggs Payne	1868-70
Edward James Roye	1870-71
James S. Smith	1871-72
Joseph Jenkins Roberts	1872-76
James Spriggs Payne	1876-78
Anthony William Gardiner	1878-83
Alfred F. Russell	1883-84
Hiliary Richard Wright Johnson	1884-91
Joseph James Cheeseman	1892-96
William David Coleman	1896-1900

Notes

Chapter 1

1. The most comprehensive examinations of the complex relationship between slavery and the founding of the American republic are found in Donald L. Robinson, *Slavery in the Structure of American Politics, 1765-1820* (New York, 1971); and David Brion Davis, *The Problem of Slavery in the Age of Revolution, 1770-1823* (Ithaca, 1975). See also Benjamin Quarles, *The Negro in the American Revolution* (Chapel Hill, 1961).

2. Joseph Wood Krutch, *Samuel Johnson* (New York, 1944), p. 244.

3. Thomas Jefferson, *Notes on the State of Virginia* (1861; reprint ed., New York, 1964), p. 139. Jefferson's fear of racial mixture was based on his suspicion that blacks were "inferior to the whites in the endowments of both body and mind" (p. 138). For an analysis of Jefferson's ambivalent racial attitudes, which sparked a heated controversy among American historians, see Fawn McKay Brodie, *Thomas Jefferson: An Intimate History* (New York, 1974).

4. William W. Freehling, "The Founding Fathers and Slavery," *American Historical Review* 77, no. 1 (February 1972): 81-93.

5. Leon F. Litwack, *North of Slavery: The Negro in the Free States, 1790-1860* (Chicago, 1961), pp. 3-29.

6. Leonard I. Sweet, *Black Images of America, 1784-1870* (New York, 1976), pp. 23-34; and Stanley K. Schultz, "The Making of a Reformer: The Reverend Samuel Hopkins As An Eighteenth-Century Abolitionist," *Proceedings of the American Philosophical Society* 115, no. 5 (1971): 350-65.

7. For an excellent account of the eighteenth-century emigrationist sentiment among New England Afro-Americans see Floyd J. Miller, *The Search for a Black Nationality: Black Colonization and Emigration, 1787-1863* (Urbana, 1975), pp. 3-20.

8. Previous to this time some Afro-Americans had reached Africa after first being resettled in Nova Scotia, Canada (see John Peterson, *Province of Freedom: A History of Sierra Leone, 1787-1870* [London, 1969]; and Ellen Gibson Wilson, *The Loyal Blacks* [New York, 1976]).

9. Sheldon H. Harris, *Paul Cuffee, Black America, and the African Return* (New York, 1972), pp. 38-39.

10. Henry Noble Sherwood, "Paul Cuffee and His Contribution to the American Colonization Society," *Proceedings of the Mississippi Valley Historical Association* 6 (1912-13): 370-402.

11. Henry Noble Sherwood, "The Formation of the American Colonization Society," *Journal of Negro History* 2, no. 3 (July 1917): 212-13.

12. Ibid., pp. 213-14.

13. For examples of colonization proposals developed before the American Colonization Society was formed see Ferdinando Fairfax, "Plan for Liberating the Negroes within the United States," *American Museum* 3 (1790): 285-87; Walter H. Fleming, "Historic Attempts to Solve the Race Problem in America by Deportation," *Journal of American History* 4, no. 2 (1910): 197-213; Gaillard Hunt, "William Thornton and Negro Colonization," *Proceedings of the American Antiquarian Society,* n.s. 30 (1920):

32-61; and Henry Noble Sherwood, "Early Negro Deportation Projects," *Mississippi Valley Historical Review* 2, no. 4 (March 1916): 484-508.

14. The best study of this reform society is Philip J. Staudenraus, *The African Colonization Movement, 1816-1865* (New York, 1961). The history of the most prominent state auxiliary society affiliated with the American Colonization Society—destined to break away, however—is given in Penelope Campbell, *Maryland in Africa: The Maryland State Colonization Society, 1831-1857* (Urbana, 1971).

15. Louis R. Mehlinger, "The Attitude of the Free Negro Toward African Colonization," *Journal of Negro History* 1, no. 3 (1916): 276-301.

16. David Walker, *Walker's Appeal, in Four Articles, Together with a Preamble, to the Coloured Citizens of the World . . . Written in Boston, in the State of Massachusetts, Sept. 28, 1829* (Boston, 1830), p. 21.

17. The literature on the pros and cons of colonization is extensive as a result of the debate that erupted over the issue, a debate sparked by the attack mounted by the forces of the abolitionist movement. See especially William Lloyd Garrison, *Thoughts on African Colonization, or, an Impartial Exhibition of the Doctrines, Principles, and Purposes of the American Colonization Society . . .* (Boston, 1832); William Jay, *An Inquiry into the Character and Tendency of the American Colonization, and Anti-Slavery Societies* (New York and Boston, 1835), and [Cyril Pearl], *Remarks on African Colonization and the Abolition of Slavery, In Two Parts: By A Citizen of New England* (Windsor, Vt., 1833).

18. E. U. Essien-Udom, *Black Nationalism: A Search for an Identity in America* (Chicago, 1962), pp. 21-23; see also Miller, *The Search for a Black Nationality*, pp. 134-69.

19. Howard Brotz, ed., *Negro Social and Political Thought, 1850-1920: Representative Texts* (New York, 1966), pp. 37-97.

20. The *Official Report of the Niger Valley Exploring Party* was written by Delany. Delany's partner, Robert Campbell, also wrote an account: *A Pilgrimage to My Motherland: An Account of a Journey among the Egbas and Yorubas of Central Africa, in 1859-60*. Both reports are now available in Martin Robinson Delany and Robert Campbell, *Search for a Place: Black Separatism and Africa, 1860* (Ann Arbor, 1969).

21. Hollis R. Lynch, *Edward Wilmot Blyden: Pan-Negro Patriot, 1832-1912* (New York and London, 1967), pp. 3-6.

22. Edward W. Blyden, "The Call of Providence to the Descendants of Africa in America," in *Negro Social and Political Thought, 1850-1920: Representative Texts*, ed. Howard Brotz (New York, 1966), pp. 112-26. The Biblical reference that begins his address comes from Deuteronomy 1:21.

23. Blyden, "The Call of Providence," p. 114.

24. Ibid., p. 115.

25. Ibid., p. 124.

26. Ibid.

27. Years later Alexander Crummell was making the same argument: "Races, like families, are the organisms and the ordinance of God; and race feeling, like the family feeling, is of divine origin. The extinction of race feeling is just as possible as the extinction of family feeling. Indeed, a race *is* a family. The principle of continuity is as masterful in races as it is in families—as it is in nation" (Alexander Crummell, "The Race Problem in America: An Address" [1888], *Africa and America: Addresses and Discourses* [Springfield, Mass., 1891], pp. 39-57).

28. Philip D. Curtin, *The Atlantic Slave Trade: A Census* (Madison, 1969), p. 92.

29. Robert William Fogel and Stanley L. Engerman, *Time on the Cross: The Economics of American Negro Slavery* (Boston, 1974), pp. 23-24.

30. Ibid., pp. 22-23. The cultural isolation fostered by the plantation structure of the British West Indies, characterized by absentee ownership, was approximated in only a few locations in the United States, such as the Sea Islands, off the coast of South Carolina and Georgia, and the Florida Everglades, where slave communities of maroons interacted with Seminole Indians (see William R. Bascom, "The Acculturation of Gullah Negroes," *American Anthropologist* 43 [January-March 1941]: 43-50; and Mary Frances Berry, *Black Resistance / White Law: A History of Constitutional Racism in America* [New York, 1971]).

31. The debate over Africanisms peaked in the 1940s, after the publication of Melville J. Herskovits's *The Myth of the Negro Past* (Boston, 1958) (see E. Franklin Frazier's review in *The Nation* 44 [February 1942], as well as his own work, *The Negro in the United States* [New York, 1949]; see also Lorenzo D. Turner, *Africanisms in the Gullah Dialect* [Chicago, 1949]).

32. It should be noted that the debate has not ended entirely (see Nathan I. Huggins, Martin Kilson, and Daniel Fox, eds., *Key Issues in the Afro-American Experience*, 2 vols. [New York, 1971], 1: 5-33).

33. John W. Blassingame, *The Slave Community: Plantation Life in the Antebellum South* (New York, 1972), pp. 39-40. Recently one historian has detailed the extent to which Afro-American culture is distinctive by exploring the underlying elements of folklore and folk culture (see Lawrence W. Levine, *Black Culture and Black Consciousness: Afro-American Folk Thought from Slavery to Freedom* [New York, 1977]).

34. Kenneth M. Stampp, *The Peculiar Institution: Slavery in the Ante-Bellum South* (New York, 1956), p. 30.

35. Two surveys of slavery in the urban environment are Richard C. Wade, *Slavery in the Cities: The South, 1820-1860* (New York, 1964); and Claudia Dale Goldin, *Urban Slavery in the American South, 1820-1860: A Quantitative History* (Chicago, 1976).

36. George Winfred Hervey, *The Story of Baptist Missions in Foreign Lands, From the Time of Carey to the Present Date* (St. Louis, 1885), p. 200; *American Missionary Register* 6 (1825): 340; and Solomon Peck, "History of the Missions of the Baptist General Convention," in *History of American Missions to the Heathen, from their Commencement to the Present Time* (Worcester, Mass., 1840).

37. Caroline Pell Gunter, "Tom Day–Craftsman," *The Antiquarian* 11, no. 2 (September 1928): 60-62; Lindsay Patterson, ed., "Negro's Art Lives in His Wrought Iron," *International Library of Negro Life and History, The Negro in Music and Art*, 2d ed., rev. (New York, 1970), pp. 207-11; and Leonard Price Stavisky, "Negro Craftsmanship in Early America," *American Historical Review* 54 (1948-49): 315-25.

38. Robert Manson Myers, *The Children of Pride: A True Story of Georgia and the Civil War* (New Haven, 1972), pp. 1068, 1100.

39. Tom W. Shick, "A Quantitative Analysis of Liberian Colonization from 1820 to 1843, with Special Reference to Mortality" (M.A. thesis, University of Wisconsin, 1970), p. 7.

40. For an extensively detailed account of manumission and colonization established in the will of a prominent American planter, see Memory F. Mitchell and Thornton W. Mitchell, "The Philanthropic Bequests of John Rex of Raleigh," *North Carolina Historical Review* 49, nos. 3 and 4 (Summer and Autumn 1972): 254-79, 353-76.

41. Manumission paper of Peyton Skipwith, 1833, Cocke Family Papers (accession no. 5680), Manuscripts Department, University of Virginia Library, Charlottesville, Va.

42. Ira Berlin, *Slaves Without Masters: The Free Negro in the Antebellum South* (New York, 1974), pp. 46-47; and John Hope Franklin, *From Slavery to Freedom: A History of Negro Americans* (New York, 1969), p. 166. For comparative data on free black populations in the New World, see David W. Cohen and Jack P. Greene, eds.,

Neither Slave Nor Free: The Freedmen of African Descent in the Slave Societies of the New World (Baltimore, 1972).

43. Wade, *Slavery in the Cities*, p. 248.

44. See Luther Porter Jackson, *Free Negro Labor and Property Holding in Virginia, 1830-1860* (New York, 1942); and Laura Foner, "The Free People of Color in Louisiana and St. Domingue: A Comparative Portrait of Two Three-Caste Societies," *Journal of Social History* 3 (Summer 1970): 406-30.

45. Foner, "The Free People of Color in Louisiana and St. Domingue," p. 411.

46. Winthrop D. Jordan, "Modern Racial Tensions and the Origins of American Slavery," *Journal of Southern History* 28 (February 1962): 28.

47. James Richardson to Henry Clay, April 28; 1832; James Richardson to R. R. Gurley, May 5, 10, 1832, American Colonization Society Papers, Manuscript Division, Library of Congress, Washington, D.C.

48. Uncle Jack, George Liele, Andrew Bryan, and John Jasper were among the outstanding examples of early Afro-American preachers (see William S. White, *The African Preacher: An Authentic Narrative* [Philadelphia, 1849] ; John W. Davis, "George Liele and Andrew Bryan: Pioneer Negro Baptist Preachers," *Journal of Negro History* 3, no. 2 [April 1918]: 119-27; and William Eldridge Hatcher, *John Jasper: The Unmatched Negro Philosopher and Preacher* [New York, 1908]).

49. Carol V. R. George, *Segregated Sabbaths: Richard Allen and the Rise of Independent Black Churches, 1760-1840* (New York, 1973). In later years the separatist church movement also developed in Africa, in response to European colonialism and Christianity (see George Shepperson and Thomas Price, *Independent African: John Chilembwe and the Origins, Setting, and Significance of the Nyasaland Native Rising of 1915* [Edinburgh, 1958]; and E. A. Ayandele, *The Missionary Impact on Modern Nigeria, 1842-1914: A Political and Social Analysis* [New York, 1967]).

50. Free Afro-American organizations are described by Ira Berlin in *Slaves Without Masters*, pp. 284-315. Despite the generally negative view Euro-Americans entertained of the free Afro-American community, there were times when the free Afro-Americans served the larger community and deserved better treatment by the public press (see Richard Allen and Absalom Jones, "Negro Service in the Philadelphia Epidemic," in *The Negro American: A Documentary History*, ed. Leslie H. Fishel and Benjamin Quarles [Glenview, Ill., 1967], pp. 164-66).

51. Quoted in Wade, *Slavery in the Cities*, p. 250.

52. Daniel Coker was already known for writing a short volume on the issue of slavery entitled *Dialogue Between a Virginian and an African Minister* (Baltimore, 1910).

53. Daniel Alexander Payne, *Recollections of Seventy Years* (Nashville, 1888), pp. 100-101.

54. William Kellogg to William McLain, October 6, 1852, American Colonization Society Papers, Washington, D.C.

55. C. Eric Lincoln, "Color and Group Identity in the United States," in *Color and Race*, ed. John Hope Franklin (Boston, 1968), p. 251.

56. Richard Wright, *American Hunger* (New York, 1977).

Chapter 2

1. Philip J. Staudenraus, *The African Colonization Movement, 1816-1865* (New York, 1961), p. 50.

2. U.S. Congress, House, *Annals of Congress*, 15th Cong., 1st sess., 1817-18, 32, pt. 2: 1771-74.

3. Special Message of President Monroe to Congress, December 19, 1819, in Charles Henry Huberich, *The Political and Legislative History of Liberia: A Documentary History of the Constitutions, Laws, and Treaties of Liberia*, 2 vols. (New York, 1947), 1:70.

4. Ibid., 1: 77. Other evidence points to the real motive of the *Elizabeth* company. Prior to their departure, the volunteers agreed to a governance pact that set forth the principles of the governmental structure in the anticipated colony (ibid., 1: 145). In 1822 Jehudi Ashmun wrote and published a commemorative biography of Samuel Bacon, *Memoir of the life and character of the Rev. Samuel Bacon . . .* (Washington, D.C., 1822).

5. Diary of Daniel Coker, February 24, 1820, in Huberich, *Political and Legislative History*, 1:80.

6. Ibid. 1: 81.

7. Samuel Bacon to Smith Thompson, March 21, 1820, American Colonization Society Papers, Chicago Historical Society, Chicago, Ill. Two representatives of the American Colonization Society, the Reverend Samuel J. Mills and Ebenezer Burgess, had visited Sierra Leone in 1818. There they met John Kizell, who had offered to welcome American settlers to his Sherbro Island settlement. Kizell had arrived in Freetown with the Nova Scotia immigrants in 1792. He became an active trader and served as the Friendly Society's first president (see Staudenraus, *The African Colonization Movement*, pp. 36-47, and Sheldon H. Harris, *Paul Cuffee, Black America, and the African Return* [New York, 1972], p. 120).

8. Daniel Coker to wife, May 26, 1820, extract reprinted in the *Maryland Gazette and Political Intelligencer*, January 4, 1821.

9. Diary of Daniel Coker, April 21-September 21, 1821, May 3, 1821, Manuscript Division, Library of Congress, Washington, D.C.

10. Ibid., May 6, 1821.

11. "Seventh Annual Report of the Baptist Board of Foreign Missions," *The Latter Day Luminary* 2 (1822): 399; *American Missionary Register* 6 (1825): 341; *The Missionary Jubilee: An Account of the Fiftieth Anniversary of the American Baptist Missionary Union*, rev. ed. (New York and Boston, 1869), pp. 214-27; and *African Repository* 5, no. 3 (March 1829): 12. The pattern of forming church congregations before leaving America became characteristic of immigration to Liberia. Eighteen immigrants on the brig *Vine*, for example, organized themselves into a church before departing from Boston in 1826 (see *African Repository* 1, no. 10 [December 1825]: 317-20).

12. Diary of Daniel Coker, May 27, 1821.

13. "Treaty between King Ben of Grand Bassa, with his Princes and Head Men on one side and Joseph R. Andrus, first Agent of the American Colonization Society on the other," April 12, 1821, American Colonization Society Papers, Chicago, Ill.

14. For the text of the final treaty agreement see Huberich, *Political and Legislative History*, 1: 195-96.

15. Willi Schulze, *A New Geography of Liberia* (London, 1973), p. 39.

16. Lott Cary to William Crane, June 15, 1825, in Adelaide Cromwell Hill and Martin Kilson, eds. *Apropos of Africa: Afro-American Leaders and the Romance of Africa* (New York, 1971), pp. 95-96.

17. J. W. Lugenbeel to William McLain, June 16, 1848, American Colonization Society Papers, Manuscript Division, Library of Congress, Washington, D.C.

18. Schulze, *New Geography of Liberia*, p. 36; see also William E. Reed, *Reconnaissance Soil Survey of Liberia* (Washington, D.C., 1951).

19. Ralph Randolph Gurley, *Life of Jehudi Ashmun . . . with a Brief Sketch of the Life of the Rev. Lott Cary* (Washington, D.C., 1835), appendix p. 131.

20. R. Mansell Prothero, *Migrants and Malaria in Africa* (London, 1965), p. 7.

21. Philip D. Curtin, *The Image of Africa: British Ideas and Action, 1780-1850* (London, 1965), pp. 177-97.

22. U.S., Congress, Senate, *U.S. Navy Department, tables showing the number of Emigrants and recaptured Africans sent to the colony of Liberia by the government of the United States . . . together with a census of the colony and a report of its commerce, &c. September, 1843: Senate Document No. 150,* 28th Cong., 2d sess., 1845. A copy of this rare primary source can be found in the Schomburg Center for Research in Black Culture, New York Public Library, New York.

23. For a detailed analysis of Liberian mortality figures of Afro-American settlers see Tom W. Shick, "A Quantitative Analysis of Liberian Colonization from 1820 to 1843, with Special Reference to Mortality," *Journal of African History* 12, no. 1 (1971): 45-59.

24. During the first twenty-five years of immigration, the following settlers had recognized medical experience: Lott Cary, Joshua Chase, Jacob W. Prout, H. J. Roberts, J. S. Smith, William H. Taylor, and Willis Williams. For basic biographical data on these individuals see Tom W. Shick, *Emigrants to Liberia, 1820 to 1843: An Alphabetical Listing,* Liberian Studies Research Working Paper No. 2 (Newark, Del., 1971). See also Penelope Campbell, "Medical Education for an African Colonist," *Maryland Historical Magazine* 65 (Summer 1970): 130-37.

25. See William Dosite Postell, *The Health of Slaves on Southern Plantations* (Baton Rouge, 1951), pp. 90-110.

26. Diary of Daniel Coker, July 29, 1821.

27. *Liberia Herald*, December 31, 1847.

28. Shick, "A Quantitative Analysis of Liberian Colonization," pp. 51-56.

29. Virtually every Liberian president has alluded to the sacrifices and perseverance of the early settlers (see, for example, William V. S. Tubman, "Independence Day Message, July 26, 1963," in *The Official Papers of William V. S. Tubman: President of the Republic of Liberia,* ed. Reginald E. Townsend [London, 1968], pp. 83-88).

30. Afro-Americans were never immune to the prevailing American prejudices about Africa in the nineteenth century. Many of the attitudes towards Africans and their culture were couched in religious terms of saving savage heathens from a barbarous lifestyle.

31. For works on the linguistic classification of Liberian languages see Joseph H. Greenberg, *The Languages of Africa* (Bloomington, 1963); David Dalby, "The Mel Languages: A Reclassification of Southern 'West Atlantic,' " *African Language Studies* 6 (1965): 1-17; and William E. Welmers, *The Mande Languages,* Georgetown University Monograph Series, no. 11 (Washington, D.C., 1958), pp. 9-24.

32. Personal communication with Svend E. Holsoe, Department of Anthropology, University of Delaware, Newark, Del. (see his "The First Vai Migration" [Paper delivered at the Liberian Studies Conference, Madison, Wis., 1974]).

33. Abner Cohen, "Cultural Strategies in the Organization of Trading Diasporas," in *The Development of Indigenous Trade and Markets in West Africa,* ed. Claude Meillassoux, (London, 1971). For a recent analysis of trade in the Senegambia region using this model see Philip D. Curtin, *Economic Change in Precolonial Africa: Senegambia in the Era of the Slave Trade* (Madison, 1975).

34. Svend E. Holsoe, "The Manding in Western Liberia: An Overview" (Paper delivered at the Conference on Manding Studies, London, 1972), p. 3.

35. The first Afro-American settler to visit Musardu was Benjamin J. K. Anderson, who made two separate journeys, in 1868-69 and in 1874. His own account of his ex-

perience is entitled *Narrative of a Journey to Musardu: The Capital of the Western Mandingoes Together with Narrative of the Expedition Dispatched to Musahdu: By the Liberian Government under Benjamin J. K. Anderson, Senior, Esq., in 1874* (London, 1971).

36. Svend E. Holsoe, "The Condo Confederation in Western Liberia," *Liberian Historical Review* 3, no. 1 (1966): 1-28. For recent data on Liberia's market system and its historical antecedents see Winston Penn Handwerker, "The Liberian Internal Market System" (Ph.D. diss., University of Oregon, 1971).

37. Holsoe, "The Manding in Western Liberia," pp. 8-9; see also S. Jangaba Johnson, "The Warrior, King Sao Boso," in *Liberian Writing: Liberia As Seen by Her Own Writers As Well As by German Authors* (Tübingen, 1970).

38. The narrative that follows relies heavily on James L. Gibbs, Jr., ed., *Peoples of Africa* (New York, 1965), pp. 197-240. Professor Gibbs's research focused on the Kpelle people, but the generalizations offered here apply to many other ethnic groups in Liberia (see Günter Schröder and Dieter Seibel, *Ethnographic Survey of Southeastern Liberia: The Liberian Kran and the Sapo,* Liberian Studies Monograph Series, no. 3 [Newark, Del., 1974]; Warren L. d'Azevedo, "Some Historical Problems in the Delineation of a Central West Atlantic Region," *Annals of the New York Academy of Sciences* 96 [1962]: 512-38; and Svend E. Holsoe "The Cassava-Leaf People: An Ethnohistorical Study of the Vai People with a Particular Emphasis on the Tewo Chiefdom" [Ph.D. diss., Boston University, 1967]).

39. The narrative that follows is based on an analysis of the Liberian census of 1843. These data, which have been coded and preserved on computer tape, are available at the Social Science Data Library, University of Wisconsin, Madison.

40. Nannie Seawell Boyd Collection, Montgomery Bell Papers, 1853-1939, Liberia Project Folder No. 8, Archives and Manuscripts Section, Tennessee State Library and Archives, Nashville, Tenn.

41. Samuel Wilkeson, *A Concise History of . . . the American Colonies in Liberia* (Washington, D.C., 1839), pp. 58-59.

42. Harry Hamilton Johnston, *Liberia,* 2 vols. (New York, 1906), 1: 157.

43. See Penelope Campbell, *Maryland in Africa: The Maryland State Colonization Society, 1831-1857* (Urbana, 1971).

44. Walter Christaller, *Central Places in Southern Germany,* trans. Carlisle W. Baskin (Englewood Cliffs, 1966).

45. Ibid., p. 18.

46. The first major challenge to Monrovia's status as the central place of Liberia came from the upriver settlements (see chapter 5).

47. J.W. Lugenbeel to William McLain, January 4, 1848, American Colonization Society Papers, Washington, D.C.

48. Ibid.

49. Ibid.

50. Stephen A. Benson to William McLain, December 27, 1850, American Colonization Society Papers, Washington, D.C.

51. R. E. Murray to William McLain, July 18, 1848, ibid.

52. Ashmun accompanied a group of recaptured Africans to Liberia on the brig *Strong* in 1822. He found the society's agents, Ayres and Wiltberger, absent from the colony and decided to assume authority as principal agent. The society's board later endorsed his position formally (see Huberich, *Political and Legislative History,* 1:277-78).

53. Ibid., 1: 296.

54. Ibid., 1: 299.

55. Jehudi Ashmun to the executive committee of the board of managers, January 15, 1825, *African Repository* 1, no. 1 (March 1825).

56. Huberich, *Political and Legislative History*, 1: 318.

57. Joseph Blake to R. R. Gurley, March 9, May 13, 1835, American Colonization Society Papers, Washington, D.C. Blake closed his letter with a request for a small plot of land by the water's edge for a shipyard.

58. James Brown to the board of managers, May 1835, ibid.

59. Ibid.

60. John B. Russwurm to R. R. Gurley, October 5, 1835, American Colonization Society Papers, Washington, D. C.

61. John B. Russwurm to Samuel Wilkeson, January 4, 1840, ibid.

62. Joseph Mechlin to American Colonization Society, April 10, 1833, Correspondence of Colonial Agents, 1833-41, Archives of the Liberian Government, Monrovia, Liberia.

63. See *Africa's Luminary*, September 18, October 2, 1840, for a history of the legal controversy from the Methodist point of view.

64. Thomas Buchanan to Samuel Wilkeson, December 13, 1840, Correspondence of Colonial Agents.

65. Anonymous to board of managers, April 7, 1841, American Colonization Society Papers, Washington, D.C.

66. Francis Burns to Samuel Wilkeson, April 2, 1841, ibid.

67. The election results gave the administration faction eight seats on the legislative council, while the Methodist faction won three seats.

68. Commonwealth Legislative Minutes, 1839-47, January 19, 1841, Archives of the Liberian Government, Monrovia, Liberia.

Chapter 3

1. Favorable and optimistic reports about Liberia are found throughout the pages of the *African Repository and Colonial Journal*. Many of these articles were reprinted in other journals and newspapers supportive of African colonization. See, for example, "The Present State of Liberia," *The Friend* 10, no. 35 (June 1837), and "Liberia and the Colonization Society," *De Bow's Review* 27 (July-December 1859). Among the most critical accounts of Liberia were Winwood Reade, *The African Sketch-Book* (London, 1873), pp. 247-61; William Nesbit, *Four Months in Liberia; or, African Colonization Exposed* (Pittsburgh, 1855); and Samuel Williams, *Four Years in Liberia: A Sketch of the Life of Rev. Samuel Williams* (Philadelphia, 1857).

2. Charles W. Thomas, *Adventures and Observations on the West Coast of Africa, and Its Islands* (New York, 1860).

3. Ibid., p. 121. Kru-speaking people, who lived all along the Liberian coast, were noted for their active involvement in maritime trade, particularly as stevedores on board ships in the coastwise trade (see Ronald W. Davis, "Historical Outline of the Kru Coast, Liberia, 1500 to the Present" [Ph.D. diss., University of Indiana, 1968]; and George E. Brooks, Jr., *The Kru Mariner in the Nineteenth Century: An Historical Compendium*, Liberian Studies Monograph Series, no. 1 [Newark, Del., 1972]. For an account of the development of the Kru-speaking community in Monrovia see Merran Fraenkel, *Tribe and Class in Monrovia* [London, 1964]).

4. Thomas, *Adventures and Observations*, p. 122.

5. Ibid., p. 154.

6. Ibid., pp. 154-55.

7. Ibid., p. 156.

8. Ibid.; see also James Wesley Smith, "The Significance of Virginians in Liberian History" (Paper delivered at the Liberian Studies Conference, Bloomington, Ind., 1976).

9. Letters from Afro-American settlers in Liberia to family and friends in America are scattered in many collections. Among the published correspondence, see Randall M. Miller, ed., *"Dear Master" Letters of a Slave Family* (Ithaca, 1978); Robert S. Starobin, ed., *Blacks in Bondage: Letters of American Slaves* (New York, 1974); and Bell Irvin Wiley, ed., *Letters from Liberia, 1833-1869* (Lexington, forthcoming).

10. For comparison, an excellent study showing the relationship between family history and society in the Gold Coast is Margaret Priestley, *West African Trade and Coast Society: A Family Study* (London, 1969). For an important study of family relations among Afro-Americans in the United States, see Herbert G. Gutman, *The Black Family in Slavery and Freedom, 1750-1925* (New York, 1976).

11. Luther Porter Jackson, *Free Negro Labor and Property Holding in Virginia, 1830-1860* (New York, 1942), p. 20. See an account of the transactions of Colson with various merchants in idem, "Free Negroes of Petersburg, Virginia," *Journal of Negro History* 12, no. 3 (July 1927): 373-75.

12. J. J. Roberts to Sarah H. Colson, January 1, 1836, reprinted in "Two Colson Family Letters," *Negro History Bulletin* 10, no. 1 (October 1946): 20.

13. N. H. Elebeck to Sarah H. Colson, June 15, 1836, in ibid., pp. 20-21.

14. *A Census of the Colony and a Report of Its Commerce, &c, September, 1843.*

15. See A. Doris Banks Henries, *The Life of Joseph Jenkins Roberts and His Inaugural Addresses* (London, 1964).

16. Will of Joseph Jenkins Roberts, Records of the Monthly and Probate Court, Montserrado County, 1874-1877, Archives of the Liberian Government, Monrovia, Liberia.

17. Petition of Sarah Ann Roberts, July 3, 1876, ibid.

18. Tom W. Shick, *Emigrants to Liberia, 1820 to 1843: An Alphabetical Listing* Liberian Studies Research Working Paper No. 2 (Newark, Del., 1971), p. 102.

19. Jackson, *Free Negro Labor and Property Holding*, p. 146.

20. American Colonization Society, *Fifteenth Annual Report* (Washington, D.C., 1832), p. 43.

21. Harriet Waring to R. R. Gurley, March 5, 1835, July 18, 1836, American Colonization Society Papers, Manuscript Division, Library of Congress, Washington, D.C.

22. Shick, *Emigrants to Liberia*, pp. 87-88.

23. Peyton Skipwith to John H. Cocke, March 6, 1835, Cocke Family (accession no. 5680) Papers, Manuscripts Department, University of Virginia Library, Charlottesville, Va. Since the writing of this book, all of the extant correspondence of the Skipwith family has been edited and published in Miller, *"Dear Master" Letters.*

24. Tom W. Shick, "A Quantitative Analysis of Liberian Colonization from 1820 to 1843, with Special Reference to Mortality," *Journal of African History* 12, no. 1 (1971): 56-57.

25. Peyton Skipwith to John H. Cocke, April 27, 1836, Cocke Family Papers.

26. Peyton Skipwith to John H. Cocke, January 30, 1838, ibid.

27. Peyton Skipwith to John H. Cocke, May 20, 1839, ibid.; *A Census of the Colony . . . September, 1843.*

28. Peyton Skipwith to John H. Cocke, April 22, December 29, 1840, Cocke Family Papers.

29. Nash Skipwith to John H. Cocke, May 15, 1851, and Matilda Lomax to John H. Cocke, October 18, 1851, ibid.

30. Matilda Lomax to S. F. Cook, July 4, 1848, ibid.

31. Matilda Lomax to John H. Cocke, September 30, 1850; January 27, 1852, ibid.

32. James Skipwith to John H. Cocke, July 17, 1858; February 11, 1859, ibid.

33. James Skipwith to Brethren Edwards, May 31, 1860, ibid.

34. Matilda Lomax to John H. Cocke, February 22, 1861, ibid.

35. Diary of J. S. Barraud, 1857, ibid.

36. *Weekly Anglo-African*, July 30, 1859.

37. "Letter to the Editor on Ladies Benevolent Society of Monrovia, in Liberia," *Liberia Herald*, July 10, 1836.

38. Hiliary Teage to R. R. Gurley, September 26, 1836, American Colonization Society Papers, Washington, D.C.

39. *Liberia Herald*, February 7, 1855.

40. Acts 9:36-42.

41. Charles Henry Huberich, *The Political and Legislative History of Liberia: A Documentary History of the Constitutions, Laws, and Treaties of Liberia*, 2 vols. (New York, 1947), 2: 1511-12. Deed Records, Montserrado County, 1847; Minutes of the House of Representatives, 1848-98, December 12, 29, 1854, January 23, 1855, and January 29, 1857, Archives of the Liberian Government, Monrovia, Liberia.

42. *Liberia Herald*, November 26, 1842.

43. A. W. Anderson to board of managers, October 10, 1841, American Colonization Society Papers, Washington, D.C. For a discussion of the history of the Lancasterian system, see Ellwood Patterson Cubberley, *Public Education in the United States* (New York, 1919), pp. 90-96; and Karl Kaestle, ed., *Joseph Lancaster and the Monitorial School Movement: A Documentary History* (New York, 1973).

44. *African Repository* 28, no. 8 (August 1852).

45. Ibid., 23, no. 5 (May 1847).

46. *Liberia Herald*, September 26, 1855.

47. Minutes of the House of Representatives, December 21, 1849; and "The Monrovia Anthaeneum, *African Repository* 40, no. 1 (January 1864).

48. *Liberia Herald*, August 9, 1855.

49. See Martin R. Delany, *The origins and objects of ancient freemasonry; its introduction into the United States, and Legitimacy among Colored Men* (Pittsburgh, 1853); and William H. Grimshaw, *Official History of Freemasonry among the Colored People in North America, Tracing the Growth of Masonry from 1717 down to the Present Day* (New York and London, 1903).

50. H. J. Roberts to J. W. Lugenbeel, Monrovia, October 1851, American Colonization Society Papers, Washington, D.C. Nineteenth-century Grand Masters who were also founders of the Restoration Grand Lodge were Thomas H. Amos, Charles B. Dunbar, Joseph Jenkins Roberts, and Beverly P. Yates.

51. "Liberian Affairs," *African Repository* 51, no. 3 (July 1875).

52. "Masonic Display," ibid., 45, no. 2 (February 1868).

53. "Cornerstone Laid" and "Masonic Celebration," ibid., 49, no. 8 (August 1873) and 51, no. 3 (July 1875), respectively.

54. "Liberia Agricultural Society," ibid., 39, no. 10 (October 1837).

55. "Union Mechanics' Association," ibid., 39, no. 12 (December 1862).

56. Minutes of the House of Representatives, January 9, 1855; January 3, 1871, and December 18, 1897, Archives of the Liberian Government, Monrovia, Liberia.

57. Minutes of the Senate, 1848-92, December 14, 1864, Archives of the Liberian Government, Monrovia, Liberia.

58. *The Statute Laws of the Republic of Liberia Passed By the Legislature from 1848 to 1879 Together with the Constitution and Amendments* (Monrovia, 1879).

59. Minutes of the Court of Quarter Sessions and Common Pleas, Montserrado County, 1886-97, December 16, 1887, Archives of the Liberian Government, Monrovia, Liberia.

60. Ibid., December 14, 1887.

Chapter 4

1. Blyden later gained respect for Islam and considered it more appropriate to the Negro race than Christianity (see his arguments in *Christianity, Islam, and the Negro Race*, 2d ed. [London, 1888]).

2. R. R. Gurley, *Life of Jehudi Ashmun . . . with a Brief Sketch of the Life of the Rev. Lott Cary* (Washington, D.C., 1835), p. 261.

3. Philip J. Staudenraus, *The African Colonization Movement, 1816-1865* (New York, 1961), pp. 234-35.

4. Harry Hamilton Johnston, *Liberia*, 2 vols. (New York, 1906), 1: 155-56; Christian Abayomi Cassell, *Liberia: History of the First African Republic* (New York, 1970), p. 107; and Samuel Wilkeson, *A Concise History of . . . the American Colonies in Liberia* (Washington, D.C., 1839), p. 61. Canot operated out of New Sesters, a site in the vicinity of the St. John's River (see Brantz Mayer, *Captain Canot or Twenty Years of an African Slaver . . .* [New York, 1854]).

5. Funds to purchase land in Liberia were raised in America and Europe by settler representatives who argued Liberia's importance in suppressing the slave trade. Philanthropists like Leeds Arthington of England contributed large sums of money with this in mind.

6. Correspondence of Colonial Agents, 1833-41, May 28, 1834, Archives of the Liberian Government, Monrovia, Liberia.

7. Commonwealth Legislative Minutes, 1839-47, September 10, 12, 1839; January 14, 15, 1840, Archives of the Liberian Government, Monrovia, Liberia.

8. *African Repository* 22, no. 5 (May 1846); Commonwealth Legislative Minutes, July 15, 1846.

9. *Liberia Herald*, July 17, 1846.

10. The first American temperance organization was the Moreau Society, formed in 1808 by Billy James Clark, a physician of Moreau, New York (see Roslyn V. Cheagle, "The Colored Temperance Movement, 1830-1860" [M.A. thesis, Howard University, 1969]).

11. *Africa's Luminary*, July 19, 1839.

12. Ibid., October 18, 1839; June 5, 1840.

13. *Liberia Herald*, June 21, 1854.

14. W. H. Davis to H. R. W. Johnson, August 15, 1885, Executive Mansion Journal of H. R. W. Johnson, 1885-88, Archives of the Liberian Government, Monrovia, Liberia.

15. *Liberia Recorder*, June 27, 1901.

16. There are many sources on missionary activity in Liberia during the nineteenth century. See, for example, George D. Browne, "History of the Protestant Episcopal Mission in Liberia up to 1838," *Historical Magazine of the Protestant Episcopal Church* 39, no. 1 (March 1970): 17-27; Harold Vink Whetstone, "The Lutheran Mission in Liberia" (M.A. thesis, Hartford Seminary Foundation, 1954); Solomon Peck, "History of the Missions of the Baptist General Convention," in *History of American Missions to the*

Heathen, from their Commencement to the Present Time (Worcester, Mass., 1840), pp. 199-207; and David Christy, *African Colonization by the Free Colored People of the United States, an Indispensable Auxiliary to African Missions: A Lecture* (Cincinnati, 1854).

17. Christy, *African Colonization*, p. 7.

18. There was an attempt to introduce Catholic missionaries to Liberia in 1841, when Father Edward Barron, vicar-general of Philadelphia, and Father John Kelly, pastor of St. John's Church in Albany, New York, arrived in Liberia aboard the ship *Harriet*. The Catholic missionaries were coolly received, and a mission was never established (see Martin J. Bane, *Catholic Pioneers in West Africa* [Dublin, 1956]).

19. *Africa's Luminary*, April 17, 1840.

20. Ibid., January 1, 1841.

21. Ibid., February 5, 1841.

22. *The Statute Laws of the Republic of Liberia Passed By The Legislature from 1848 to 1879 Together with the Constitution and Amendments* (Monrovia, 1879). The apprentice law was first passed in 1838 by the Colonial Legislative Council.

23. Apprentice contract, December 4, 1839, Deed Records, Grand Bassa County, 1839-43, Archives of the Liberian Government, Monrovia, Liberia.

24. Ibid.

25. August session, 1840, Commonwealth Court Records, 1838-42, Archives of the Liberian Government, Monrovia, Liberia.

26. November session, 1838, Commonwealth Court Records.

27. See, for example, J. Gus Liebenow, *Liberia: The Evolution of Privilege* (Ithaca, 1969), pp. 16-17.

28. Tom W. Shick, "A Quantitative Analysis of Liberian Colonization from 1820 to 1843, with Special Reference to Mortality" (M.A. thesis, University of Wisconsin, 1970), p. 5.

29. *African Repository* 10, no. 3 (May 1834), pp. 89-90. See also ibid., 34, no. 10 (October 1858); and Charles Henry Huberich, *The Political and Legislative History of Liberia: A Documentary History of the Constitutions Laws, and Treaties of Liberia*, 2 vols. (New York, 1947), 1: 630-37.

30. *African Repository* 16, no. 19 (October 1840).

31. Ibid., 15, no. 15 (September 1839).

32. Ibid., 15, no. 19 (October 1840).

33. Ibid., 37, no. 1 (January 1861).

34. Ibid.

35. Journal of John Moore McCalla, July 18, 1860, West Virginia and Regional History Collection, West Virginia University Library, Morgantown, W. Va. For comparative data on recaptured Africans in other places in West Africa see John Peterson, *Province of Freedom: A History of Sierra Leone, 1787-1870* (London, 1969); Jean Herskovits Kopytoff, *A Preface to Modern Nigeria: The "Sierra Leonians" in Yoruba, 1830-1890* (Madison, 1965); and Johnson U. J. Asiegbu, *Slavery and the Politics of Liberation, 1787-1861: A Study of Liberated African Emigration and British Anti-Slavery Policy* (London and Harlow, 1969).

36. Journal of John Moore McCalla, July 19, 1860.

37. Ibid., July 24, 1860.

38. Many entries in McCalla's journal show his negative racial attitudes toward Africans. At one point he noted: "As usual a dull day at sea but not a quiet one on board of our ship for the constant gibberish of the African sounds like the chattering of one hundred monkies" (ibid., July 22, 1860). The next day McCalla stated: "Amused myself this morning watching the negroes eat. Their greedy, animal like manner was

disgusting to behold" (ibid., July 23, 1860).

39. Ibid., August 7, 8, 1860. The *Liberia Herald* carried an account regarding the activities of a "witch doctor" in the settlement of New Georgia (see *African Repository* 23, no. 1 [January 1847]).

40. Journal of John Moore McCalla, August 5, 1860.

41. Ibid., July 25, 1860. Buchanan was governor of Liberia, and McLain was a member of the board of managers of the American Colonization Society.

42. John Seys to Jacob Thompson, October 31, 1860, U.S. Congress, House, Executive Documents, *Report of John Seys, 1856-1863: House Executive Document No. 28*, 37th Cong., 3d sess., 1863; John Seys to the Secretary of State, November 1, 1860, "Dispatches from United States Consuls in Monrovia," Roll 2, February 14, 1858-February 22, 1864, National Archives, Washington, D.C.; and John H. Lewis, to the Secretary of State, August 22, 1860, *House Executive Document No. 28*, 37th Cong., 3d sess, 1863.

43. John Seys to Isaac Toucey, September 3, 1860, and John Seys to Jacob Thompson, October 31, 1860, U.S., Congress, House, Executive Documents, *Report of John Seys, 1856-1863: House Executive Document No. 28*, 37th Cong., 3d sess., 1863.

44. John Seys to Isaac Toucey, October 31, 1860, ibid.

45. John Seys to R. R. Gurley, December 5, 1860, in *African Repository* 37, no. 2 (February 1861).

46. Ibid.

47. "Report of the African Mission to the Board of Missions of the P. E. Church in the U.S.A., Assembled October, 1862," in *African Repository* 39, no. 1 (January 1863).

48. "Report of the Presbyterian Board of Foreign Missions," ibid., 39, no. 8 (August 1863).

49. Stephen A. Benson to R. R. Gurley, October 31, 1860, in ibid., 37, no. 1 (January 1861).

50. Reprinted from *Liberia Herald* in *African Repository* 37, no. 3 (March 1861).

51. John Seys to Isaac Toucey, October 16, 1862, U.S. Congress, House, Executive Documents, *Report of John Seys, 1856-1863: House Executive Document No. 28*, 37th Cong., 3d sess., 1863.

52. J. W. Lugenbeel to William McLain, February 8, 1847, in *African Repository* 23, no. 5 (May 1847).

53. *African Repository* 23, no. 6 (June 1847).

54. Minutes of the House of Representatives, 1848-98, January 5, 1864, Archives of the Liberian Government, Monrovia, Liberia. Congo settlements developed adjacent to the Afro-American settlements of Virginia and Brewerville in Montserrado County (see Minutes of the Senate, 1848-92, January 3, 11, 1884, Archives of the Liberian Government, Monrovia, Liberia).

55. Minutes of the House of Representatives, February 1, 1864; Minutes of the Senate, February 2, 1864.

56. Minutes of the House of Representatives, December 30, 1864.

57. Ibid.

Chapter 5

1. For a geographic description of the St. Paul River see Stefan von Gnielinski, *Liberia in Maps: Graphic Perspectives of a Developing Country* (New York, 1972), p. 20.

2. "History of the St. Paul's Settlement," Jehudi Ashmun Papers, 1826-28, Archives of the Liberian Government, Monrovia, Liberia.

3. "Private Instructions to the Settlers," ibid.

4. All the elected officials of the Caldwell settlement in 1825 and 1826 were originally free Afro-Americans (See "Officers Civil and Military of Caldwell for the Year Commencing September 1, 1826," ibid.).

5. "Temporary Regulations for the Government of the St. Paul's Settlement," ibid. These regulations were all suspended by the comprehension of the Caldwell settlement within the General Organization, Civil, Military, and Judiciary of the Colony.

6. R. Randall to board of managers, American Colonizaton Society, December 28, 1828, in *African Repository* 5, no. 1 (March 1829): 1-8.

7. Ibid.

8. Harry Hamilton Johnston, *Liberia*, 2 vols. (New York, 1906), 1: 146. Eight years after its founding, Millsburg was described as "at the fall of the St. Paul's river about twenty miles from the sea, and boats ascend without difficult to its wharf. This settlement is beautiful, healthy, occupied by industrious farmers, and has a soil very productive" (*The Friend*, [June 3, 1837], p. 279; see also Joseph Mechlin to R. R. Gurley, March 30, 1830, in *African Repository* 6, no. 2 [April 1830] : 49-62).

9. A. W. Anderson to R. R. Gurley, March 15, 1830, in *African Repository* 6, no. 2 (April 1830): 49-62. Agent Mechlin made the same point to the American Colonization Society: "One of the chief obstacles to the more general cultivation of the soil, is the mania for trading which pervades all classes" (Joseph Mechlin to the American Colonization Society, July 21, 1831, in *African Repository* 7, no. 9 [November 1831] : 257-71).

10. "Manuscript History of Clay Ashland," author unknown, mimeographed, in the possession of Major M. Branch, Monrovia, Liberia.

11. Interview with the Hon. Julius Winifred Alaric Richards, August 11, 1973, Clay Ashland, Liberia, in the Shick Oral Data Collection. This collection of oral data tapes is on deposit at the Archives of Traditional Music, Folklore Institute, Indiana University, Bloomington, Ind.

12. Jessie Oliver Haynes, "A Brief History of the Founding of the Township of Brewerville, Montserrado County, Republic of Liberia, 1869-1970," Mimeographed (Monrovia, n.d.). Like Arthington, Brewerville was named in honor of a philanthropist who contributed money to the American Colonization Society (see "Manuscript History of Arthington," author unknown, mimeographed, in the possession of Major M. Branch, Monrovia, Liberia). The settlement was named in honor of Robert Arthington, of Leeds, England, who made a donation of one thousand pounds to the American Colonization Society, which made possible the establishment of the new settlement.

13. The full list of names in the Richards family genealogy appears in appendix B. The genealogy was constructed on the basis of data collected during a twelve-month research trip.

14. "List of Emigrants by the Liberia Packet," *African Repository* 26, no. 8 (August 1850): 247-48.

15. Ibid.

16. *African Repository* 40, no. 8 (August 1864).

17. In the courtyard of the St. Peter's Methodist Church is a small graveyard that includes several members of the Richards family—Sarah L. Richards, Philip Collins Simpson, Martha Ora Simpson, R. Van Richards, and Philip Francis Simpson. Four members of the family—R. Van Richards, W. David Richards, S. T. A. Richards, and presently, the Reverend Mark Richards, Jr.—have served over the years as pastor of the church.

18. An Act Pertaining to Bounty Land, *The Statute Laws of the Republic of Liberia Passed By the Legislature from 1848 to 1879 Together with the Constitution and Amendments (Monrovia, 1879)*.

19. Deed Record for Othello Richards, July 23, 1869, Deed Records, Montserrado County, 1865-69, Archives of the Liberian Government, Monrovia, Liberia.

20. Charles Henry Huberich, *The Political and Legislative History of Liberia: A Documentary History of the Constitutions, Laws, and Treaties of Liberia*, 2 vols. (New York, 1947), 2: 1346.

21. An Act Regulating the Sale of Public Lands, *Statute Laws of Liberia*.

22. The sale of real estate for debts by the courts was controversial even before independence. Lewis Crook protested the sale of his town lot in Monrovia to pay an outstanding debt while he was at Millsburg working on his farm (see Lewis Crook to the American Colonization Society, March 3, 1835, American Colonization Society Papers, Manuscript Division, Library of Congress, Washington, D.C.).

23. *Liberia Herald*, May 15, 1856, reprinted in *African Repository* 32, no. 8 (August 1856).

24. Report of the Attorney General of the Republic of Liberia to the Legislature, September 30, 1892, Department of Justice Correspondence, 1892-1904, Archives of the Liberian Government, Monrovia, Liberia.

25. J. T. Gibson to J. J. Roberts, June 12, 1872, Executive Mansion Correspondence, 1856-99, Archives of the Liberian Government, Monrovia, Liberia.

26. Ibid.

27. Minutes of the House of Representatives, 1848-98, December 13, 1855, Archives of the Liberian Government, Monrovia, Liberia.

28. The civil case of S. D. Richards versus Sarah Richards (widow of W. M. Richards) and S. T. Prout (brother of the widow) appears in Minutes of the Court of Quarter Sessions and Common Pleas, Montserrado County, 1886-1897, Archives of the Liberian Government, Monrovia, Liberia.

29. Answer of Sarah Richards and S. T. Prout to the Bill in Equity, December 11, 1887, ibid.

30. Bill of Complaint in Equity: Samuel D. Richards versus Sarah Richards and S. T. Prout, September 26, 1887, ibid.

31. Ibid.

32. Personal communication with Dr. Mary Frances Berry, Office of Health, Education and Welfare, Washington, D.C. I am grateful to Dr. Berry for her assessment of the legal implications of this decision.

33. Bill of Complaint in Equity: Samuel D. Richards versus Sarah Richards and S. T. Prout, March 30, 1887, Court of Quarter Sessions and Common Pleas. For a parallel account of the judicial function of the Afro-American church in the United States see Patricia Guthrie, "Catching Sense: The Meaning of Plantation Membership among Blacks on St. Helena Island, South Carolina" (Ph.D. diss., University of Rochester, 1977).

34. Minutes of the House of Representatives, December 17, 1866. For a petition from Clay Ashland asking for a charter for the Union Association of Clay Ashland, see Minutes of the Senate, 1848-92, January 22, 1862, Archives of the Liberian Government, Monrovia, Liberia.

35. Petition from Brewerville, Executive Mansion Correspondence.

36. Petition from Virginia Settlement to President H. R. W. Johnson, August 27, 1885, Executive Mansion Journal of H. R. W. Johnson, 1885-88, Archives of the Liberian Government, Monrovia, Liberia. Twenty-one years earlier a similar boundary dis-

pute had developed between Upper Virginia and Clay Ashland (see Minutes of the House of Representatives, December 21, 1864).

37. Petition from Virginia Settlement to President H. R. W. Johnson.

38. President Johnson to Messrs. Holderness, Miller, Snorton, Capehart and others, Virginia, September 18, 1885, Executive Mansion Journal H. R. W. Johnson.

39. *Liberia Herald*, October 20, 1852.

40. Ibid.

41. Protest against the Election Returns from Clay Ashland, Minutes of the Senate, December 7, 10, 1875.

42. An Act to Regulate the Militia, organization, discipline, pay, *Statute Laws of Liberia*.

43. D. E. Howard to Captain of the Virginia Militia, September 18, 1885, Executive Mansion: Journal of His Excellency H. R. W. Johnson. The use of indigenous Africans in militia companies set a precedent that was to be followed more extensively once the Liberia Frontier Force was organized at the turn of the century (See Dalvan M. Coger, "Americans in the Liberian Frontier Force" [Paper delivered at the African Studies Association Meeting. San Francisco, 1974]).

44. For example: "The Captains and Commanders of the different companies in Monrovia, New Georgia, Caldwell, Virginia, Clay Ashland, Louisiana, Millsburg, and North Carolina, are hereby notified to parade their respective companies, in the Settlement of Caldwell, on Friday, the 5th, of October next, at the hour of 9 o'clock A.M. at the usual place of rendezous, armed and equipped as the Law directs; the line will form at 10 o'clock A.M." (*Liberia Herald*, October 1, 1862).

45. For an interesting account of the problem of tracing the identity of the heroine of the battle, Matilda Newport, see Jane J. Martin and Rodney Carlisle, "The Search for Matilda Newport" (Paper delivered at the Liberian Studies Conference, Bloomington, Ind., 1976).

46. *Liberia Herald*, November 7, 1845.

Chapter 6

1. Abayomi Winfrid Karnga, *Liberia before the New World* (London, 1923), p. 23. For a fascinating piece of historical detection on the identity of Matilda Newport see Jane J. Martin and Rodney Carlisle, "The Search for Matilda Newport" (Paper delivered at the Liberian Studies Conference, Bloomington, Ind., 1976).

2. This assertion has been reinforced by the research of other historians. Jane Martin has found similar patterns in Maryland County, while Mary Jo Sullivan documents this for Sinoe Court in "Settlers in Sinoe County, Liberia, and Their Relations with the Kru, c. 1835-1920" (Ph.D. diss., Boston University, 1978).

3. Reuben Dongey, a tanner by trade, came to Liberia from Virginia in 1824. In 1833 he died of consumption (see Tom W. Shick, *Emigrants to Liberia, 1820 to 1843: An Alphabetical Listing*, Liberian Studies Research Working Paper No. 2 [Newark, Del., 1971], p. 29). On March 17, 1842, the *Liberia Herald* published an account of the arrival in Monrovia of a caravan from the interior comprising Kondah and Mandingo traders.

4. R. Randall to the American Colonization Society, December 28, 1828, reprinted in *African Repository*, 5 no. 1 (March 1829): 1-8.

5. Ibid.

6. Accounts of the Gatumbe War appear in *Africa's Luminary* and the *Liberia*

Herald. The best secondary account is Svend E. Holsoe, "Settler-Indigenous Relations in Western Liberia," *African Historical Studies* 4, no. 2 (1971): 350-52.

7. C. C. Hoffman to R. R. Gurley, December 11, 1860, reprinted in *African Repository* 37, no. 5 (May 1861).

8. *African Repository* 32, no. 10 (October 1856). The first steamboat on the St. Paul River was the *Sarah Ann Irons*, built by Clement Irons and Scipio A. Givens and launched in the 1880s (see, State Department Correspondence, Foreign and Local, 1886-1906, Archives of the Liberian Government, Monrovia, Liberia).

9. Petition from Clay Ashland, September 15, 1885, Executive Mansion Journal of H. R. W. Johnson, 1885-88, Archives of the Liberian Government, Monrovia, Liberia. Hereafter, all citations of correspondence in this chapter comes from the Executive Mansion Journal of H. R. W. Johnson, unless otherwise stated.

10. H. R. W. Johnson to Messrs. Dixon, Jones, King, Coleman, Lomax, and other citizens of Clay Ashland, October 22, 1885.

11. Writs issued by Justice Bracewell, in the Matter of Dwallah Zeppie, c. 1887.

12. T. J. Bracewell to H. R. W. Johnson, July 18, 1887.

13. Thomas Mitchell to H. R. W. Johnson, July 17, 1887.

14. H. R. W. Johnson to T. J. Bracewell, July 19, 1887; see also H. R. W. Johnson to Thomas Mitchell, July 19, 1887.

15. H. R. W. Johnson to T. J. Bracewell, July 19, 1887.

16. Petition from Arthington to H. R. W. Johnson, July 26, 1887.

17. T. C. Lomax, John H. Ricks, et al. to H. R. W. Johnson, July 16, 1887.

18. Thomas Mitchell to H. R. W. Johnson, August 1, 1887.

19. Petition from Dwallah Zeppie presented by S. E. F. Codogans, Attorney, to H. R. W. Johnson, July 18, 1887.

20. In Liberia African settlements generally are referred to as towns, even when their size would classify them as villages elsewhere. "Half-towns" are smaller settlements, usually established near farms. It is at half-towns that farm workers live when there is agricultural work to be done, thereby eliminating long, daily walks to cultivation sites (see Stefan von Gnielinski, *Liberia in Maps: Graphic Perspectives of a Developing Country* [New York, 1972], pp. 48-49).

21. A Report Made by the Messengers Sent to Zeppy by Native African Commissioners, August 1, 1887.

22. Statement of One of the Captured Parties, Which Statement Agrees With the Other Two, n.d.

23. Hill and John Moore to H. R. W. Johnson, August 4, 1887.

24. H. R. W. Johnson to J. P. Washington and Cornelius Miller, September 18, 1887.

25. H. R. W. Johnson to Thomas Mitchell, J. P. Washington, and Cornelius Miller, September 17, 1887.

26. Thomas A. Sims to H. R. W. Johnson, November 22, 1887.

27. H. R. W. Johnson to Thomas A. Sims, November 25, 1887.

28. Thomas A. Sims to H. R. W. Johnson, November 30, 1887.

29. Ibid.

30. See D. W. Urey to H. R. W. Johnson; Padmore, Hunter, and Sims to H. R. W. Johnson; and John Moore to H. R. W. Johnson—all dated April 29, 1890.

31. H. R. W. Johnson to James D. Jones, May 15, 1890.

32. James D. Jones to H. R. W. Johnson, May 21, 1890. If based on an American model, regimental strength could be close to five hundred men under arms.

33. Ibid.

34. James D. Jones to H. R. W. Johnson, May 22, 1890.
35. James D. Jones to H. R. W. Johnson, May 24, 26, 1890.
36. James D. Jones to H. R. W. Johnson, May 26, 1890.
37. James D. Jones to H. R. W. Johnson, May 27, 1890.
38. H. R. W. Johnson to J. D. Jones, June 6, 1890.
39. T. W. Haynes to H. R. W. Johnson, September 3, 1891.
40. Petition from Clay Ashland to H. R. W. Johnson, September 15, 1885.
41. T. W. Smith to H. R. W. Johnson, March 25, 1892, Executive Mansion Correspondence, 1856-99, Archives of the Liberian Government, Monrovia, Liberia.
42. Last Will and Testament of Catherine L. Mills, executed on October 23, 1905, Records of the Monthly and Probate Court, Montserrado County, Archives of the Liberian Government, Monrovia, Liberia.
43. Last Will and Testament of Samuel R. Hoggard, executed on December 28, 1903, ibid.
44. Last Will and Testament of Samuel C. Cokes, executed on January 5, 1904, ibid.
45. Last Will and Testament of Samson Lambirth, executed on December 27, 1881, in Deed Records, Montserrado County, 1882-84, Archives of the Liberian Government, Monrovia, Liberia.
46. Complaint of Patsey Gordon, March 14, 1893, Court of Quarter Sessions and Common Pleas, Montserrado County, 1892-93, Archives of the Liberian Government, Monrovia, Liberia.
47. Act Passed by the 19th Legislature at their second session, 1884-85, State Department Correspondence, Foreign and Local, 1886-1906, Archives of the Liberian Government, Monrovia, Liberia.
48. Warren L. d'Azevedo, "A Tribal Reaction to Nationalism (Part One)," *Liberian Studies Journal* 1 no. 2 (Spring 1969): 19.

Chapter 7

1. The British colony at Freetown was established by the chartered Sierra Leone Company with the dual object of resettling Africans rescued from the slave trade and developing an economic base that would not only make the colony self-sufficient but also return a reasonable profit to the company's shareholders (See John Peterson, *Province of Freedom: A History of Sierra Leone, 1787-1870* [London, 1969]).
2. Charles Henry Huberich, *The Political and Legislative History of Liberia: A Documentary History of the Constitutions, Laws, and Treaties of Liberia*, 2 vols. (New York, 1947), 1: 365.
3. For a general account of American traders operating on the West African coast see George E. Brooks, Jr., *Yankee Traders, Old Coasters, and African Middlemen: A History of American Legitimate Trade with West Africa in the Nineteenth Century* (Brookline, Mass., 1970). For a preview of a larger study of the Liberian coasting trade forthcoming see Dwight N. Syfert, "The Liberian Coasting Trade, 1822-1900," *Journal of African History* 18, no. 2 (1977): 217-35.
4. Huberich, *Political and Legislative History*, 1: 812; see also pp. 772-84 for an 1845 message of Joseph Jenkins Roberts to the legislative council in which he details, at length, the difficulties with British subjects trading along the Liberian coast.
5. For an example of an early colonial ordinance that attempted to restrict the trading operations of foreigners on the Liberian coast see "An Ordinance Prohibiting

Foreigners to Trade with the Native Inhabitants of a District of Coast Therein Limited, and Fixing the Compensation and Explaining the Duties of Commission Merchants," in Huberich, *Political and Legislative History*, 2: 1312-14.

6. Minutes of the Senate, 1848-92, December 15, 1849, Archives of the Liberian Government, Monrovia, Liberia.

7. Laurie, Hamilton, and Company to Lord Palmerston, August 16, 1848, F.O. 47/1, Public Record Office, London (hereinafter references to Public Record Office documents in London will be cited by record group and piece numbers only).

8. Laurie, Hamilton and Company to Lord Palmerston, August 29, 1849, F.O. 47/2.

9. Lord Palmerston to Laurie, Hamilton and Company, October 22, 1849, F.O. 47/2.

10. Laurie, Hamilton and Company to Lord Palmerston, May 13, 1850, F.O. 47/3.

11. Ibid.

12. J. J. Roberts to Lord Palmerston, September 2, 1848, F.O. 47/1. For the resolutions of appreciation extended to the British government by the Liberian legislature, see J. J. Roberts to Thomas Hodgkin, January 23, 1850, F.O. 47/3.

13. A. W. Hanson to Lord Palmerston, November 21, 1850, F.O. 47/3.

14. J. J. Roberts to Lord Palmerston, July 5, 1850, F.O. 47/3. It should be noted that some advocates of immigration and colonization by Afro-Americans argued that by devoting attention to cotton cultivation, it might be possible to hurt the economic stability of the American South, thereby undermining the institution of slavery (see Floyd J. Miller, *The Search for a Black Nationality: Black Colonization and Emigration, 1787-1863* [Urbana, 1975], pp. 219-20.

15. See Boothman to Henry Addington, January 7, 1851, F.O. 47/5; A. W. Hanson to Lord Palmerston, April 11, 1851, F.O. 47/4; Lord Palmerston to A. W. Hanson, November 11, 1851, F.O. 47/4; and A. D. Williams to A. W. Hanson, January 14, 1852, F.O. 47/6.

16. A. W. Hanson to Lord Palmerston, November 21, 1850, F.O. 47/3. Hanson also wrote to David Murray warning him against engaging in illicit commerce, while informing him of the likely modification of Liberian laws relating to commerce and revenue (A. W. Hanson to David Murray, December 26, 1850, F.O. 47/3).

17. A. W. Hanson to Lord Palmerston, December 31, 1850, F.O. 47/3. Apparently the legislature's decision met with some objections. A resolution requesting the president to grant no special license to foreigners to trade within twelve miles of ports of entry won approval in the legislature but failed to get the endorsement of Roberts (see Minutes of the Senate, December 12, 19, 1850).

18. A. W. Hanson to Lord Palmerston, April 9, 1850, F.O. 47/3.

19. Foreign Office to A. W. Hanson, September 28, 1850, F.O. 47/3. The possibility that Hanson tried to supplement his annual salary of five hundred pounds seems likely, since he wrote frequently to the Foreign Office concerning the expense of maintaining an official residence in Monrovia. All of his requests for additional funds were turned down (see, for example, A. W. Hanson to Bidwell, December 31, 1850, F. O. 47/3; and A. W. Hanson to Lord Palmerston, October 29, 1851, F.O. 47/4).

20. A. W. Hanson to Samuel Gurney, February 25, 1851, F.O. 47/4.

21. See *Liberia Herald*, December 3, 1851; January 28, 1852.

22. Minutes of the Senate, December 23, 1851.

23. A. W. Hanson to Lord Palmerston, February 18, 1852, F.O. 47/6. Three months later Hanson reported that his house was surrounded by a mob throwing stones through

the windows and that rumors circulated that his assassination had been ordered by high government officials (see A. W. Hanson to the Earl of Malmesbury, April 20, 1852, F.O. 47/6).

24. John N. Lewis to William McLain, April 20, 1852, American Colonization Society Papers, Manuscript Division, Library of Congress, Washington, D.C.

25. A. W. Hanson to Lord Palmerston, November 7, 24, 1851, F.O. 47/4.

26. Hiliary Teage to H. W. Bruce, April 20, 1852, Miscellaneous State Department Correspondence, Archives of the Liberian Government, Monrovia, Liberia.

27. King Bowyah to A. W. Hanson, October 31, 1851, F.O. 47/4. The Afro-American settlers represented the first serious threat to the middleman role played by coastal African groups. The settlers claimed sovereignty, and thus the Africans believed they were trying to usurp their commercial preeminence. Thus the issue of treaties and the transfer of sovereignty rights were fundamentally an economic issue to the Africans on the coast. The settlers proved to be a poor substitute for the British merchants, so many African leaders wanted to withdraw from earlier agreements—thus the conflict over settler authority, particularly after the republic was formed.

28. J. J. Roberts to the Earl of Malmesbury, May 17, 1852, F.O. 47/7.

29. Henry Addington to the Earl of Malmesbury, July 24, 1852, F.O. 47/7.

30. Governor Hill to Lord J. Russell, January 1, 1861, F.O. 403/6.

31. Commander Smith to John N. Lewis, December 17, 1860 (enclosure in Governor Hill to Lord J. Russell, January 1, 1861, F.O. 403/6).

32. John N. Lewis to Commander Smith, December 17, 1860 (enclosure in Governor Hill to Lord J. Russell, January 1, 1861, F.O. 403/6).

33. Gerard Ralston to Lord J. Russell, March 28, 1861, F.O. 403/6. The funds used to purchase the land were donated by Samuel Gurney, of London, and an American benefactor from Cincinnati. See also "Extract from Chamber's Repository on Liberia." Further Correspondence Respecting Negotiations with Liberia for the Establishment of Conterminous Boundaries (African, No. 282), #174, 1879-86, Sierra Leone Archives, Freetown, Sierra Leone.

34. Governor Hill to Lord J. Russell, January 1, 1861, F.O. 403/6.

35. Extract from the Minutes of Council Chambers, Sierra Leone, May 29, 1862, F.O. 403/6. The Mercantile Association of Freetown apparently lobbied for this position (see Lieutenant Governor Hill to the Duke of Newcastle, September 21, 1862 [enclosure in Mr. Elliott to E. Hammond, October 15, 1862, F.O. 403/6]). One dissenting voice from Sierra Leone came from Lieutenant Governor Blackall in 1863. He declared: "I do not share the prejudice which I acknowledge exists among both Europeans and natives against it [the Liberian government], but I wish to see its own authority within its own limits, whatever they may be" (Lieutenant Governor Blackall to the Duke of Newcastle, January 15, 1863 [enclosure in Mr. Elliott to E. Hammond, April 30, 1863, F.O 403/6]).

36. "Proceedings of the Commissioners appointed by the Respective Government of Great Britain and the Republic of Liberia to investigate the question relating to the North-West Boundary of the said Republic, and to fix upon a Line which shall be recognized by the two Governments as comprising, for the present, the Northern limit of the Liberian Government," April 27-May 4, 1863, F.O. 403/6.

37. Memorandum by W. H. Wylde on the Liberian boundary question, Foreign Office, October 15, 1863, F.O. 403/6.

38. Edward W. Blyden to Gerard Ralston, August 5, 1864, F.O. 403/6.

39. See Mr. Egarton to Gerard Ralston, March 29, 1867, F.O. 403/6.

40. Isaac T. Pratt, Nathaniel A. Palmer, Joseph F. Hamilton, John T. Thomas, Margaret Faulkner, Phoebe Palmer, and Mary Brown to Sir Arthur E. Kennedy, August

28, 1868, Liberian Boundary Papers, Box No. 30, 1862-86, Sierra Leone Government Archives, Freetown, Sierra Leone.

41. In 1868 Prince Mannah asked for British intervention: "I write to inform you that you must write to their [the Liberian] Governor not to disturb me because I do not know when they bought this Country. My great Grandfather never tell me say that they sold any part of our land to them . . ." (Prince Mannah to Sierra Leone government, October 12, 1868, ibid.)

42. Isaac Thomas Pratt and Nathaniel A. Palmer to Sir Arthur E. Kennedy, February 15, 1869, ibid.; see also Deposition of Isaac Thomas Pratt, May 29, 1869, ibid.

43. See James S. Payne to George M. Macaulay, March 13, 1869, ibid.

44. Extracts from the *Republican*, June 11, 1869, F.O. 403/6. Anti-Sierra Leone sentiment persisted in Liberia. In 1882 the *West African Reporter* charged that an anti-Sierra Leone organization called the Society of Black Things had been formed in Liberia (see *West African Reporter*, April 29, 1882).

45. Republic of Liberia versus George M. Macaulay and others named in the indictment charged with conspiracy, June 17, 1869, Liberian Boundary Papers, Box No. 30, 1862-86, Sierra Leone Government Archives, Freetown, Sierra Leone.

46. Sentence of the Court Passed on George M. Macaulay, June 19, 1869, ibid.

47. Bond for Goerge M. Macaulay, June 19, 1869, and Affadavit of George M. Macaulay, July 12, 1869, ibid.

48. Confidential draft from Sierra Leone government to Lord Granville, July 13, 1869, ibid.

49. President Payne's appeal to Her Majesty's government, October 6, 1869, F.O. 403/6.

50. Ibid.

51. Draft from Sierra Leone government to the president or other officer administering the government of Liberia, August 18, 1870, Liberian Boundary Papers, Box No. 30, 1862-86, Sierra Leone Government Archives, Freetown, Sierra Leone.

52. The decision to contract a major loan came only after the English refused to release Liberia from the indemnification obligation (see President Roye to Sir Arthur E. Kennedy, May 6, 1870, and Sir Arthur E. Kennedy to President Roye, May 11, 1870, F.O. 403/6).

53. For example, Reverend Richmond Sampson established an experimental indigo plantation to determine the profitability of extracting dye for sale abroad (see Ralph Randolph Gurley, *Life of Jehudi Ashmun . . . with a Brief Sketch of the Life of the Rev. Lott Cary [Washington, D.C., 1835]*, appendix p. 133).

54. In 1851 an agricultural society was formed in Clay Ashland with the object of encouraging the raising of ginger for export. Each member of the society was obligated to plant and cultivate at least one quarter acre of ginger (see Erskine to J. W. Lugenbeel, October 16, 1851, American Colonization Society Papers, Washington, D.C.).

55. A very different argument for the slow agricultural development in Liberia has been put forth by several scholars. J. Gus Liebenow and M. B. Akpan, for example, attribute slow agricultural development to the settlers' slavery background; to their deep attachment to American food, which caused them to favor imported foodstuffs; to their unfamiliarity with African farming methods; and to their general dislike for manual labor (see J. Gus Liebenow, *Liberia: The Evolution of Privilege* [Ithaca, 1969], pp. 12-13; and M. B. Akpan, "The Liberian Economy in the Nineteenth Century: The State of Agriculture and Commerce," *Liberian Studies Journal* 6, no. 1 [1975]: 1-24).

56. *Liberia Herald*, March 17, 1842. Six years later Cyrus Willis had increased his yield to three thousand pounds. He would have had a yield of *eight* thousand pounds of sugar and a considerable quantity of syrup but for an accident that left him bedridden

for several weeks just before his cane was to be processed (see *African Repository* 24, no. 9 [September 1848]).

57. "To the Sugar Growers," *Liberia Herald*, January 21, 1857; see also *African Repository* 32, no. 10 (October 1856), and 37, no. 6 (June 1861).

58. Abraham Blackledge to J. W. Lugenbeel, May 18, 1851, American Colonization Society Papers, Washington, D.C.

59. *African Repository* 30, no. 10 (October 1854).

60. Ibid., 40, no. 10 (October 1864).

61. "Sugar Making on the St. Paul River," ibid., 39, no. 1 (January 1863).

62. Ibid.

63. Ibid. Local Africans often proved unreliable because they would leave the employ of the settler farmers to tend their own farms or to defend their villages in times of war. Upriver farmers made some efforts to bring in Africans from distant areas as a way of minimizing this problem. "A few days ago a small boat came in from Bassa, with fifty Bassa natives, who had been hired in that country to labor on a farm on the St. Paul's. Since then, two other planters have secured a number of Kroomen for the same purpose, from Palmas" ibid., 40, no. 10 [October 1864]).

64. Interview with John B. Morris, Clay Ashland, Liberia, December 14, 1974.

65. B. V. R. James to R. R. Gurley, September 8, 1863, in *African Repository* 40, no. 1 (January 1864).

66. "Coffee Cultivation Along the St. Paul's," *Liberia Herald*, reprinted in *African Repository* 28, no. 2 (February 1852).

67. Charles Starkes to the editor, February 18, 1859, in *African Repository* 35, no. 6 (June 1859).

68. See Alexander Crummell Papers, Schomburg Center for Research in Black Culture, New York Public Library, for extensive correspondence between Crummell and Morris relating to Morris's coffee-cultivation schemes.

69. *African Repository* 39, no. 5 (May 1863), and 39, no. 12 (December 1863).

70. M. B. Akpan, "Liberian Economy in the Nineteenth Century," p. 18. See also V. Boutilly, *Le Caféier de Libéria: Sa Culture et sa manipulation* (Paris, 1900); and G. A. Crüwell, *Liberian Coffee in Ceylon: The History of the Introduction and Progress of the Cultivation up to April 1878* (Colombo, 1878).

71. *African Repository* 39, no. 4 (April 1863).

72. William C. Burke to R. R. Gurley, September 29, 1863, reprinted in ibid., 30, no. 1 (January 1864).

73. See, for example, John H. Smith to the assistant secretary of state, December 7, 1878, "Depatches from United States Consuls in Monrovia, 1852-1906," U.S., National Archives, Microcopy 169, Washington, D.C.

74. In 1892 a charge of "domestic slavery" in the St. Paul River area prompted Liberian president Joseph J. Cheeseman to write several prominent citizens in the area asking them to "say in writing if you know of any instance where any person is directly or indirectly engaged in 'domestic slavery' in violation of the Constitution and Laws of Liberia" (see J. J. Cheeseman to Messrs. Ferguson, Gibson, Moore, and Day, May 23, 1892, Executive Mansion Correspondence, 1856-99, Archives of the Liberian Government, Monrovia, Liberia).

75. John H. Smith to the assistant secretary of state, October 8, 1885, "Despatches from United States Consuls in Monrovia, 1852-1906," U.S., National Archives, Microcopy 169, Washington, D.C.

76. Franklin W. Knight, *Slave Society in Cuba During the Nineteenth Century* (Madison, 1970), p. 44. Knight argues that the United States became Cuba's major trade partner after 1850.

77. "Coffee at Low-Water Mark," *The Liberian Recorder*, December 9, 1897. For an excellent study of Brazilian coffee cultivation in the nineteenth century see Stanley J. Stein, *Vassouras: A Brazilian Coffee County, 1850-1900* (Cambridge, Mass., 1957).

78. J. J. Roberts to the Earl of Malmesbury, June 15, 1859, F.O. 47/15.

79. "From Our Correspondent, Clay Ashland, October 26, 1852," *Liberia Herald*, November 3, 1852.

80. Advertus A. Hoff, *A Short History of Liberia College and the University of Liberia* (Monrovia, 1962), p. 53.

81. See Township of Clay Ashland versus President and Trustees of Liberia College, Injunction Case, Court of Quarter Sessions and Common Pleas, March Term 1858, Monrovia, Liberia.

82. Ibid. In the same year the legislature received a petition from ninety-three upriver settlers supporting the Clay Ashland site for Liberia College (see Minutes of the House of Representatives, January 15, 1858, Archives of the Liberian Government, Monrovia, Liberia).

83. Hoff, *A Short History of Liberia College*, p. 54. The issue has not completely died. More than one hundred years later, President William R. Tolbert has ordered the relocation of the campus of the University of Liberia from its present site in Monrovia to a site outside of the city.

84. "Letter from D. A. Wilson, Monrovia, December 11, 1857," *Colonization Herald*, February 12, 1858.

85. See, Minutes of the House of Representatives, January 22, 1862. For additional references to the removal of the seat of government see Minutes of the Senate, January 14, 1864; and Minutes of the House of Representatives, January 25, 29, 1870.

86. Minutes of the Senate, December 23, 28, 1863.

87. "The Seat of Government," *African Repository* 40, no. 5 (May 1864).

88. One classic example of this pattern is the Johnson family. Elijah Johnson was a pioneer settler who arrived in the 1820s. His son Hiliary Richard Wright Johnson became Liberia's tenth president, and his grandson Frederick E. R. Johnson served Liberia as a supreme court justice.

89. The charge of caste distinction was made most sharply by Edward Wilmot Blyden. He considered mulattoes to be a divisive group among the Liberian settlers (see Edward W. Blyden, *On Mixed Races in Liberia*, Smithsonian Institution Annual Report, 1870 [Washington, D.C., 1871], pp. 386-89).

90. The *Liberia Herald*, for example, was pleased when the first organized opposition to the Republican Party had to endorse the Republican candidate for president because they had no possible winning candidate of their own: "The instance marks the good sense so far of the people; and we trust that every citizen will use his influence to the end, that partyism in a great measure, if continued, will be deprived of much of its latent rancor" (*Liberia Herald*, February 4, 1857, enclosure in F.O. 47/13).

91. The present True Whig Party traces its founding to a meeting of partisans in the Clay Ashland settlement home of John Henry William Good in 1860. Among the participants at the meeting were Samuel David Richards, James David Simpson, Augustus Houston, Edward Wilmot Blyden, Reverend Debric Simpson, and Severin George. See the speech of President William V. S. Tubman, "On the Occasion of the Laying of the Cornerstone of the Edward J. Roye Memorial Headquarters of the True Whig Party," in *The Official Papers of William V. S. Tubman: President of the Republic of Liberia*, ed. Reginald E. Townsend (Monrovia, 1968).

92. See Christian Abayomi Cassell, *Liberia: History of the First African Republic* (New York, 1970), pp. 264-65.

93. See Minutes of the House of Representatives, January 20, 31, 1870.

94. Cassell, *Liberia*, p. 275; and Hollis R. Lynch, *Edward Wilmot Blyden: Pan-Negro Patriot, 1832-1912* (New York and London, 1967), pp. 49-50.

95. Roye and his supporters believed that since he had secured the loan, his administration should be allowed to carry out the policy that the loan made possible (see Minutes of the Senate, February 10, 1872).

96. Minutes of the Senate, February 14, 1872.

97. The story of the coup d'etat has been embellished over time. One account states that Roye attempted to flee Monrovia by swimming to a ship in the harbor but was drowned by the weight of the gold he was carrying; thus the popular saying "weight [or wait] killed Roye." The double meaning here implies that Roye delayed his departure too long! Another account—probably more accurate—indicates that Roye was stopped before he could escape by sea and that he was beaten and left for dead in the Monrovia prison—which once occupied the site of the E. J. Roye Building (see the 1872-73 minutes of the House of Representatives and the Senate for details).

98. The manifesto listed the specific grievances against Roye and the constitutional rationale for deposing him. The provisional government was directed by a three-member executive committee that including Charles D. Dunbar, R. A. Sherman, and Amos Herring (see Manifesto, October 27, 1871, F.O. 403/9).

99. Alexander Crummell to _____ , January 31, 1872, Liberia Papers of the Domestic and Foreign Missionary Society, Church Historical Society Library, Austin, Tex. Crummell wrote several interesting letters about the Roye episode to the missionary society (see Crummell to Dennison, July 20, September 18, 1871).

100. The Liberia Annual Conference, representing an important cross-section of settler leadership, made its position public by declaring: "We the members of the Liberia Annual Conference in session assembled in view of the unprecedented difficulties that are now upon us involving the vitals of our common Country, and jeopardizing its very existence, feel it behooves us at this juncture, and in this war to give some expression declaratory of our sympathies with the officers of Government, Executive, Judiciary, and Legislative in their indefatigable effort to arrest the potent evils threatening our very dissolution as a nation and to thus restore peace and safety to our new happy home" (Minutes of the Senate, February 9, 1872).

Chapter 8

1. Edward W. Blyden to J. J. Cheeseman, February 9, 1894, Executive Mansion Correspondence, 1856-99, Archives of the Liberian Government, Monrovia, Liberia.

2. Between 1820 and 1900 approximately ten thousand Afro-Americans immigrated to Liberia. In contrast, between 1820 and 1850 over two hundred thousand European immigrants reached Australia with the assistance of the British government. In the Australian case, the massive immigration enabled settlers to expand inland to exploit the pastoral opportunities on the interior plains (see Peter J. Murdza, "The American Colonization Society and Emigration to Liberia, 1865 to 1904" [M.A. thesis, University of Wisconsin, 1972] ; and Gordon Greenwood, ed., *Australia: A Social and Political History* [Sydney, 1966] , p. 12).

3. T. Harry Williams, *Lincoln and the Radicals* (Madison, 1960), p. 4.

4. John George Nicolay and John Hay, *Abraham Lincoln: A History*, 10 vols. (New York, 1890), 6: 354.

5. Abraham Lincoln, "First Inaugural Address," in *A Compilation of the Messages and Papers of the Presidents, 1789-1897*, ed. James Daniel Richardson, 10 vols. (Washington, D.C., 1899), 6: 5.

6. Abraham Lincoln. "First Annual Message to Congress," in ibid., 6: 47. The congressional bill to authorize "the President to appoint Diplomatic Representatives to the Republics of Haiti and Liberia" was introduced by Charles Sumner on February 4, 1862. In 1864 the United States signed treaties of friendship, commerce, and navigation with Haiti and Liberia (see Charles H. Wesley, "The Struggle for the Recognition of Haiti and Liberia As Independent Republics," *Journal of Negro History* 2, no. 4 [1917]: 369-83).

7. John Seys to Caleb B. Smith, December 23, 1861, U.S., Congress, House, Executive Documents, *Report of John Seys, 1856-1863: House Executive Document No. 28*, 37th Cong., 3d sess., 1863.

8. "Address on Colonization to a Deputation of Negroes," in *The Collected Works of Abraham Lincoln*, 1809-1865, ed. Roy Prentice Basler, 8 vols. (New Brunswick, N.J., 1953-55, vol. 5.

9. Marvin R. Cain, *Lincoln's Attorney General: Edward Bates of Missouri* (Columbia, Mo., 1965), p. 220.

10. See Johnson U. J. Asiegbu, *Slavery and the Politics of Liberation, 1787-1861: A Study of Liberated African Emigration and British Anti-Slavery Policy* (London and Harlow, 1969); and Monica Schuler, "Yarri, Yarri Koongo: A Social History of Liberated African Immigration into Jamaica, 1841-1867" (Ph.D. diss., University of Wisconsin, 1977).

11. Lieutenant Governor Eyre to the Duke of Newcastle, July 5, 1862, Confidential Prints, West Indies: Correspondence Respecting the Emigration of Free Negroes from the United States to the West Indies, C.O. 884/2, Public Record Office, London (hereinafter cited to be as C.O. 884/2).

12. William Stuart to Earl Russell, June 17, 1862, C.O. 884/2.

13. Sir F. Rogers to E. Hammond, August 12, 1862, C.O. 884/2.

14. A. H. Layard to Sir F. Roger, August 19, 1862, C.O. 884/2.

15. William Stuart to Earl Russell, September 4, 1862, C.O. 884/2.

16. William Stuart to Earl Russell, September 15, 1862, C.O. 884/2.

17. William Stuart to Earl Russell, September 28, 1862, C.O. 884/2.

18. The Duke of Newcastle to the governors of Jamaica, British Guiana, and Trinidad, October 16, 1862, C.O. 884/2.

19. Lieutenant Governor Eyre to the Duke of Newcastle, September 20, October 24, 1862, C.O. 884/2.

20. The Duke of Newcastle to Lieutenant Governor Eyre, October 31, 1862, C.O. 884/2.

21. John Hodge to Sir F. Rogers, November 18, 1862, C.O. 884/2.

22. Lord Lyons to Earl Russell, December 26, 1862, C.O. 884/2.

23. Sir F. Rogers to E. Hammond, January 16, 1863, C.O. 884/2.

24. Ephraim Douglass Adams, *Great Britain and the American Civil War* (New York, 1958).

25. Ibid., p. 60.

26. David Donald, ed., *Inside Lincoln's Cabinet: The Civil War Diaries of Salmon P. Chase* (New York, 1954), p. 112.

27. Gideon Welles, *Diary*, ed. Howard K. Beale, 3 vols. (New York, 1960), 2: 150-53.

28. For Lincoln's view on the competition of white labor against black labor, see Abraham Lincoln, "Second Annual Message," in Richardson, *Messages and Papers of the Presidents*, 6: 126-42.

29. Wells, *Diary*, 1: 150-53.

30. See Nathan L. Ferris, "The Relations of the United States with South America During the American Civil War," *Hispanic American Historical Review* 21 (February 1941: 51-78; Paul J. Scheips, "Lincoln and the Chiriqui Colonization Project," *Journal of Negro History* 37, no. 4 (October 1952): 418-53; and Walter A. Payne, "Lincoln's Caribbean Colonization Plan," *Pacific Historian* 7 (1963): 65-72.

31. Lincoln, "Second Annual Message."

32. The narrative on the Ile A 'Vache episode comes from Bernard Kock, *Statement of Facts in Relation to the Settlement on the Island of A'Vache . . .* (New York, 1864).

33. Ibid., p. 19.

34. Ibid., p. 22.

35. Abraham Lincoln to Edwin M. Stanton, in Richardson, *Messages and Papers of the Presidents,* 6: 232-33.

36. See Willie Lee Rose, *Rehearsal for Reconstruction: The Port Royal Experiment* (Indianapolis, 1964).

37. For details of Afro-American participation in the military during the Civil War see Thomas Wentworth Higginson, *Army Life in a Black Regiment* (Boston, 1900); and Dudley Taylor Cornish, *The Sable Arm: Negro Troops in the Union Army, 1861-1865* (New York, 1956).

38. T. Harry Williams, ed., *Abraham Lincoln: Selected Speeches, Messages, and Letters* (New York, 1957), pp. 261-63.

39. See Thomas Holt, *Black over White: Negro Political Leadership in South Carolina During Reconstruction* (Urbana, 1977), pp. 74-75.

40. The statistics on Liberian emigration were published in the *African Repository* throughout the nineteenth century. The figures represented those emigrants sent out by or through the influence of the American Colonization Society.

41. For general treatment of the fall of Reconstruction governments in the South and the aftermath, see Rayford W. Logan, *The Betrayal of the Negro: From Rutherford B. Hayes to Woodrow Wilson* (New York, 1965); and C. Vann Woodward, *The Strange Career of Jim Crow* (New York, 1974).

42. George Brown Tindall, *South Carolina Negroes, 1877-1900* (Columbia, S.C., 1952), p. 159.

43. See Alfred B. Williams, *The Liberian Exodus: An Account of the Voyage of the First Emigrants in the Bark "Azor" and Their Reception in Monrovia With a Description of Liberia—Its Customs and Civilization, Romances and Prospects* (Charleston, S.C., 1878).

44. The best single account of emigration at the turn of the century is Edwin S. Redkey, *Black Exodus: Black Nationalist and Back-to-Africa Movements, 1890-1910* (New Haven, 1969), esp. pp. 47-72.

45. Ibid., pp. 150-251.

46. Two excellent studies of the migration period are Nell Irvin Painter, *Exodusters: Black Migration to Kansas after Reconstruction* (New York, 1977); and Florette Henri, *Black Migration: Movement North, 1900-1920* (New York, 1975).

47. The details concerning the increased British pressure on Liberia after 1871 can be found in Confidential Prints, Africa, of the British Foreign Office, London: F.O. 403/9, and F.O. 403/11, Liberian Boundary Question, Correspondence; Liberian Boundary Question, Further Correspondence. For the French-Liberian boundary disputes in the nineteenth century see F.O. 403/162, French Claim to the Coast of Africa between Grand Lahou and Cape Palmas, Memorandum.

48. Edward W. Blyden to J. J. Cheeseman, February 9, 1894, Executive Mansion Correspondence, 1856-99.

49. Ibid.

50. The ongoing boundary controversy with England served to reinforce the view among Liberians that larger designs on Liberian sovereignty were a part of British colonial plans (Hollis R. Lynch, *Edward Wilmot Blyden: Pan-Negro Patriot, 1832-1912* [New York and London, 1967], pp. 178-79).

51. George Washington to J. J. Cheeseman, n.d., and J. J. Cheesman to George Washington, October 5, 1892, Executive Mansion Correspondence, 1892-93; Proposition 1 and 2 submitted to the chairman of the Senate, November 26, 1897, Miscellaneous State Department Correspondence, Archives of the Liberian Government, Monrovia, Liberia.

Chapter 9

1. See M. B. Akpan, "Black Imperialism: Americo-Liberian Rule over the African Peoples of Liberia, 1841-1964," *Canadian Journal of African Studies* 7, no. 2 (1973): 217-36; and J. K. Obatala, "Liberia: The Meaning of Dual Citizenship," *Black Scholar* 4, no. 10 (July-August 1973): 16-19.

2. Tom W. Shick, "Liberia Reconsidered: A Reply to J. K. Obatala," *Black Scholar* 5, no. 2 (October 1973): 53-56.

3. William H. Sewell, Jr., "Marc Bloch and the Logic of Comparative History," *History and Theory* 6 (1967): 210.

4. Minutes of the Board of Managers, October 16, 1820, American Colonization Society Papers, Manuscript Division, Library of Congress, Washington, D.C.

5. C. W. DeKiewiet, *A History of South Africa: Social and Economic* (London and New York, 1957), p. 8.

6. Geoffrey Blainey, *The Tyranny of Distance: How Distance Shaped Australia's History* (Melbourne, 1966).

7. Philip D. Curtin, *The Image of Africa: British Ideas and Action, 1780-1850* (London, 1965), pp. 343-62; idem, "The White Man's Grave: Image and Reality, 1780-1850," *Journal of British Studies* 1 (1961): 94-110; and K. G. Davies, "The Living and the Dead: White Mortality in West Africa, 1684-1732," in *Race and Slavery in the Western Hemisphere: Quantitative Studies*, ed. Stanley L. Engerman and Eugene D. Genovese (Princeton, 1975), pp. 83-98.

8. Raymond Maxwell Crawford, *Australia* (London and New York, 1952), p. 13.

9. DeKiewiet, *History of South Africa*, p. 19.

10. See, for example, Ezequiel Gallo, *Farmers in Revolt: The Revolutions of 1893 in the Province of Sante Fe, Argentina* (London, 1976), pp. 5-23; and Carl C. Taylor, *Rural Life in Argentina* (Baton Rouge, 1948).

11. James R. Scobie, *Argentina: A City and A Nation* (New York, 1964), p. 47.

12. DeKiewiet, *History of South Africa*, p. 21.

13. Gordon Greenwood, ed., *Australia: A Social and Political History* (Sydney, 1966), p. 12.

14. Ibid., p. 21.

15. Ibid., p. 55.

16. See Harold Edward Hockly, *The Story of the British Settlers of 1820 in South Africa* (Cape Town, 1957).

17. DeKiewiet, *History of South Africa*, pp. 46-47.

18. Ibid., p. 54.

19. Greenwood, *Australia*, p. 47.

20. See Edward Gibbon Wakefield, *A Letter from Sydney and Other Writings* (London, 1929).

21. Robert Bowden Madgwick, *Immigration into Eastern Australia*, 1788-1851 (Sydney, 1969), p. 51.

22. Brian Fitzpatrick, *The Australian People, 1788-1945* (Melbourne, 1946), p. 51.

23. The major analyses of the dynamics of frontier are Frederick Jackson Turner, *The Significance of Frontier in American History* (New York, 1963); Frederick Alexander, *Moving Frontiers: An American Theme and Its Application to Australian History* (Melbourne, 1947); and Owen Lattimore, *Inner Asian Frontiers of China* (Boston, 1962).

24. The first historian to argue for the economic interdependence of the South African frontiersmen and coastal urban settlements during the years of expansion was S. David Neumark in his study, *Economic Influences on the South African Frontier, 1652-1836* (Stanford, 1957).

25. Ibid., pp. 145-51.

26. Ibid., p. 186.

27. Scobie, *Argentina*, p. 72.

28. See Tulio Halperín-Donghi, *Politics, Economics, and Society in Argentina in the Revolutionary Period* (Cambridge, 1975).

29. DeKiewiet, *History of South Africa*, p. 102.

30. Martin Lowenkopf, *Politics in Liberia: The Conservative Road to Development* (Stanford, 1976), pp. 38-40.

31. Quoted in ibid., p. 55.

Selected Bibliography

Bibliographical Guides

Duignan, Peter. *Handbook of American Resources for African Studies.* Stanford: Hoover Institution Press, 1967.

Foley, David M. "Liberia's Archival Collection." *African Studies Bulletin* 2, no. 2 (September 1969): 217-20.

Hogg, Peter C. *The African Slave Trade and Its Suppression: A Classified and Annotated Bibliography of Books, Pamphlets, and Periodical Articles.* London: Frank Cass, 1973.

Holsoe, Svend E. "A Bibliography of Liberian Government Documents." *African Studies Bulletin* 2, nos. 1 and 2 (1968): 39-62, 149-94.

_____. *A Bibliography on Liberia: Books.* Liberian Studies Research Working Paper No. 1. Newark, Del.: Department of Anthropology, University of Delaware, 1971.

_____. *A Bibliography on Liberia: Periodicals Concerning Colonization.* Liberian Studies Research Working Paper No. 3. Newark, Del.: Department of Anthropology, University of Delaware, 1971.

Schatz, Walter, ed. *Directory of Afro-American Resources.* New York: R. R. Bowker Co., 1970.

Shick, Tom W. "Catalog of the Liberian Government Archives." *Africa in History* 3 (1976): 193-202.

Solomon, Marvin D., and d'Azevedo, Warren L. *A General Bibliography of the Republic of Liberia.* Evanston: Northwestern University Press, 1962.

Williams, Ethel L., and Brown, Clifton L. *Afro-American Religious Studies: Comprehensive Bibliography with Locations in American Libraries.* Metuchen, N.J.: Scarecrow Press, 1972.

Primary Sources

Archival Collections

Austin, Tex. Church Historical Society Library. Liberia Papers of the Domestic and Foreign Missionary Society.

Bloomington, Ind. Indiana University. Folklore Institute. Archives of Traditional Music: Shick Oral Data Collection.

Charlottesville, Va. University of Virginia Library. Manuscripts Department, Cocke Family Papers: Correspondence with the Skipwith Family in Liberia.

Chicago, Ill. Chicago Historical Society. American Colonization Society Papers: Correspondence from American Colonization Society Agents in Liberia; Joseph Jenkins Roberts Papers.

Monrovia, Liberia. University of Liberia Library. Jesse and Mars Lucas Correspondence.

Morgantown, W. Va. West Virginia University Library. West Virginia and Regional History Collection. Journal of John Moore McCalla, 1860.

Nashville, Tenn. Disciples of Christ Historical Society Library. Minutes of the Ninth Street Christian Church, 1853.

Nashville, Tenn. Tennessee State Library and Archives. Archives and Manuscripts Section. Nannie Seawell Boyd Collection, Montgomery Bell Papers, 1853-1939; John S. Russwurm Papers: Family Correspondence, Box 2, no. 7; William Slatter Papers.

New York, N.Y. New York Public Library. Schomburg Center for Research in Black Culture. Alexander Crummell Papers.

Washington, D.C. Library of Congress. Manuscript Division. American Colonization Society Papers; Diary of Daniel Coker, April 21-September 21, 1821; Peter Force Papers.

Government Documents

England

Confidential Prints, Africa.

F.O. 403/6, 1861-71. Boundary of the Republic of Liberia, Correspondence.

F.O. 403/9, 1871-78. Liberian Boundary Question, Correspondence.

F.O. 403/11, 1878-79. Liberian Boundary Question, Further Correspondence.

F.O. 403/129, 1890. Right of Liberia to Claim a Frontier up to the San Pedro River, Memorandum.

F.O. 403/162, 1891. French Claim to the Coast of Africa between Grand Lahou and Cape Palmas, Memorandum.

Confidential Prints, West Indies.
C.O. 884/2. Correspondence Respecting the Emigration of Free Negroes from the United States to the West Indies.
General Correspondence, Liberia. F.O. 47/1-16, 1848-1905.

Liberia

Monrovia. Archives of the Liberian Government (under the custody of the Ministry of Foreign Affairs).
Colonial Council Minutes, 1838-39.
Commonwealth Court Records, 1838-42.
Commonwealth Legislative Minutes, 1839-47.
Correspondence of Colonial Agents, 1833-41.
Deed Records, Montserrado County, 1847.
Department of Justice Correspondence, 1892-1904.
Executive Mansion Correspondence, 1856-99.
Executive Mansion Journal of H. R. W. Johnson, 1885-88.
Jehudi Ashmun Papers, 1826-28.
Miscellaneous State Department Correspondence.
Minutes of the Court of Quarter Sessions and Common Pleas, Montserrado County, 1866-97.
Minutes of the House of Representatives, 1848-98.
Minutes of the Monthly and Probate Court, Montserrado County, 1874-77.
Minutes of the Senate, 1848-92.
Records of the Monthly and Probate Court, Montserrado County, 1874-77.
State Department Correspondence, Foreign and Local, 1886-1906.

Sierra Leone

Freetown. Fourah Bay University Library.
Sierra Leone Collection. Further Correspondence Respecting Negotiations with Liberia for the Establishment of Conterminous Boundaries (African 282), #174, 1879-86.
Sierra Leone Collection. Further Correspondence Respecting Negotiations with Liberia for the Establishment of Conterminous Boundaries (African, 251), 1881-86.
Freetown, Sierra Leone Government Archives.
Liberian Boundary Papers. Box No. 30, 1862-86.

United States

U.S., Congress, House, Emigration Office, *Report on Colonization and Emigration*. Washington, D.C.: U.S. Government Printing Office, 1862.

U.S., Congress, House, Executive Documents, *Report of John Seys, 1856-1863: House Executive Document No. 28*, 37th Cong., 3d sess., 1863.

U.S., Congress, House, Executive Documents, *Report of the Rev. R. R. Gurley: House Executive Document No. 75*, 31st Cong., 1st sess., 1849-50.

U.S., Congress, House, Executive Documents, *The Colony of Liberia in Africa: House Executive Document No. 162*, 28th Cong., 1st sess., 1843-44.

U.S., Congress, Senate, *Roll of the Emigrants That Have Been Sent to the Colony of Liberia, West Africa, by the American Colonization Society and Its Auxiliaries to September, 1843 &c.: Public Document No. 9*, 28th Cong., 2d sess., 1845.

U.S., Congress, Senate, *U.S. Navy Department, tables showing the number of Emigrants and recaptured Africans sent to the colony of Liberia by the government of the United States: also the number of emigrants freeborn, number that purchased their freedom, number emancipated, &c: together with a census of the colony and a report of its commerce, &c. September, 1843: Senate Document No. 150*, 28th Cong., 2d sess., 1845.

U.S., National Archives, Microcopy 169, "Despatches from United States Consuls in Monrovia, 1852-1906."

U.S., National Archives, Microcopy 170, "Despatches from United States Ministers to Liberia, 1863-1906."

Newspapers and Journals

African Repository and Colonial Journal. Washington, D.C.
Africa's Luminary. Monrovia.
Liberia Herald. Monrovia.
Liberian Recorder. Monrovia.
The Friend. Philadelphia.
Weekly Anglo-African. New York.

Books, Pamphlets, Articles, and Edited Collections of Documents

A Brief Historical Account of the Settlement of Arthington, Covering Thirty-Five Years. Monrovia: College of West Africa Press, 1905.

Anderson, Benjamin J. K. *Narrative of a Journey to Musardu: The Capital of the Western Mandingoes Together with Narrative of the Expedition Dispatched to Musahdu: By the Liberian Government under Benjamin J. K. Anderson, Senior, Esq., in 1874.* 2d. ed. London: Frank Cass & Co., 1971.

Ashmun, Jehudi. *Memoir of the life and character of the Rev. Samuel Bacon, A.M., late an officer of marines in the United States' service: afterwards, attorney at law in the state of Pennsylvania: and subsequently, a minister of the Episcopal church, and principal agent of the American government for persons liberated from slave-ships, on the coast of Africa; where he terminated his life in the month of May, 1820.* Washington, D.C.: J. Gideon, Jr., 1822.

Blyden, Edward Wilmot. *Christianity, Islam, and the Negro Race.* 2d ed. London: W. B. Whittingham & Co., 1888.

_____. *Liberia's Offering.* New York: John A. Gray, 1862.

_____. *On Mixed Races in Liberia.* Smithsonian Institution Annual Report, 1870. Washington, D.C., 1871.

_____. "The Call of Providence to the Descendants of Africa in America." Reprinted in *Negro Social and Political Thought, 1850-1920: Representative Texts,* edited by Howard Brotz. New York: Basic Books, 1966.

Boutilly, V. *Le Caféier de Libéria: Sa Culture et sa manipulation.* Paris: A. Challamel, 1900.

Christy, David. *African Colonization by the Free Colored People of the United States, an Indispensable Auxiliary to African Missions: A Lecture.* Cincinnati: J. A. & U. P. James, 1854.

Coker, Daniel. *A Dialogue Between a Virginian and an African Minister.* Baltimore: Benjamin Edes, 1810.

Crummell, Alexander. *Africa and America: Addresses and Discourses.* Springfield, Mass.: Willey & Co., 1891.

Crüwell, G. A. *Liberian Coffee in Ceylon: The History of the Introduction and Progress of the Cultivation up to April 1878.* Colombo: A. M. & J. Ferguson, 1878.

Delany, Martin Robinson. *Official Report of the Niger Valley Exploring Party.* New York: T. Hamilton, 1861.

_____. *The condition, elevation, emigration, and destiny of the colored people of the United States politically considered.* Philadelphia: privately printed, 1852.

_____. *The origin and objects of ancient Freemasonry; its introduction into the United States, and legitimacy among colored men.* Pittsburgh: W. S. Haven, 1853.

_____, and Campbell, Robert. *Search for a Place: Black Separatism and Africa, 1860.* Ann Arbor: University of Michigan Press, 1969, reprint.

Donald, David, ed. *Inside Lincoln's Cabinet: The Civil War Diaries of Salmon P. Chase.* New York: Longmans, Green, 1954.

Fairfax, Ferdinando. "Plan for Liberating the Negroes within the United States." *American Museum* 3 (1790): 285-87.

Fishel, Leslie H., and Quarles, Benjamin. *The Negro American: A Documentary History*. 2d. ed. Glenview, Ill.: Scott, Foresman and Co., 1967.

Garrison, William Lloyd. *Thoughts on African Colonization, or, an Impartial Exhibition of the Doctrines, Principles, and Purposes of the American Colonization Society Together with the Resolutions, Addresses, and Remonstrances of the Free People of Color*. Boston: Garrison & Knapp, 1832.

Gurley, Ralph Randolph. *Life of Jehudi Ashmun, late Colonial Agent in Liberia. With an Appendix, containing Extracts from His Journal and Other Writings; with a Brief Sketch of the Life of the Rev. Lott Cary*. Washington, D.C.: J. C. Dunn, 1835.

Hervey, George Winfred. *The Story of Baptist Missions in Foreign Lands, From the Time of Carey to the Present Date*. St. Louis: C. R. Barns, 1885.

Jay, William. *An Inquiry into the Character and Tendency of the American Colonization, and American Anti-Slavery Societies*. New York: Leavitt, Lord & Co.; Boston: Crocker & Brewster, 1835.

Jefferson, Thomas. *Notes on the State of Virginia*. 1861. Reprint. New York: Harper & Row, Publishers, Harper Torchbook, 1964.

Jones, Absalom, and Allen, Richard. *A Narrative of the Proceedings of the Black People During the Late Awful Calamity in Philadelphia in the Year 1793, and a Refutation of Some Censures Thrown Upon Them in Some Late Publications*. Philadelphia: W. W. Woodward, 1794.

Kock, Bernard. *Statement of Facts in Relation to the Settlement on the Island of A'Vache, Near Hayti, W.I., of a Colony under Bernard Kock, with Documentary Evidence and Affidavits*. New York: William C. Bryant & Co., 1864.

Lincoln, Abraham. *The Collected Works of Abraham Lincoln, 1809-1865*. Edited by Roy Prentice Basler. 8 vols. New Brunswick, N.J.: Rutgers University Press, 1953-55.

Lugenbeel, James Washington. *Sketches of Liberia: Comprising a Brief Account of the Geography, Climate, Productions, and Diseases, of the Republic of Liberia*. Washington, D.C.: C. Alexander, 1850.

Mayer, Brantz. *Captain Canot, or, Twenty Years of an African Slaver; being an Account of His Career and Adventures on the Coast, In the Interior, on Shipboard, and in the West Indies*. New York: D. Appleton, 1854.

Nesbit, William. *Four Months in Liberia; or, African Colonization Exposed*. Pittsburgh: J. T. Shryock, 1855.

Nicolay, John George, and Hay, John. *Abraham Lincoln: A History*. 10 vols. New York: The Century Co., 1890.

Payne, Daniel Alexander. *Recollections of Seventy Years*. Nashville: Publishing House of the A.M.E. Sunday School Union, 1888.

[Pearl, Cyril.] *Remarks on African Colonization and the Abolition of Slavery,*

In Two Parts: By a Citizen of New England. Windsor, Vt.: Richards & Tracy, 1833.

Peck, Solomon. "History of the Missions of the Baptist General Convention." In *History of American Missions to the Heathen, from their Commencement to the Present Time*. Worcester, Mass.: Spooner & Howland, 1840.

Reade, Winwood. *The African Sketch-Book*. London: Smith, Elder & Co., 1873.

Richardson, James Daniel, ed. *A Compilation of the Messages and Papers of the Presidents, 1789-1897*. 10 vols. Washington, D.C.: U.S. Government Printing Office, 1899.

Shick, Tom W. *Emigrants to Liberia, 1820 to 1843: An Alphabetical Listing*. Liberian Studies Research Working Paper No. 2. Newark, Del.: Department of Anthropology, University of Delaware, 1971.

The Missionary Jubilee: An Account of the Fiftieth Anniversary of the American Baptist Missionary Union. New York: Sheldon and Company; Boston: Gould and Lincoln, 1869 (revised edition).

The Statute Laws of the Republic of Liberia Passed by the Legislature from 1848 to 1879 Together with the Constitution and Amendments. Monrovia: T. W. Howard, 1879.

Thomas, Charles W. *Adventures and Observations on the West Coast of Africa, and Its Islands*. New York: Derby and Jackson, 1860.

Tubman, William V. S. *The Offical Papers of William V. S. Tubman: President of the Republic of Liberia*. Edited by Reginald E. Townsend. London: Longmans, Green, 1968.

Wakefield, Edward Gibbon. *A Letter from Sydney and Other Writings*. London, 1929.

Walker, David. *Walker's Appeal, in Four Articles, Together with a Preamble, to the Coloured Citizens of the World, But in Particular, and Very Expressly, to Those of the United States of America, written in Boston, in the State of Massachusetts, Sept. 28, 1829*. Boston: privately printed, 1830.

Welles, Gideon. *Diary*. Edited by Howard K. Beale. New York: W. W. Norton, 1960.

White, William S. *The African Preacher: An Authentic Narrative*. Philadelphia: Presbyterian Board of Publication, 1849.

Wilkeson, Samuel. *A Concise History of the Commencement, Progress and Present Condition of the American Colonies in Liberia*. Washington, D.C.: Madisonian Office, 1839.

Williams, Alfred B. *The Liberian Exodus: An Account of the Voyage of the First Emigrants in the Bark "Azor" and Their Reception in Monrovia With a Description of Liberia—Its Customs and Civilization, Romances and Prospects*. Charleston, S.C.: News and Courier Book Presses, 1878.

Williams, Samuel. *Four Years in Liberia: A Sketch of the Life of Rev. Samuel Williams*. Philadelphia, 1857.

Secondary Works

Adams, Ephraim Douglass. *Great Britain and the American Civil War*. New York: Russell & Russell, 1958.

Akpan, M. B. "Black Imperialism: Americo-Liberian Rule over the African Peoples of Liberia, 1841-1964." *Canadian Journal of African Studies* 7, no. 2 (1973)ː 217-36.

―――― . "The African Policy of the Liberian Settlers, 1841-1932: A Study of the 'Native' Policy of a Non-Colonial Power in Africa." Ph.D. diss., Ibadan University, 1968.

―――― . "The Liberian Economy in the Nineteenth Century: The State of Agriculture and Commerce." *Liberian Studies Journal* 6, no. 1 (1975): 1-24.

Alexander, Frederick. *Moving Frontiers: An American Theme and Its Application to Australian History*. Melbourne: Melbourne University Press, 1947.

Asiegbu, Johnson U. J. *Slavery and the Politics of Liberation, 1787-1861: A Study of Liberated African Emigration and British Anti-Slavery Policy*. London and Harlow: Longmans, 1969.

Ayandele, E. A. *The Missionary Impact on Modern Nigeria, 1842-1914: A Political and Social Analysis*. New York: Humanities Press, 1967.

Bane, Martin J. *Catholic Pioneers in West Africa*. Dublin: Clonmore & Reynolds, 1956.

Bascom, William R. "The Acculturation of Gullah Negroes." *American Anthropologist* 43 (January-March 1941): 43-50.

Berlin, Ira. *Slaves Without Masters: The Free Negro in the Antebellum South*. New York: Pantheon Books, 1974.

Berry, Mary Frances. *Black Resistance / White Law: A History of Constitutional Racism in America*. New York: Appleton-Century-Crofts, 1971.

Blainey, Geoffrey. *The Tyranny of Distance: How Distance Shaped Australia's History*. Melbourne: Sun Books, 1966.

Blassingame, John W. *The Slave Community: Plantation Life in the Antebellum South*. New York: Oxford University Press, 1972.

Brodie, Fawn McKay. *Thomas Jefferson: An Intimate History*. New York: Norton, 1974.

Brooks, George E., Jr. *The Kru Mariner in the Nineteenth Century: An Historical Compendium*. Liberian Studies Monograph Series, no. 1. Newark, Del.: University of Delaware, Department of Anthropology, 1972.

―――― . *Yankee Traders, Old Coasters, and African Middlemen: A History of American Legitimate Trade with West Africa in the Nineteenth Century*. Brookline, Mass.: Boston University Press, 1970.

Browne, George D. "History of the Protestant Episcopal Mission in Liberia up to 1838." *Historical Magazine of the Protestant Episcipal Church* 39, no. 1 (March 1970): 17-27.

Cain, Marvin R. *Lincoln's Attorney General: Edward Bates of Missouri.* Columbia, Mo.: University of Missouri Press, 1965.

Campbell, Penelope. *Maryland in Africa: The Maryland State Colonization Society, 1831-1857.* Urbana: University of Illinois Press, 1971.

————. "Medical Education for an African Colonist." *Maryland Historical Magazine* 65 (Summer 1970): 130-37.

Cassell, Christian Abayomi. *Liberia: History of the First African Republic.* New York: Fountainhead Publishers, 1970.

Cheagle, Roslyn V. "The Colored Temperance Movement, 1830-1860." M.A. thesis, Howard University, 1969.

Christaller, Walter. *Central Places in Southern Germany.* Translated by Carlisle W. Baskin. Englewood Cliffs, N.J.: Prentice-Hall, 1966.

Coger, Dalvan M. "Americans in the Liberian Frontier Force." Paper delivered at the African Studies Association Meeting, San Francisco, Calif., 1974.

Cohen, Abner. "Cultural Strategies in the Organization of Trading Diasporas." In *The Development of Indigenous Trade and Markets in West Africa,* edited by Claude Meillassoux. London: Oxford University Press, 1971.

Cohen, David W., and Greene, Jack P., eds. *Neither Slave Nor Free: The Freedmen of African Descent in the Slave Societies of the New World.* Baltimore: Johns Hopkins University Press, 1972.

Cornish, Dudley Taylor. *The Sable Arm: Negro Troops in the Union Army, 1861-1865.* New York: Longmans, Green, & Co., 1956.

Crawford, Raymond Maxwell. *Australia.* London and New York: Hutchinson's University Library, 1852.

Cubberley, Ellwood Patterson. *Public Education in the United States.* New York: Houghton Mifflin Co., 1919.

Curtin, Philip D. *Economic Change in Precolonial Africa: Senegambia in the Era of the Slave Trade.* Madison: University of Wisconsin Press, 1975.

————. *The Atlantic Slave Trade: A Census.* Madison: University of Wisconsin Press, 1969.

————. *The Image of Africa: British Ideas and Action, 1780-1850.* London: Macmillan & Co., 1965.

————. "The White Man's Grave: Image and Reality, 1780-1850." *Journal of British Studies* 1 (1961): 94-110.

Dalby, David. "The Mel Languages: A Reclassification of Southern 'West Atlantic.' " *African Language Studies* 6 (1965): 1-17.

Davies, K. G. "The Living and the Dead: White Mortality in West Africa, 1684-1732." In *Race and Slavery in the Western Hemisphere: Quantitative Studies,* edited by Stanley L. Engerman and Eugene D. Genovese. Princeton: Princeton University Press, 1975.

Davis, David Brion. *The Problem of Slavery in the Age of Revolution, 1770-1823.* Ithaca: Cornell University Press, 1975.

Davis, John W. "George Liele and Andrew Bryan: Pioneer Negro Baptist Preachers." *Journal of Negro History* 3, no. 2 (April 1918): 119-27.

Davis, Lenwood G. "Black American Images of Liberia, 1877-1914." *Liberian Studies Journal* 6, no. 1 (1975): 53-72.

Davis, Ronald W. "Historical Outline of the Kru Coast, Liberia, 1500 to the Present." Ph.D. diss., University of Indiana, 1968.

d'Azevedo, Warren L. "A Tribal Reaction to Nationalism, (Part One)." *Liberian Studies Journal* 1, no. 2 (Spring 1969): 1-22.

————. "Some Historical Problems in the Delineation of a Central West Atlantic Region." *Annals of the New York Academy of Sciences* 96 (1962): 512-38.

————. "The Setting of Gola Society and Culture: Some Theoretical Implications of Time and Space." *Kroeber Anthropological Society Papers* 21 (Fall 1959): 43-125.

DeKiewiet, C. W. *A History of South Africa: Social and Economic.* London and New York: Oxford University Press, 1957.

Engerman, Stanley L., and Genovese, Eugene D., eds. *Race and Slavery in the Western Hemisphere: Quantitative Studies.* Princeton: Princeton University Press, 1975.

Essien-Udom, E. U. *Black Nationalism: A Search for an Identity in America.* Chicago: The University of Chicago Press, 1962.

Farley, Reynolds. *Growth of the Black Population: A Study of Demographic Trends.* Chicago: Markham Publishing Co., 1970.

Ferris, Nathan L. "The Relations of the United States with South America During the American Civil War." *Hispanic American Historical Review* 21 (February 1941): 51-78.

Fitzpatrick, Brian. *The Australian People, 1788-1945.* Melbourne: Melbourne University Press, 1946.

Fleming, Walter H. "Historic Attempts to Solve the Race Problem in America by Deportation." *Journal of American History* 4, no. 2 (1910): 197-213.

Fogel, Robert William, and Engerman, Stanley L. *Time on the Cross: Economics of American Negro Slavery.* Boston: Little, Brown, 1974.

Foner, Laura. "The Free People of Color in Louisiana and St. Domingue: A Comparative Portrait of Two Three-Caste Societies." *Journal of Social History* 3 (Summer 1970): 406-30.

Fraenkel, Merran. *Tribe and Class in Monrovia.* London: Oxford University Press, 1964.

Franklin, John Hope. *From Slavery to Freedom: A History of Negro Americans.* 4th ed. New York: Vintage Books, 1969.

————, ed. *Color and Race.* Boston: Houghton Mifflin Co., 1968.

Frazier, E. Franklin. *The Negro in the United States.* New York: Macmillan Co., 1949.

Freehling, William W. "The Founding Fathers and Slavery." *American Historical Review* 77, no. 1 (February 1972): 81-93.

Gallo, Ezequiel. *Farmers in Revolt: The Revolutions of 1893 in the Province of Santa Fe, Argentina.* London: Athlone Press, 1976.

George, Carol V. R. *Segregated Sabbaths: Richard Allen and the Rise of Independent Black Churches, 1760-1840.* New York: Oxford University Press, 1973.

Gibbs, James L., Jr., ed. *Peoples of Africa.* New York: Holt, Rhinehart and Winston, 1965.

Gnielinski, Stefan von. *Liberia in Maps: Graphic Perspectives of a Developing Country.* New York: Africana Publishing Corp., 1972.

Goldin, Claudia Dale. *Urban Slavery in the American South, 1820-1860: A Quantitative History.* Chicago: University of Chicago Press, 1976.

Greenberg, Joseph H. *The Languages of Africa.* Bloomington: Indiana University Press, 1963.

Greenwood, Gordon, ed. *Australia: A Social and Political History.* Sydney: Angus & Robertson, 1966.

Griffith, Cyril Edgar. "Martin R. Delany and the African Dream, 1812-1885." Ph.D. diss., Michigan State University, 1973.

Grimshaw, William H. *Official History of Freemasonry among the Colored People in North America, Tracing the Growth of Masonry from 1717 down to the Present Day.* New York and London: Broadway Publishing Co., 1903.

Gunter, Caroline Pell. "Tom Day—Craftsman." *The Antiquarian* 11, no. 2 (September 1928): 60-62.

Guthrie, Patricia. "Catching Sense: The Meaning of Plantation Membership among Blacks on St. Helena Island, South Carolina." Ph.D. diss., University of Rochester, 1977.

Gutman, Herbert G. *The Black Family in Slavery and Freedom, 1750-1925.* New York: Pantheon Books, 1976.

Halperín-Donghi, Tulio. *Politics, Economics, and Society in Argentina in the Revolutionary Period.* Cambridge: Cambridge University Press, 1975.

Handwerker, Winston Penn. "The Liberian Internal Market System." Ph.D. diss., University of Oregon, 1971.

Harris, Sheldon H. *Paul Cuffee, Black America, and the African Return.* New York: Simon & Schuster, 1972.

Hatcher, William Eldridge. *John Jasper: The Unmatched Negro Philosopher and Preacher.* New York: F. H. Revell Co., 1908.

Haynes, Jesse Oliver. "A Brief History of the Founding of the Township of Brewerville, Montserrado County, Republic of Liberia, 1869-1970." Mimeographed. Monrovia: Historical Committee of Brewerville, n.d.

Henri, Florette. *Black Migration: Movement North, 1900-1920.* New York: Anchor Press, 1975.

Henries, A. Doris Banks. *The Life of Joseph Jenkins Roberts, and His Inaugural Addresses.* London: Macmillan & Co., 1964.

Herskovits, Melville J. *The Myth of the Negro Past.* Boston: Beacon Press, 1958.

————, and Herskovits, Frances S. *Trinidad Village.* New York: Octagon Books, 1964.

Higginson, Thomas Wentworth. *Army Life in a Black Regiment.* Boston: Houghton Mifflin, 1900.

Hill, Adelaide Cromwell, and Kilson, Martin, eds. *Apropos of Africa: Afro-American Leaders and the Romance of Africa.* New York: Anchor Books, 1971.

Hockly, Harold Edward. *The Story of the British Settlers of 1820 in South Africa.* Cape Town: Juta, 1957.

Hoff, Advertus A. *A Short History of Liberia College and the University of Liberia.* Monrovia: Consolidated Publications, 1962.

Holder, Burleigh. "A History of Crozierville." *Liberian Studies Journal* 3, no. 1 (1970-71): 21-30.

Holsoe, Svend E. "A Study of Relations Between Settlers and Indigenous Peoples in Western Liberia, 1821-1847." *African Historical Studies* 4, no. 2 (1971): 331-62.

————. "Economic Activities in the Liberian Areas: The Pre-European Period to 1820." Paper delivered at the Liberian Studies Conference, Bloomington, Ind., 1976.

————. "The Cassava-Leaf People: An Ethnohistorical Study of the Vai People with a Particular Emphasis on the Tewo Chiefdom." Ph.D. diss., Boston University, 1967.

————. "The Condo Confederation in Western Liberia." *Liberian Historical Review* 3, no. 1 (1966): 1-28.

————. "The First Vai Migration." Paper delivered at the Liberian Studies Conference, Madison, Wis., 1974.

————. "The Manding in Western Liberia: An Overview." Paper delivered at the Conference on Manding Studies, London, 1972.

Holt, Thomas. *Black over White: Negro Political Leadership in South Carolina During Reconstruction.* Urbana: University of Illinois Press, 1977.

Howard, Warren S. *American Slavers and the Federal Law, 1837-1862.* Berkeley and Los Angeles: University of California Press, 1963.

Huberich, Charles Henry. *The Political and Legislative History of Liberia: A Documentary History of the Constitutions, Laws, and Treaties of Liberia.* 2 vols. New York: Central Book Co., 1947.

Huggins, Nathan I.; Kilson, Martin; and Fox, Daniel, eds. *Key Issues in the Afro-American Experience.* 2 vols. New York: Harcourt Brace Jovanovich, 1971.

Hunt, Gaillard. "William Thornton and Negro Colonization." *Proceedings of the American Antiquarian Society*, n.s. 30 (1920): 36-61.

Jackson, Luther Porter. "Free Negroes of Petersburg, Virginia." *Journal of Negro History* 12, no. 3 (July 1930): 365-88.

————. *Free Negro Labor and Property Holding in Virginia, 1830-1860.* New York: Appleton-Century Co., 1942.

Johnston, Harry Hamilton. *Liberia.* 2 vols. New York: Dodd, Mead & Co., 1906.

Jones, Hannah A. B. "The Struggle for Political and Cultural Unification in Liberia, 1847-1930." Ph.D. diss., Northwestern University, 1962.

Jordan, Winthrop D. "Modern Racial Tensions and the Origins of American Slavery." *Journal of Southern History* 28 (February 1962): 18-30.

Kaestle, Karl, ed. *Joseph Lancaster and the Monitorial School Movement: A Documentary History.* New York: Teachers College Press, 1973.

Karnga, Abayomi Winfrid. *Liberia before the New World.* London: F. I. Phillips, 1923.

Knight, Franklin W. *Slave Society in Cuba During the Nineteenth Century.* Madison: University of Wisconsin Press, 1970.

Kopytoff, Jean Herskovits. *A Preface to Modern Nigeria: The "Sierra Leonians" in Yoruba, 1830-1890.* Madison: University of Wisconsin Press, 1965.

Lattimore, Owen. *Inner Asian Frontiers of China.* Boston: Beacon Press, 1962.

Leach, Edmund. "Polyandry, Inheritance and the Definitions of Marriage." *Man* 55 (December 1955): 182-86.

Levine, Lawrence W. *Black Culture and Black Consciousness: Afro-American Folk Thought from Slavery to Freedom.* New York: Oxford University Press, 1977.

Liberian Writing: Liberia As Seen by Her Own Writers As Well As by German Authors. Tübingen: Erdmann, 1970.

Liebenow, J. Gus. *Liberia: The Evolution of Privilege.* Ithaca: Cornell University Press, 1969.

Litwack, Leon F. *North of Slavery: The Negro in the Free States, 1790-1860.* Chicago: University of Chicago Press, 1961.

Logan, Rayford W. *The Betrayal of the Negro: From Rutherford B. Hayes to Woodrow Wilson.* New York: Collier Books, 1965.

Lowenkopf, Martin. *Politics in Liberia: The Conservative Road to Development.* Stanford: Hoover Institution Press, 1976.

Lynch, Hollis R. *Edward Wilmot Blyden: Pan-Negro Patriot, 1832-1912.* New York and London: Oxford University Press, 1967.

————. *Pan-Negro Nationalism in the New World before 1862.* Boston University Papers on Africa, no. 2, pp. 149-79. Boston, 1966.

Madgwick, Robert Bowden. *Immigration into Eastern Australia, 1788-1851.* Sydney: Sydney University Press, 1969.

"Manuscript History of Arthington." Monrovia, Liberia: mimeographed, n.d.

"Manuscript History of Clay Ashland." Monrovia, Liberia: mimeographed, n.d.

Martin, Jane J. "The Dual Legacy: Government Authority and Mission Influence Among the Glebo of Eastern Liberia, 1834-1910." Ph.D. diss., Boston University, 1968.

————, and Carlisle, Rodney. "The Search for Matilda Newport." Paper delivered at the Liberian Studies Conference, Bloomington, Ind., 1976.

Mehlinger, Louis R. "The Attitude of the Free Negro Toward African Coloni-
zation." *Journal of Negro History* 1, no. 3 (1916): 276-301.
Miller, Floyd J. *The Search for a Black Nationality: Black Colonization and
Emigration, 1787-1863.* Urbana: University of Illinois Press, 1975.
Miller, Randall M., ed. *"Dear Master" Letters of a Slave Family.* Ithaca:
Cornell University Press, 1978.
Mitchell, Memory F. "Off to Africa–With Judicial Blessings." Mimeographed.
n.d.
Mitchell, Memory F. and Mitchell, Thornton W. "The Philanthropic Bequests
of John Rex of Raleigh." *North Carolina Historical Review* 49, nos.
3 and 4 (Summer and Autumn 1972): 254-79, 353-76.
Myers, Robert Manson. *The Children of Pride: A True Story of Georgia and
the Civil War.* New Haven: Yale University Press, 1972.
Neumark, S. David. *Economic Influences on the South African Frontier,
1652-1836.* Stanford: Stanford University Press, 1957.
Obatala, J. K. "Liberia: The Meaning of Dual Citizenship." *Black Scholar* 4,
no. 10 (July-August 1973): 16-19.
Omer-Cooper, J. D. *The Zulu Aftermath: A Nineteenth-Century Revolution
in Bantu Africa.* Evanston: Northwestern University Press, 1966.
Murdza, Peter J. "The American Colonization Society and Emigration to
Liberia, 1865 to 1904." M.A. thesis, University of Wisconsin, 1972.
Painter, Nell Irvin. *Exodusters: Black Migration to Kansas after Reconstruc-
tion.* New York: Alfred A. Knopf, 1977.
Patterson, Lindsay, ed. *International Library of Negro Life and History: The
Negro in Music and Art.* 2d ed., rev. New York: Publishers Co.,
1970.
Payne, Walter A. "Lincoln's Caribbean Colonization Plan." *Pacific Historian*
7 (1963): 65-72.
Peterson, John. *Province of Freedom: A History of Sierra Leone, 1787-1870.*
London: Farber, 1969.
Poe, William Allen. "Georgia Influence in the Development of Liberia."
Georgia Historical Review 57, no. 1 (Spring 1973): 1-16.
Porter, Dorothy. "The Organized Educational Activities of Negro Literary
Societies, 1828-1846." *Journal of Negro Education* 5, no. 4 (Octo-
ber 1936): 555-76.
Porter, Philip W. "Population Distribution and Land Use in Liberia." Ph.D.
diss., London School of Economics and Political Science, 1956.
Postell, William Dosite. *The Health of Slaves on Southern Plantations.* Baton
Rouge: Louisiana State University Press, 1951.
Priestley, Margaret. *West African Trade and Coast Society: A Family Study.*
London: Oxford University Press, 1969.
Prothero, R. Mansell. *Migrants and Malaria in Africa.* London: Longmans,
1965.
Quarles, Benjamin. *The Negro in the American Revolution.* Chapel Hill:
University of North Carolina Press, 1961.

Redkey, Edwin S. *Black Exodus: Black Nationalist and Back-to-Africa Movements, 1890-1910.* New Haven: Yale University Press, 1969.

Reed, William E. *Reconnaissance Soil Survey of Liberia.* Washington, D.C.: U.S. Government Printing Office, 1951.

Robinson, Donald L. *Slavery in the Structure of American Politics, 1765-1820.* New York: Harcourt Brace Jovanovich, 1971.

Rose, Willie Lee. *Rehearsal for Reconstruction: The Port Royal Experiment.* Indianapolis: Bobbs-Merrill, 1964.

Sabin, James J. "The Making of the Americo-Liberian Community." Ph.D. diss., Columbia University, 1974.

Scheips, Paul J. "Lincoln and the Chiriqui Colonization Project." *Journal of Negro History* 37, no. 4 (October 1952): 418-53.

Schroder, Günter, and Seibel, Dieter. *Ethnographic Survey of Southeastern Liberia: The Liberian Kran and the Sapo.* Liberian Studies Monograph Series, no. 3. Newark, Del.: University of Delaware, Department of Anthropology, 1974.

Schuler, Monica. "Yarri, Yarri Koongo: A Social History of Liberated African Immigration into Jamaica, 1841-1867." Ph.D. diss., University of Wisconsin, 1977.

Schultz, Stanley K. "The Making of a Reformer: The Reverend Samuel Hopkins as an Eighteenth-Century Abolitionist."*Proceedings of the American Philosophical Society* 115, no. 5 (1971): 350-65.

Schulze, Willi. *A New Geography of Liberia.* London: Longmans, 1973.

Scobie, James R. *Argentina: A City and A Nation.* New York: Oxford University Press, 1964.

Sewell, William H., Jr. "Marc Bloch and the Logic of Comparative History." *History and Theory* 6 (1967): 208-18.

Shepperson, George, and Price, Thomas. *Independent African: John Chilembwe and the Origins, Setting, and Significance of the Nyasaland Native Rising of 1915.* Edinburgh: Edinburgh University Press, 1958.

Sherwood, Henry Noble. "Early Negro Deportation Projects." *Mississippi Valley Historical Review* 2, no. 4 (March 1916): 484-508.

————. "Paul Cuffee and His Contribution to the American Colonization Society." *Proceedings of the Mississippi Valley Historical Association* 6 (1912-13): 370-402.

————. "The Formation of the American Colonization Society." *Journal of Negro History* 2, no. 3 (July 1917): 209-27.

Shick, Tom W. "A Quantitative Analysis of Liberian Colonization from 1820 to 1843 with Special Reference to Mortality." *Journal of African History* 12, no. 1 (1971): 45-59.

————. "A Quantitative Analysis of Liberian Colonization from 1820 to 1843 with Special Reference to Mortality." M.A. thesis, University of Wisconsin, 1970.

_____. "Liberia Reconsidered: A Reply to J. K. Obatala." *Black Scholar* 5, no. 2 (October 1973): 53-56.

_____. "Preliminary Analysis of the 1843 Liberian Census." Paper delivered at the Liberian Studies Conference, Madison, Wis., 1974.

_____. "The Social and Economic History of Afro-American Settlers in Liberia, 1820 to 1900." Ph.D. diss., University of Wisconsin, 1976.

Sigler, Phil. "Attitudes of Free Blacks Towards Emigration." Ph.D. diss., Northwestern University, 1969.

Smith, James Wesley. "The Significance of Virginians in Liberian History." Paper delivered at the Liberian Studies Conference, Bloomington, Ind., 1976.

Stampp, Kenneth M. *The Peculiar Institution: Slavery in the Ante-Bellum South*. New York: Vintage Books, 1956.

Starobin, Robert S. *Industrial Slavery in the Old South*. New York: Oxford University Press, 1970.

_____, ed. *Blacks in Bondage: Letters of American Slaves*. New York: New Viewpoints, 1974.

Staudenraus, Philip J. *The African Colonization Movement, 1816-1865*. New York: Columbia University Press, 1961.

Stavisky, Leonard. "Negro Craftsmanship in Early America." *American Historical Review* 54 (1948-49): 315-25.

Stein, Stanley J. *Vassouras: A Brazilian Coffee County, 1850-1900*. Cambridge, Mass.: Harvard University Press, 1957.

Sullivan, Jo Mary. "Settlers in Sinoe County, Liberia, and Their Relations with the Kru, c. 1835-1920." Ph.D. diss., Boston University, 1978.

Sundiata, I. K. "Prelude to Scandal: Liberia and Fernando Po, 1880-1930." *Journal of African History* 15, no. 1 (1974): 97-112.

Sweet, Leonard I. *Black Images of America, 1784-1870*. New York: Norton & Co., 1976.

Syfert, Dwight N. "A Survey of the Liberian Coasting Trade, 1822-1900." Paper delivered at the Liberian Studies Conference, Bloomington, Ind., 1976.

_____. "The Liberian Coasting Trade, 1822-1900." *Journal of African History* 18, no. 2 (1977): 217-35.

Taylor, Carl C. *Rural Life in Argentina*. Baton Rouge: Louisiana State University Press, 1948.

Tindall, George Brown. *South Carolina Negroes, 1877-1900*. Columbia, S.C.: University of South Carolina Press, 1952.

Turner, Frederick Jackson. *The Significance of Frontier in American History*. New York: Ungar, 1963.

Turner, Lorenzo D. *Africanisms in the Gullah Dialect*. Chicago: University of Chicago Press, 1949.

Turner, J. Michael. "Les Bresiliens—The Impact of Former Brazilian Slaves on Dahomey." Ph.D. diss., Boston University, 1972.

"Two Colson Family Letters." *Negro History Bulletin* 10, no. 1 (October 1946): 20-21.

Uya, Okon E., ed. *Black Brotherhood: Afro-Americans and Africa.* Lexington, Mass.: D. C. Heath & Co., 1971.

Wachter, G. Joseph. "Early Negro Colonization and America's West African Settlers of 1820-1822." M.A. thesis, Morgan State College, 1972.

Wade, Richard C. *Slavery in the Cities: The South, 1820-1860.* New York: Oxford University Press, 1964.

Welmers, William E. *The Mande Languages.* Georgetown University Monograph Series, no. 11, pp. 9-24. Washington, D.C., 1958.

Wesley, Charles H. "The Struggle for the Recognition of Haiti and Liberia As Independent Republics." *Journal of Negro History* 2, no. 4 (1917): 369-83.

Whetstone, Harold Vink. "The Lutheran Mission in Liberia." M.A. thesis, The Hartford Seminary Foundation, 1954.

Wiley, Bell Irvin, ed. *Letters from Liberia, 1833-1869.* Lexington, Ky.: University of Kentucky Press, forthcoming.

Williams, T. Harry. *Lincoln and the Radicals.* Madison: University of Wisconsin Press, 1960.

_____, ed. *Abraham Lincoln: Selected Speeches, Messages, and Letters.* New York: Rinehart, 1957.

Williams, Walter Lee. "Black American Attitudes Towards Africa: The Missionary Movement, 1877-1900." Ph.D. diss., University of North Carolina, 1974.

Wilson, Ellen Gibson. *The Loyal Blacks.* New York: G. P. Putnam's Sons, Capicorn Books, 1976.

Woodward, C. Vann. *The Strange Career of Jim Crow.* 3d rev. ed. New York: Oxford University Press, 1974.

Wright, Richard. *American Hunger.* New York: Harper & Row Publishers, 1977.

Index